The CREATION of HUMAN ABILITY

A Handbook for Scientologists

The Creation of Human Ability

A Handbook for Scientologists

L. RON HUBBARD

Bridge Publications, Inc.

A
HUBBARD®
PUBLICATION

Published by
Bridge Publications, Inc.
4751 Fountain Avenue
Los Angeles, California 90029

ISBN 978-1-4031-4421-8

Printed in the United States of America

IMPORTANT NOTE

In reading this book, be very certain you never go past a word you do not fully understand. The only reason a person gives up a study or becomes confused or unable to learn is because he or she has gone past a word that was not understood.

The confusion or inability to grasp or learn comes AFTER a word the person did not have defined and understood. It may not only be the new and unusual words you have to look up. Some commonly used words can often be misdefined and so cause confusion.

This datum about not going past an undefined word is the most important fact in the whole subject of study. Every subject you have taken up and abandoned had its words which you failed to get defined.

Therefore, in studying this book be very, very certain you never go past a word you do not fully understand. If the material becomes confusing or you can't seem to grasp it, there will be a word just earlier that you have not understood. Don't go any further, but go back to BEFORE you got into trouble, find the misunderstood word and get it defined.

GLOSSARY

To aid reader comprehension, L. Ron Hubbard directed the editors to provide a glossary. This is included in the Appendix, *Editor's Glossary of Words, Terms and Phrases*. Words sometimes have several meanings. The *Editor's Glossary* only contains the definitions of words as they are used in this text. Other definitions can be found in standard language or Dianetics and Scientology dictionaries.

If you find any other words you do not know, look them up in a good dictionary.

*O*o your ways: behold,
I send you forth as lambs among wolves.

Carry neither purse, nor scrip,
nor shoes: and salute no man by the way.

And into whatsoever house ye enter, first say,
Peace be to this house.

And if the son of peace be there,
your peace shall rest upon it:
if not, it shall turn to you again.

And in the same house remain,
eating and drinking such things as they give:
for the laborer is worthy of his hire.
Go not from house to house.

And in whatsoever city ye enter,
and they receive you, eat such things
as are set before you:

And heal the sick that are therein,
and say unto them, The kingdom of God
is come nigh unto you.

———

And he turned him unto his
disciples, and said privately,
Blessed are the eyes
which see the things that ye see:

For I tell you, that many prophets and kings
have desired to see those things which ye see,
and have not seen them;
and to hear those things which ye hear,
and have not heard them.

St. Luke 10: 3-9, 23-24

THE CREATION OF HUMAN ABILITY
CONTENTS

"The goal of Intensive Procedure is to bring about a complete tolerance and comfort on the part of the preclear for the physical universe, his exteriorization and general rehabilitation."

PREFACE

PREFACE

Dear Auditor,

I have written this book for you to help you with your processing.

It combines all the procedures of major workability developed and tested during seven Advanced Clinical Course units. As processes were developed and tested, I discovered that more and more workability was to be found in communication alone. Thus Intensive Procedure was not developed straight from theory, but was evolved out of theory where it agreed with workability.

The stress is upon certainty of communication on the part of the preclear with objects in the physical universe. The Formula of Communication itself, in all of its parts, must be entirely rehabilitated with the preclear in the physical universe before the preclear can then begin with his own universe.

The goal of Intensive Procedure is to bring about a complete tolerance and comfort on the part of the preclear for the physical universe, his exteriorization and general rehabilitation.

Best Regards,

L. Ron Hubbard

July 1954

THE

"An auditor must observe the Auditor's Code
if he intends to produce beneficial
results in a preclear."

One

AUDITOR'S
CODE
1954

Chapter One

THE
AUDITOR'S CODE
1954

 N AUDITOR MUST observe the Auditor's Code if he intends to produce beneficial results in a preclear.

The auditor's attention is very strongly called to sections 12 and 13. Section 13 contains the difference between a bad auditor and a good auditor. Whereas the whole Code is important, section 13 is vitally important. So much so that an auditor not understanding it will not produce good results in a preclear. Section 13 means that an auditor must not change the process just because the preclear's perception or communication is changing. A bad auditor will change the process every time the preclear starts to change. This is the auditor obsessively duplicating the preclear. A good auditor will run a process until it no longer produces change in the preclear and only then will go to a new process. A bad auditor can always be estimated by the number of processes he uses on a preclear, for any process in modern procedures, consistently used, will produce considerable change. When the auditor changes a process just because the preclear starts to change, we call this "Auditor Q and Aing." It is a very bad manifestation.

1 Do not evaluate for the preclear.

2 Do not invalidate or correct the preclear's data.

3 Use the processes which improve the preclear's case.

4 Keep all appointments once made.

5 Do not process a preclear after 10:00 P.M.

6 Do not process a preclear who is improperly fed.

7 Do not permit a frequent change of auditors.

8 Do not sympathize with the preclear.

9 Never permit the preclear to end the session on his own independent decision.

10 Never walk off from a preclear during a session.

11 Never get angry with a preclear.

12 Always reduce every communication lag encountered by continued use of the same question or process.

13 Always continue a process as long as it produces change and no longer.

14 Be willing to grant beingness to the preclear.

15 Never mix the processes of Scientology with those of various other practices.

16 Maintain two-way communication with the preclear.

The Auditor's Code of 1954 has been evolved from four years of observing processing. It is the technical code of Scientology. It contains the important errors which harm cases. It could be called the moral code of Scientology.

The Code

"Never regret yesterday.
Life is in you today and you make
your tomorrow."

Two

OF HONOR

The Code
of Honor

NO ONE EXPECTS the Code of Honor to be closely and tightly followed.

An ethical code cannot be enforced. Any effort to enforce the Code of Honor would bring it into the level of a moral code. It cannot be enforced simply because it is a way of life which can exist as a way of life only as long as it is not enforced. Any other use but self-determined use of the Code of Honor would, as any Scientologist could quickly see, produce a considerable deterioration in a person. Therefore its use is a luxury use, and which is done solely on self-determined action, providing one sees eye to eye with the Code of Honor.

1 Never desert a comrade in need, in danger or in trouble.

2 Never withdraw allegiance once granted.

3 Never desert a group to which you owe your support.

4 Never disparage yourself or minimize your strength or power.

5 Never need praise, approval or sympathy.

6 Never compromise with your own reality.

7 Never permit your affinity to be alloyed.

8 Do not give or receive communication unless you yourself desire it.

9 Your self-determinism and your honor are more important than your immediate life.

10 Your integrity to yourself is more important than your body.

11 Never regret yesterday. Life is in you today and you make your tomorrow.

12 Never fear to hurt another in a just cause.

13 Don't desire to be liked or admired.

14 Be your own adviser, keep your own counsel and select your own decisions.

15 Be true to your own goals.

This is the ethical code of Scientology, the code one uses not because he has to but because he can afford such a luxury.

chapter

THE CODE OF A

"To use the best I know of Scientology,
to the best of my ability, to better my preclears,
groups and the world."

SCIENTOLOGIST

1954

The Code
of a Scientologist
1954

 HE CODE OF A SCIENTOLOGIST was evolved to safeguard Scientologists in general and is subscribed to by leading Scientologists.

As a Scientologist, I pledge myself to the Code of Scientology for the good of all.

1   To hear or speak no word of disparagement to the press, public or preclears concerning any of my fellow Scientologists, our professional organization or those whose names are closely connected to this science.

2   To use the best I know of Scientology, to the best of my ability, to better my preclears, groups and the world.

3   To refuse to accept for processing and to refuse to accept money from any preclear or group I feel I cannot honestly help.

4   To deter to the fullest extent of my power anyone misusing or degrading Scientology to harmful ends.

5   To prevent the use of Scientology in advertisements of other products.

6   To discourage the abuse of Scientology in the press.

7   To employ Scientology to the greatest good of the greatest number of dynamics.

8   To render good processing, sound training and good discipline to those students or peoples entrusted to my care.

9 To refuse to impart the personal secrets of my preclears.

10 To engage in no unseemly disputes with the uninformed on the subject of my profession.

C h a p t e r

A Summary

"The freedom of an individual depends upon
that individual's freedom to alter his
considerations of space, energy, time and forms
of life, and his roles in it."

f o u r

OF SCIENTOLOGY

A SUMMARY OF SCIENTOLOGY

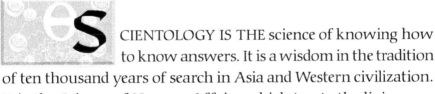

SCIENTOLOGY IS THE science of knowing how to know answers. It is a wisdom in the tradition of ten thousand years of search in Asia and Western civilization. It is the Science of Human Affairs which treats the livingness and beingness of Man and demonstrates to him a pathway to greater freedom.

Subjects which were consulted in the organization and development of Scientology include the *Veda*; the *Tao*, by Lao-tzu; the *Dharma* and the *Discourses* of Gautama Buddha; the general knowingness about life extant in the lamaseries of the Western Hills of China; the technologies and beliefs of various barbaric cultures; the various materials of Christianity, including *St. Luke*; the mathematical and technical methodologies of the early Greeks, Romans and Arabians; the physical sciences, including what is now known as nuclear physics; the various speculations of Western philosophers such as Kant, Nietzsche, Schopenhauer, Herbert Spencer and Dewey; and the various technologies extant in the civilizations of both the Orient and Occident in the first half of the twentieth century.

Scientology is an organization of the pertinencies which are mutually held true by all men in all times and the development of technologies which demonstrate the existence of new phenomena, not hitherto known, which are useful in creating states of beingness considered more desirable by Man.

There are two distinct divisions in Scientology. The first is philosophic, the second is technical. Under the philosophic heading one discovers the ways and means of forming new ways of life and of evaluating or creating standards of livingness and beingness. By this knowingness alone, and without processing, it should be understood clearly that a new way of life could be created or an old way of life could be understood and better endured or altered. Under the technical division we have a long series of developed processes which, applied immediately and directly to life or an organism thereof, produce changes at the will of the practitioner.

Scientology concludes and demonstrates certain truths. These truths might be considered to be the highest common denominators of existence itself.

The following summary of these truths has the aspect of precision observations rather than philosophic hazardings. When treated as precision observations, many results occur. When regarded as philosophic opinions, only more philosophy results.

CONSIDERATIONS TAKE RANK OVER THE MECHANICS OF SPACE, ENERGY AND TIME.

By this it is meant that an idea or opinion is, fundamentally, superior to space, energy and time or organizations of form, since it is conceived that space, energy and time are themselves broadly agreed-upon considerations. That so many minds agree brings about reality in the form of space, energy and time.

These mechanics, then, of space, energy and time, are the product of agreed-upon considerations mutually held by life.

The aspect of existence when viewed from the level of Man, however, is a reverse of the greater truth above. For Man works on the secondary opinion that mechanics are real and that his own personal considerations are less important than space, energy and time. This is an inversion. These mechanics of space, energy and time, the forms, objects and combinations thereof, have taken such precedence in Man that they have become more important than considerations, as such, and so his ability is overpowered and he is unable to act freely in the framework of mechanics. Man, therefore, has an inverted view. Whereas considerations, such as those he daily makes, are the actual source of space, energy, time and forms, Man is operating so as not to alter his basic considerations. He, therefore, invalidates himself by supposing an Other-determinism of space, energy, time and form. Although he is part of that which created these, he gives them such strength and validity that his own considerations thereafter must fall subordinate to space, energy, time and form, and so he cannot alter the universe in which he dwells.

The freedom of an individual depends upon that individual's freedom to alter his considerations of space, energy, time and forms of life, and his roles in it. If he cannot change his mind about these, he is then fixed and enslaved amidst barriers such as those of the physical universe and barriers of his own creation. Man thus is seen to be enslaved by barriers of his own creation. He creates these barriers himself or by agreeing with things which hold these barriers to be actual.

There is a basic series of assumptions in processing, which assumptions do not alter the philosophy of Scientology. The first of these assumptions is that Man can have a greater freedom.

The second is that so long as he remains relatively sane, he desires a greater freedom. And the third assumption is that the auditor desires to deliver a greater freedom to that person with whom he is working. If these assumptions are not agreed upon and are not used, then auditing degenerates into "the observation of effect," which is, of course, a goalless, soulless pursuit and is, indeed, a pursuit which has degraded what is called "modern science."

The goal of processing is to bring an individual into such thorough communication with the physical universe that he can regain the power and ability of his own considerations (postulates).

A Scientologist is one who understands life. His technical skill is devoted to the resolution of the problems of life.

The technical information of the Scientologist includes the following Axioms, which are a list of usable or self-evident truths as revised from the earlier Logics and Axioms.

1   *Life is basically a Static.*

Definition:

A Life Static has no mass, no motion, no wavelength, no location in space or in time. It has the ability to postulate and perceive.

2   *The Static is capable of considerations, postulates and opinions.*

3   *Space, energy, objects, form and time are the result of considerations made and/or agreed upon or not by the Static, and are perceived solely because the Static considers that it can perceive them.*

4   *Space is a viewpoint of dimension.*

5   *Energy consists of postulated particles in space.*

6   *Objects consist of grouped particles.*

7   *Time is basically a postulate that space and particles will persist.*

8   *The apparency of time is the change of position of particles in space.*

9   *Change is the primary manifestation of time.*

10   *The highest purpose in the Universe is the creation of an effect.*

11 *The considerations resulting in conditions of existence are fourfold:*

> *a. As-isness is the condition of immediate creation without persistence, and is the condition of existence which exists at the moment of creation and the moment of destruction, and is different from other considerations in that it does not contain survival.*

> *b. Alter-isness is the consideration which introduces change, and therefore time and persistence, into an As-isness to obtain persistency.*

> *c. Isness is an apparency of existence brought about by the continuous alteration of an As-isness. This is called, when agreed upon, Reality.*

> *d. Not-isness is the effort to handle Isness by reducing its condition through the use of force. It is an apparency and cannot entirely vanquish an Isness.*

12 *The primary condition of any universe is that two spaces, energies or objects must not occupy the same space. When this condition is violated (perfect duplicate) the apparency of any universe or any part thereof is nulled.*

13 *The Cycle-of-Action of the physical universe is: Creation, Survival, Destruction.*

14 *Survival is accomplished by Alter-isness and Not-isness, by which is gained the persistency known as time.*

15 *Creation is accomplished by the postulation of an As-isness.*

16 *Complete destruction is accomplished by the postulation of the As-isness of any existence and the parts thereof.*

17 *The Static, having postulated As-isness, then practices Alter-isness, and so achieves the apparency of Isness and so obtains Reality.*

18 *The Static, in practicing Not-isness, brings about the persistence of unwanted existences, and so brings about unreality, which includes forgetfulness, unconsciousness and other undesirable states.*

19 *Bringing the Static to view As-is any condition devaluates that condition.*

20 *Bringing the Static to create a perfect duplicate causes the vanishment of any existence or part thereof.*

A perfect duplicate is an additional creation of the object, its energy and space, in its own space, in its own time, using its own energy. This violates the condition that two objects must not occupy the same space, and causes vanishment of the object.

21 *Understanding is composed of Affinity, Reality and Communication.*

22 *The practice of Not-isness reduces Understanding.*

23 *The Static has the capability of total Knowingness. Total Knowingness would consist of total ARC.*

24 *Total ARC would bring about the vanishment of all mechanical conditions of existence.*

25 *Affinity is a scale of attitude which falls away from the co-existence of Static, through the interpositions of distance and energy, to create identity, down to close proximity but mystery.*

By the practice of Isness (Beingness) and Not-isness (refusal to Be) individuation progresses from the Knowingness of complete identification down through the introduction of more and more distance and less and less duplication, through Lookingness, Emotingness, Effortingness, Thinkingness, Symbolizingness, Eatingness, Sexingness, and so through to Not-Knowingness (Mystery). Until the point of Mystery is reached, some communication is possible, but even at Mystery an attempt to communicate continues. Here we have, in the case of an individual, a gradual falling-away from the belief that one can assume a complete Affinity down to the conviction that all is a complete Mystery. Any individual is somewhere on this Know to Mystery Scale. The original Chart of Human Evaluation was the Emotion section of this scale.

26 *Reality is the agreed-upon apparency of existence.*

27 *An Actuality can exist for one individually, but when it is agreed with by others it can then be said to be a Reality.*

The anatomy of Reality is contained in Isness, which is composed of As-isness and Alter-isness. Isness is an apparency, it is not an Actuality. The Actuality is As-isness altered so as to obtain a persistency.

Unreality is the consequence and apparency of the practice of Not-isness.

28 *Communication is the consideration and action of impelling an impulse or particle from source-point across a distance to receipt-point, with the intention of bringing into being at the receipt-point a duplication of that which emanated from the source-point.*

The Formula of Communication is: Cause, Distance, Effect, with Attention and Duplication.

The component parts of Communication are Consideration, Intention, Attention, Cause, Source-point, Distance, Effect, Receipt-point, Duplication, the Velocity of the impulse or particle, Nothingness or Somethingness. A non-Communication consists of Barriers. Barriers consist of Space, Interpositions (such as walls and screens of fast-moving particles) and Time. A communication, by definition, does not need to be two-way. When a communication is returned, the Formula is repeated, with the Receipt-point now becoming a Source-point and the former Source-point now becoming a Receipt-point.

29 *In order to cause an As-isness to persist, one must assign other authorship to the creation than his own. Otherwise, his view of it would cause its vanishment.*

Any space, energy, form, object, individual or physical universe condition can exist only when an alteration has occurred of the original As-isness so as to prevent a casual view from vanishing it. In other words, anything which is persisting must contain a "lie" so that the original consideration is not completely duplicated.

30 *The general rule of auditing is that anything which is unwanted and yet persists must be thoroughly viewed, at which time it will vanish.*

If only partially viewed, its intensity, at least, will decrease.

31 *Goodness and Badness, Beautifulness and Ugliness, are alike considerations and have no other basis than opinion.*

32 *Anything which is not directly observed tends to persist.*

33 *Any As-isness which is altered by Not-isness (by force) tends to persist.*

34 *Any Isness, when altered by force, tends to persist.*

35 *The Ultimate Truth is a Static.*

A Static has no mass, meaning, mobility, no wavelength, no time, no location in space, no space.

This has the technical name of "Basic Truth."

36 *A lie is a second postulate, statement or condition designed to mask a primary postulate which is permitted to remain.*

Examples:

Neither truth nor a lie is a motion or alteration of a particle from one position to another.

A lie is a statement that a particle having moved did not move, or a statement that a particle not having moved did move.

The basic lie is that a consideration which was made was not made, or that it was different.

37 *When a primary consideration is altered but still exists, persistence is achieved for the altering consideration.*

All persistence depends on the Basic Truth, but the persistence is of the altering consideration, for the Basic Truth has neither persistence nor impersistence.

38 1: *Stupidity is the unknownness of consideration.*

2: Mechanical Definition: *Stupidity is the unknownness of time, place, form and event.*

1: Truth is the exact consideration.

2: Truth is the exact time, place, form and event.

Thus we see that failure to discover Truth brings about stupidity.

Thus we see that the discovery of Truth would bring about an As-isness by actual experiment.

Thus we see that an Ultimate Truth would have no time, place, form or event.

Thus, then, we perceive that we can achieve a persistence only when we mask a truth.

Lying is an alteration of time, place, event or form.

Lying becomes Alter-isness, becomes stupidity.

(The blackness of cases is an accumulation of the case's own or another's lies.)

Anything which persists must avoid As-isness. Thus, anything to persist must contain a lie.

39 *Life poses problems for its own solution.*

40 *Any problem, to be a problem, must contain a lie. If it were truth, it would unmock.*

An "unsolvable problem" would have the greatest persistence. It would also contain the greatest number of altered facts.

To make a problem, one must introduce Alter-isness.

41 *That into which Alter-isness is introduced becomes a problem.*

42 *MEST (Matter, Energy, Space, Time) persists because it is a problem.*

It is a problem because it contains Alter-isness.

43 *Time is the primary source of untruth.*

Time states the untruth of consecutive considerations.

44 *Theta (the Static) has no location in Matter, Energy, Space or Time. It is capable of consideration.*

45 *Theta can consider itself to be placed, at which moment it becomes placed, and to that degree a problem.*

46 *Theta can become a problem by its considerations but then becomes MEST.*

A problem is to some degree MEST. MEST *is* a problem.

47 *Theta can resolve problems.*

48 *Life is a game wherein Theta as the Static solves the problems of Theta as MEST.*

49 *To solve any problem it is only necessary to become theta the solver rather than theta the problem.*

50 *Theta as MEST must contain considerations which are lies.*

51 *Postulates and live communication not being MEST and being senior to MEST can accomplish change in MEST without bringing about a persistence of MEST. Thus auditing can occur.*

The above is a summary of states of being which can be used to create, cause to persist or destroy.

HAVING AGREED TO THE MECHANICS AND RETAINING THE AGREEMENTS, THE THETAN CAN YET MAKE INNUMERABLE POSTULATES WHICH, BY THEIR CONTRADICTION AND COMPLEXITY, CREATE, CAUSE TO PERSIST AND DESTROY HUMAN BEHAVIOR.

c h a p t e r

INTENSIVE

"The sole criterion of the case is whether or not
it can be exteriorized."

f i v e

PROCEDURE

Chapter five

INTENSIVE PROCEDURE

Outline

NTENSIVE PROCEDURE consists of a special series of processes which, when used by a skilled auditor as designed, produce optimum results upon preclears as of this date of release.

In the use of this procedure, only two types of case are considered and the procedure is adapted to these two types. The sole criterion of the case is whether or not it can be exteriorized. This is promptly established by the use of ARC Straightwire. When there is no noticeable communication lag, then Route 1 is employed in this procedure. When there is any noticeable communication lag, Route 2 is employed.

All sessions begin with the first three identical steps. Then, if he has established that there is no noticeable communication lag with ARC Straightwire (the third step), the auditor proceeds on Route 1. However, if a noticeable communication lag exists when using ARC Straightwire, the auditor (having flattened this lag for the moment) proceeds on Route 2. The amount of occlusion on the case is not the test.

1: Get into two-way communication with the preclear.

2: Discuss the present time problem, if any.

3: Get the preclear into session with ARC Straightwire.

Route 1:

R1-4:   Be Three Feet Back of Your Head

R1-5:   Copying

Whatever the preclear happens to be looking at (do not direct his attention to anything), have him copy it one at a time, many, many times. Then have him locate a nothingness and copy it many, many times.

R1-6:   Back Anchor Points

Have preclear hold the two upper back anchor points of the room for at least two minutes by the clock.

R1-7:   Where He Is Not

Have preclear let go and find many places where he is not.

R1-8:   Safe to Look At

Have preclear discover many things, one after another, which he considers safe to look at.

R1-9:   Grand Tour

R1-10: Occupying the Same Space

Have preclear discover things he wouldn't mind occupying the same space with him.

R1-11: Problems and Solutions in Havingness

Have preclear be problems and solutions in havingness.

R1 12:   A Complete Remedy of Havingness of Energy

Have preclear mock-up generators, power plants and suns to give him energy, on that gradient scale, until he is totally convinced that he does not have to receive energy from an outside source (a complete remedy of havingness).

R1-13:   GE Anchor Points

Have preclear adjust GE anchor points.

R1-14:   Thetan Machines

Have preclear create and destroy various kinds of thetan machines.

R1-15:   Physical Universe Copying

Repair preclear's ability to communicate by having him copy many scenes in the physical universe.

Now have preclear run each and every Route 2 step until the auditor is convinced that he can do these easily and ably.

Route 2:

If the preclear had any appreciable communication lag, as established in the third step above (ARC Straightwire), all Route 1 steps are omitted and the case is entered into Route 2 – the first step of which is R2-16.

R2-16: Opening Procedure of 8-C

Run preclear through Opening Procedure of 8-C Parts (a) (b) (c), each one until the physical communication lag stabilizes.

R2-17: Opening Procedure by Duplication

Opening Procedure by Duplication until preclear feels good about it.

R2-18: Spotting Spots in Space (and Remedy of Havingness)

Have preclear spot spots in space until he can do it easily, meanwhile remedying his havingness.

R2-19: Spotting Spots in Room

Have preclear spot spots in room and move body into them and move body out into new spots.

R2-20: Use of Problems and Solutions

R2-21: Granting of Beingness

Granting of Beingness (life) to something.

R2-22: Spanning Attention

R2-23: Attention by Duplication

R2-24: Exteriorization by Distance,
　　　 extroverted and introverted alternately

R2-25: Viewpoint and Viewpoint ARC Straightwire

R2-26: Remedy of Laughter

R2-27: Resolve Dangerousness of Environment,
　　　 Cause and Effect

R2-28: Nothing-Something

R2-29: Time Tolerance

R2-30: Position by Security (SOP 8-D)

R2-31: Beingness Processing

R2-32: Assignment of Attributes

R2-33: Perfect Duplication

R2-34: Description Processing

R2-35: Location Processes

R2-36: Self-determinism

R2-37: Yelling

R2-38: Holding Anchor Points

R2-39: Conceiving Something Interesting

R2-40: Conceiving a Static

R2-41: Via

R2-61: Good and Evil

R2-62: Overt Acts and Motivators

R2-63: Accept-Reject

R2-64: Touching

R2-65: Alteration

R2-66: Electing Cause

R2-67: Objects

R2-68: Incomprehensibility

R2-69: Please Pass the Object

R2-70: Expectance Level

R2-71: Answers

R2-72: Security Processing

R2-73: Making Something for the Future

R2-74: Processing (self-auditing)

R2 75: Knowingness

R2-76: Communication Processing

R2-77: Games

Now take a Route 2 preclear
through Route 1.

Chart of Processes

Where they are on the ARC Tone Scale.

Exteriorized

Spot Spots in Space	4.0
Spot Spots in Space	3.6
Remedy of Havingness	3.5
Remedy of Havingness	3.1
Opening Procedure by Duplication	3.0
Opening Procedure by Duplication	2.6
Opening Procedure 8-C	2.5
Opening Procedure 8-C	
Elementary Straightwire	1.8
Elementary Straightwire	1.1
Two-way Communication	1.0
Two-way Communication	–8.0

Cautions

Follow the Auditor's Code.

The procedure which turns on a condition will turn it off.

Run a procedure as long as it produces communication changes (perception, changes in altering communication lag).

It has been found by long practice that the only things which spin a preclear are:

1. Too many auditors;

2. Not enough food; and

3. Processing between 10:00 P.M. and 8:00 A.M.

When in doubt, remedy havingness.

When choosing between two procedures, use the simpler one.

For all cases who have any psychosomatic ills, or who are neurotic or psychotic, use only R2–16 anywhere from ten to a hundred hours or until the person is no longer ill, neurotic or psychotic.

INTENSIVE PROCEDURE: Auditing Commands

"One can be
comfortable
in communicating
only when one is
willing to be Cause
and is willing
to be an Effect."

AUDITING COMMANDS FOR INTENSIVE PROCEDURE

1: Get into two-way communication with the preclear.

Axiom 28: *Communication is the consideration and action of impelling an impulse or particle from source-point across a distance to receipt-point, with the intention of bringing into being at the receipt-point a duplication of that which emanated from the source-point.*

The Formula of Communication is: Cause, Distance, Effect, with Attention and Duplication.

The component parts of Communication are Consideration, Intention, Attention, Cause, Source-point, Distance, Effect, Receipt-point, Duplication, the Velocity of the impulse or particle, Nothingness or Somethingness. A non-Communication consists of Barriers. Barriers consist of Space, Interpositions (such as walls and screens of fast-moving particles) and Time. A communication, by definition, does not need to be two-way. When a communication is returned, the Formula is repeated, with the Receipt-point now becoming a Source-point and the former Source-point now becoming a Receipt-point.

One can be comfortable in communicating only when one is willing to be Cause and is willing to be an Effect. As the distance factor in communication lessens, or as mass increases in the particle, one views the condensing manifestation of the Know to Sex Scale and a deterioration of affinity. As the communication is less and less willingly duplicated, one observes the deterioration of the reality factor of the ARC Triangle. To improve communication, one must lessen mass, increase velocity and increase the distance factor, improve the quality of duplication, remedy attention, and bring about a willingness on the part of Cause to be an Effect and on the part of Effect to be Cause. To reach toward a theoretical perfection in communication, one should be willing to tolerate, in any form, any of the component parts of communication itself—with the understanding that these include affinity and reality. Any sensory perceptic can be utilized in communication in establishing a two-way communication.

Communication lag is the interval of time intervening between a posed question and the actual and precise answer to that question. Communication lag is a manifestation of two-way communication. Whether the interval is filled with speech or silence, the definition of communication lag still holds true. An auditor must go by the rule that all questions posed must receive answers and therefore must be careful that he poses questions which can be answered by a person in the condition of the preclear.

This is the most important step of any auditing session and its achievement by any perception, with affinity and reality, is a specific goal of the auditor. If a preclear for any reason drags under processing, it is because the auditor was not sure that the preclear was in communication with anything and was not in communication, actually, with the things to which the auditor directed his attention.

2: Discuss the present time problem, if any.

Discussion of the present time problem is necessary each session so as to discover whether or not the preclear has had a disturbance between sessions which has so fixed his attention that he is unable to give his complete presence to auditing.

3: Get the preclear into session with ARC Straightwire.

ARC Straightwire is used to determine the communication lag of the preclear.

The steps of ARC Straightwire are:

"Can you recall something that is quite real to you?"
"Can you recall a time when you were in good communication with someone?"
"Can you recall a time when someone was in good communication with you?"
"Can you recall a time when you felt some affinity for someone?"
"Can you recall a time when someone felt some affinity for you?"

In actual practice, to establish the communication lag it is only necessary to use the first question, *"Can you recall something that is quite real to you?"* and then use this question enough more times to bring the communication lag to a constancy before proceeding on with further steps.

Intensive Procedure: Route 1

"A thetan located in a space is less than theta itself, but a thetan located is much greater than Homo sapiens."

ROUTE 1

R1-4:
Be Three Feet Back of Your Head

The command *"Be three feet back of your head"* should be given casually. And if immediately obeyed, the auditor, with no further discussion, should then go on to R1-5. If there is any argument after this command is given, or if the preclear cannot quite understand what is occurring and does not do so, then it is indicated that the auditor switch Routes and, without further argument on the subject of exteriorization, continue the session with R2-16.

Note

A thetan located in a space is less than theta itself, but a thetan located is much greater than Homo sapiens.

R1-5:
Copying

Whatever the preclear happens to be looking at (do not direct his attention to anything), have him copy it one at a time, many, many times. Then have him locate a nothingness and copy it many, many times.

Without directing the preclear's attention to anything, ask him:

"What (he is) *looking at?"*

And then have him mock-up a copy of whatever he sees, whether it is the room, a picture or blackness. Have him then make another copy of what he saw, and another one, and another one, and another one, and another one. These copies are all the same as the original sight which he perceived when asked what he was looking at.

Acquaint the preclear with the word "copy" by first asking him to:

"Make another one just like it," and then for this phrase substitute the word *"copy."*

When the preclear has made some two dozen copies, have him do something, anything, with these copies so as to dispose of them. They can be used to supplement havingness, in which case he would be asked to push them all together and pull them in upon himself. In any event, do not leave him with these copies.

When the copies are disposed of, have the preclear locate a nothingness by saying:

"Can you find a nothingness somewhere around you?"

And then have him copy it by saying:

"Now make another one just like it,"
"Make another one just like it,"
"Now copy that first nothingness again," and so forth, until he has copied this a couple of dozen times.

Then have him dispose of these nothingnesses.

R1-6:
Back Anchor Points

Have preclear hold the two upper back anchor points of the room for at least two minutes by the clock.

"Locate the two upper back corners of the room (those behind the preclear's body), *hold on to them and don't think.*"

Do this for at least two minutes.

The preclear could be alternately asked to:

"*Find two nothingnesses and hold on to them* (for two minutes) *without thinking.*"

The length of time is not mentioned to the preclear.

When this has been done, do not neglect to tell the preclear to let go. Do not run the next step with him still holding on to the two back corners of the room.

R1-7:
Where He Is Not

Have preclear let go and find many places where he is not.

"Now find a place where you are not."

Repeat this command many times until any communication lag developed by the question has been rendered constant.

Repeat the Copying (R1-5), Back Anchor Points (R1-6) and Where He Is Not (R1-7), one after the other, many times.

R1-8:
Safe to Look At

Have preclear discover many things, one after another, which he considers safe to look at.

This step is the basic theory behind R2-25, Viewpoint Straightwire. Its intention is to render the preclear comfortable while looking at anything. The keynote here is to use the goal of Viewpoint Straightwire directly. One is interested in having him look at actual things, in the MEST universe, from Look down to Sex on the Know to Sex Scale. One should include, in particular, turbulent masses and mysteries.

The most important part of this process, and the one which should be stressed while others are neglected, is to get the preclear to actually look at actual things. Then, to have him look at actual Emotions. And finally, to make very certain that he can be very comfortable in looking at all manner of Efforts. To do this one sends the preclear, as a thetan, out into the world and has him actually find things which it is comfortable for him to look at in the bands of plain Lookingness, then Emotion, then Effort.

One starts with the command:

"What would it be all right for you to look at here in this room?"

This is done with the body's eyes closed. The preclear is made to give as many things in the room, which it would be all right for him to look at, as is necessary to bring to constant any communication lag involved. Run the command:

"Now find something it is safe to look at outside this room."

When it is ascertained that, in this exercise of discovering things which are all right for him to look at, the preclear is wandering rather far afield with some confidence, the auditor should tell him:

"Now go and find some emotional states which it would be all right for you to look at."

The preclear actually goes around to various parts of the world and sees people and animals in various states of Emotion until he discovers he can be completely comfortable in viewing all the emotions on the Tone Scale in action–Apathy, Grief, Fear, Resentment, Anger, Antagonism, Boredom, Enthusiasm and Serenity.

When this has been accomplished, have the preclear find some Efforts being engaged in by something, anywhere, which it would be comfortable for the preclear to view. It may take some little time to discover something in the line of Effort which he can really comfortably perceive. He finds various Efforts which he can view and the process should be continued until he can look very comfortably upon wild and turbulent motion.

The keynote of this process is to get the preclear completely certain that he can view anything in the universe, with aplomb, particularly Emotion and Effort. The process can be continued, if with less benefit, with the remainder of the Know to Sex Scale plus Mystery:

Know
Look
Emote
Effort
Think
Symbols
Eat
Sex
Mystery

If in doubt, the auditor should run the entire band from Know to Sex including Mystery.

It should be clearly understood by the auditor that the preclear does not simply think about these things or mock them up and view them. The auditor wants the preclear, exteriorized, to go around various places in the actual physical universe and *look* at things and so build his tolerance on the physical universe.

IT IS IMPORTANT THAT IT MAY BE NECESSARY TO REMEDY THE PRECLEAR'S HAVINGNESS AT INTERVALS WHILE THIS STEP IS IN PROGRESS.

R1-9:
Grand Tour

The commands of the Grand Tour are as follows:

"Be near Earth,"
"Be near the Moon,"
"Be near the Sun."

"Be near the Earth,"
"Be near the Moon,"
"Be near the Sun."

"Earth,"
"Moon,"
"Sun," giving the last three commands many times.

Each time the auditor must wait until the preclear signifies that he has completed the command. The preclear is supposed to move near these bodies or simply be near them, it does not matter which.

The Grand Tour continues with:

"Now find a rock."

"Be inside of it,"
"Be outside of it."

"Inside,"
"Outside."

"Inside,"
"Outside."

"Be in the center of the Earth,"
"Be outside of Earth."

"Inside,"

"Outside," and back and forth until the preclear is able to do this very rapidly.

Then the Grand Tour continues:

"Be near Mars,"
"Be at the center of Mars."

"Outside of Mars,"
"Center."

"Outside,"
"Now move down slowly toward the surface."

The preclear will probably question this, for he has run into a force screen or thinks he has.

"All right then, be on the surface of Mars,"
"Be above Mars."

"Be on the surface,"
"Be above Mars."

"Move down to the surface of Mars."

He is shifted into various positions in the vicinity of Mars until he is entirely used to that planet.

When the preclear is entirely comfortable in the solar system by reason of running the Grand Tour, do Change of Space with him (as below): First, on all the locations where he has received auditing, therapy or treatment of any kind here on Earth. Next, do all the key locations mentioned in *History of Man*, such as the entrance point of the MEST universe, the place where he made his first facsimile, etc.

This is run in this fashion:

"Be at the place where you entered the MEST universe,"
"Be at the center of this room."

"Be at the place where you entered the MEST universe,"
"Center of this room."

"Entrance point,"
"Room."

"Entrance point,"
"Room," and so forth, until the entrance point is in present time.

The preclear should be made to run Change of Space on any area until that area is in present time. Originally it could be conceived that only the place where the preclear is, *is* in present time–that all other places are in past time to the degree that they are far from the preclear. The object is to get all areas into present time.

CAUTION: Change of Space is never run with the commands *"Be here," "Be there."* For when the preclear is "there," it has become "here" to him. Thus the actual designation, in brief, should be given each time.

IMPORTANT: WHILE RUNNING CHANGE OF SPACE OR ANY PART OF THE GRAND TOUR, IT MAY BE NECESSARY TO REMEDY THE HAVINGNESS OF THE PRECLEAR.

This is done with the commands:

"Put up eight anchor points as though they were the corners of a cube around you,"
"Now pull them in on you."

"Put up eight more,"
"Pull them in on you."

Any dopiness, or increasing sadness, or a feeling of degradation on the part of the preclear, comes about from lack of havingness. In the Grand Tour, it is more important for the preclear to locate and occupy exact locations in space and in objects than it is for him to examine the surrounding area.

R1-10:
Occupying the Same Space

Have preclear discover things he wouldn't mind occupying the same space with him.

AGREEMENT WITH THE PHYSICAL UNIVERSE BRINGS ABOUT THE CONSIDERATION ON THE PART OF THE PRECLEAR THAT TWO THINGS CANNOT OCCUPY THE SAME SPACE.

It is this basic rule which keeps the physical universe "stretched."

It is not, however, true that two things cannot occupy the same space. And it is particularly untrue when the two "things" are an object and a thetan, since a thetan can occupy the space any object is occupying.

The process is run with the question:

"Now tell me something you wouldn't mind having occupy the same space you are in,"

or

"Give me something you wouldn't mind having occupy your space."

The auditor must ascertain, in any answer the preclear gives, whether or not the preclear is absolutely certain he wouldn't object to this mutual occupation of the same space. The preclear is made to get item after item, until he recognizes a high reality on it, and then is made to occupy the same space as many things. (This is comparable to the Step I processes of earlier SOPs, where the preclear was made to be in many things.)

When it has been clearly established that the preclear, with absolute certainty, is perfectly able to tolerate anything occupying his same space, the auditor goes on to the next step.

R1-11:
Problems and Solutions in Havingness

Have preclear be problems and solutions in havingness.

Ask the preclear:

"What kind of a problem can you be in havingness?"
"What kind of a problem can you be in not-havingness?" many times, until he has isolated many Problems for many people.

"What kind of a problem can others be to you in havingness?"
"What kind of a problem can others be to you in not-havingness?"

After this has been well worked over, advance into Solutions with:

"What kind of a solution can you be to havingness?"
"What kind of a solution can you be to not-havingness?" and so forth.

It may be necessary to explain what is meant by "havingness," but it has been my experience this has not been so.

R1-12:
A Complete Remedy of Havingness of Energy

Have preclear mock-up generators,
power plants and suns to give him energy,
on that gradient scale, until he is totally
convinced that he does not have to
receive energy from an outside source
(a complete remedy of havingness).

Having run R1-10 and R1-11, the preclear should be able to get good mock-ups. The main object of this step, however it is done, is to get the preclear to recognize that he himself creates the energy which he uses. One of the methods of doing this is having him mock-up generators (of various sizes, on a gradient scale), then larger generators, then power plants, lightning bolts and, finally, suns to give him energy.

At this step, a complete remedy of havingness should be accomplished. If it is not adequately accomplished with this step, the auditor should return to R1-10, do that and R1-11, and then repeat R1-12.

R1-13:
GE Anchor Points

Have preclear adjust GE anchor points.

Early in processing, never direct the preclear's attention to his body. If he happens to be looking at his body, this is all right. But do not tell him to look at his body.

To begin R1-13, have preclear copy his body many, many times and push the mock-ups into it. Have him pretend that, by mock-ups, he is exteriorizing from various other kinds of bodies. Have him interiorize and exteriorize many times from his present body. Then have him mock-up the electronic structure of his body until he can see it easily.

Now ask him:

"Do you see any gold balls in your head?"

If he does not, have him mock-up gold balls until his head's golden balls appear. Now have him move any golden balls he finds which are out of position in his head until they are in the proper position. When an anchor point (golden ball) will not move back into position, have the preclear mock-up many anchor points in that area–which is to say, remedy the body's havingness in that area. Then, and only then, will it be found that the anchor point of the body itself will go back into that position.

CAUTION: Never let the preclear mock-up an anchor point of his own and put it into position in the body. The GE can tolerate only its own anchor points.

Ask the preclear:

"Can you find any more of these golden balls which are out of position?" and have him move them back into position, or assemble them, or remedy them, until all the anchor points of the body are in excellent condition and in the proper position.

R1-14:
Thetan Machines

Have preclear create and destroy various kinds of thetan machines.

A thetan is always equipped with various kinds of machinery. Remedying of havingness should make it very easy for him to dispense with or create new machinery.

He has machines which send him places, machines which hide things and machines which zap him. There are two types of machines: those that mock things up and those that unmock things. But there can be a great variety of considerations in this machinery. Machines are actually machines. He makes them up of tubes and other electronic equipment. Sometimes they look like huge teletypewriters. Simply duplicating a machine many times will at last reduce it to nothingness. A thetan whose havingness has been remedied, has relatively little difficulty with machinery as he is not keeping it around to supply him with energy. He has set up machinery which will "zap" him when he gets into certain positions. This, in life, as a Homo sapiens, is manifested by fear of self-invalidation. It comes from the machine, since invalidation on the upper echelon is by force.

Have him make machinery which actually works, make the machinery work, and destroy the machinery, until he is totally confident of his ability to make and destroy any and all types of machines. It is important that the machinery he mocks-up actually works. The process of making a machine is to make a postulate, fit it into a machine, hide the machine and forget it. The machine is keyed against something the thetan may think. When the thetan thinks something, the machine goes into action.

Be very wary of destroying all of a thetan's machinery. Be also very wary of leaving a thetan with no mass as he feels very unhappy about being only a thought.

R1-15:
Physical Universe Copying

Repair preclear's ability to communicate by having him copy many scenes in the physical universe.

This step is actually the same step as R1-5, but it is run on a wider basis. The thetan is sent around to various parts of the world and the universe and asked to copy things. He copies each one, many times, until he is satisfied that his copy is exact in all respects with the original in the physical universe. When the thetan has accomplished this, he will be able to make things with adequate density and mass.

Now have preclear run each and every Route 2 step until the auditor is convinced that he can do these easily and ably.

INTENSIVE PROCEDURE: Route 2

"If the preclear had any appreciable communication lag, as established in the third step above (ARC Straightwire), all Route 1 steps are omitted and the case is entered into Route 2—the first step of which is R2–16."

ROUTE 2

R 2-16:
Opening Procedure of 8-C

Run preclear through Opening Procedure of 8-C Parts (a) (b) (c), each one until the physical communication lag stabilizes.

The auditor should make sure at first, while running Step (a), that the spots he designates are highly generalized and are not small areas, until the preclear can be directed to small and precise spots.

The entire modus operandi of Opening Procedure of 8-C consists in having the preclear move his body around the room under the auditor's direction until:

a. He finds he is in actual communication with many spots on the surface of things in the room;

b. He can select spots in the room and know that he is selecting them and can communicate with them; and

c. He can select spots and move to them, decide when to touch them and when to let go.

Each one of these steps is done until the auditor is well assured that the preclear has no communication lag.

The auditing commands are as follows:

"Do you see that chair?"
"Go over to it and put your hand on it."

"Now look at that lamp,"
"Now walk over to it and put your hand on it."

This is done with various objects (without specifically designating spots of a more precise nature than an object) until the preclear is very certain that he is in good communication with these objects and the walls and other parts of the room. The auditor can say anything he pleases, or seemingly introduce any significance he wishes to, so long as he hews very closely to the actual thing in this method which makes it work–which is to say, perceiving the physical universe and making contact with it.

Part (a) has been enlarged by the auditor's selecting exact spots:

"Do you see that black mark on the left arm of that chair?"
"All right. Go over to it and put your finger on it,"
"Now take your finger off it."

"Do you see the lower bolt on that light switch?"
"All right. Go over to it and put your finger on it,"
"Take your finger off of it," and so forth, until the preclear has a *uniform perception* of any and all objects in the room including the walls, the floor and the ceiling.

This step can be kept up for a long time. It has an infinity of variations. But it is not the variations which work, it is the making and breaking of communication with the actual designated spots.

IF AT ANY TIME THERE IS ANY DOUBT ABOUT THE PRECLEAR'S CASE, DO THIS STEP, PART (a) UNTIL SATISFIED THAT COMMUNICATION IS GOOD.

CHAPTER FIVE
INTENSIVE PROCEDURE: ROUTE 2

A CASE WHICH WILL NOT OBEY OPENING PROCEDURE 8-C (a) ORDERS WILL ALWAYS PERVERT OR ALTER COMMANDS TO BE PERFORMED WITH LESS SUPERVISION THAN PERCEPTION OF HIS BODY.

Part (b) has these auditing commands:

"Find a spot in this room."

No further designation is necessary for this spot. Spotting procedure gives the preclear determinism of selection.

When the preclear has done so, the auditor says:

"Go over to it and put your finger on it."

When the preclear has done this, the auditor says:

"Now let go of it."

It must be emphasized that the preclear is not to act upon a command until the command is given. And must not let go until told to let go. The preclear is permitted to select spots until such time as all communication lag is flat and until he is freely selecting spots on the walls, objects, chairs, etc., with no specialization whatsoever–which means that his perception of the room has become uniform. Many things turn up in running this procedure, such as the fact that the preclear cannot look at walls, etc.

Part (c) of this procedure is run with these auditing commands:

"Find a spot in the room,"
"Make up your mind when you are going to touch it and then touch it,"
"Make up your mind when you are going to let go of it and let go."

A variation of this process is to have the preclear make up his mind about a spot and then have him change his mind and select another spot.

Rule

The trouble with most cases, and the trouble with any case which is hung up and is not progressing, is that an insufficient quantity of Opening Procedure 8-C has been used by the auditor. This has been found to be an invariable rule.

Preclears will pretend to run commands of a subjective nature, but not run them at all. In other words, the auditor is saying do one thing and the preclear is doing quite another. Thus the process is not actually being used on the preclear. The difficulty in this case is a specific difficulty in communication, where the preclear cannot duplicate. But more important than that, any preclear whose case is hanging up is out of touch with reality and the environment to such an extent that he has begun to do processes on mock-ups rather than on the actual physical universe. It will be discovered that doing processes on mock-ups, such as finding spots in them, finding distances to them and so forth, is productive of no gain and even negative gain. Only processes which directly address the physical universe are found to raise the tone of the preclear. He has to come up to full tolerance of it before he can get out of it. Thus, any case bogging down somewhere in more intricate procedures can be relieved and brought into present time by 8-C.

Caution

The only caution on the part of the auditor is that he must be very precise about giving his orders (and must insist on the preclear being very *certain* that he is actually seeing spots and touching them) and inhibiting the preclear from executing the commands before they are given.

Important

IN PROCESSING PSYCHOTICS AND NEUROTICS OF WHATEVER DEGREE, USE ONLY R2–16, OPENING PROCEDURE 8-C, EACH PART UNTIL THE PERSON IS SURE WHO IS DOING IT. USE ONLY R2–16 UNTIL CASE IS FULLY SANE. USE NO OTHER PROCESS OF ANY KIND.

R 2-17:
Opening Procedure by Duplication

Opening Procedure by Duplication until preclear feels good about it.

Opening Procedure by Duplication is begun only after the preclear has some reality on his environment. Until the preclear's reality on his environment is good, Opening Procedure by Duplication should not be done—for the preclear only turns on an unreality circuit and goes through it mechanically.

The first part of Opening Procedure by Duplication is to get the preclear to examine, communicate with and own (somewhat on the order of Opening Procedure of 8-C) two dissimilar objects.

These objects are then placed several feet apart and at a level so that the preclear can pick them up without bending over, but so that he has to walk between them. Once the auditor is entirely satisfied that the preclear has reality on these objects and can own them, he then begins Opening Procedure by Duplication with the following commands (supposing that one of the objects was a book and the other was an ashtray):

"Go over to the book,"
"Look at it,"
"Pick it up,"
"What is its color?"

At this point the preclear must give an answer.

"What is its temperature?"

Here the preclear must answer again.

"What is its weight?"

Here again the preclear must answer.

"Put it down in exactly the same place."

When the preclear has executed:

"Go over to the ashtray,"
"Look at it,"
"Pick it up,"
"What is its color?"

The preclear says an answer.

"What is its temperature?"

The preclear says his answer.

"What is its weight?"

The preclear says his answer.

"Put it down in exactly the same place."

When the preclear has executed:

"Go over to the book."

And the same words and the same formula are used, over and over, until the preclear has had a sufficient number of hours of Opening Procedure by Duplication to enable him to do it without communication lag, without protest, without Apathy, but only Cheerfulness, each time seeing the items newly. This is a process which is done by the hour. The process is better when done consecutively for so many hours, rather than done an hour apiece each day for several days.

This procedure is the first step of Procedure 30.

R 2-18:
Spotting Spots in Space (and Remedy of Havingness)

Have preclear spot spots in space until he can do it easily, meanwhile remedying his havingness.

As briefly as Spotting Spots in Space and Remedying Havingness can be stated, this is one of the key processes of Scientology and has an infinity of variations.

It is actually two processes stemming from one: While the preclear is still interiorized, Spotting Spots and Remedying Havingness is done by the preclear remaining where he is and simply indicating (by pointing) where the spot is which he is designating. When it is done with the preclear exteriorized, it becomes Change of Space (R1-9).

This process has an infinity of uses and is one of the best processes in rendering an assist. Here, in Intensive Procedure, we use it in its simplest form.

The auditor says:

"Spot a spot in the space of this room."

The preclear does so.

The auditor ascertains whether or not the spot has color, mass, or if it is simply a location in space. A spot should be simply a location in space, it should not have color or mass.

The preclear is asked to locate several such spots in the room. It is important that he walk over to them and that he put his finger on them.

After he has done this for a very short time, it will be discovered that his havingness has decreased markedly. The auditor has him mock-up something which is acceptable to him and has him pull it in on his body until any queasiness or physical upset is remedied.

As soon as this is accomplished, the auditor has him spot more spots in the space of the room.

R 2-19:
Spotting Spots in Room

Have preclear spot spots in room and move body into them and move body out into new spots.

Only when the preclear can do R2-18 comfortably and actually locate locations independent of the objects in the room itself, does the auditor go on to the next phase of this process, which is:

"Locate a spot in the room which you can then move into your body."

When the preclear has done so, the auditor says:

"Move your body over the spot."

When the preclear has done this:

"Move your body off that spot."

It will be discovered that the preclear may find that the spot moves along with his body. One simply wants the location in space and this, of course, does not itself move. Only the body moves.

This is done many times, until the preclear is adept at moving his body over these spots and moving his body off of them. It is understood, of course, that the location simply moves on into the body as the body is moved over it and that the location moves out of the body as the body is moved away from it. In other words, the location is stable, the body is moving. This is done until the preclear is absolutely sure that it is he who is moving his body over such spots. It may be necessary to remedy havingness while this step is being done.

The third part of this step is done as follows:

"Spot a spot in the space of this room,"
"Now move your body around it,"
"Fix your body on that spot,"
"Now change your mind about staying there."

And without the preclear moving off the spot:

"Pick out a new spot,"
"Now move your body around the new spot."

This process has many variations. One can have a preclear move a chronic somatic around such spots, fix it there and unfix it. One can have a preclear find a spot and then appear there and then disappear there, find a new spot and appear there and disappear there. The main thing is to have the preclear spot spots and move his body around them and then move his body off the spot.

R 2-20:
Use of Problems and Solutions

The use of Problems and Solutions is the second step for Procedure 30 and includes the steps already given in R1-11 (Problems and Solutions in Havingness). The auditor asks the preclear:

"What kind of a problem could you be to your mother?"

And when the preclear has found one:

"All right. Can you be that problem?"

And when the preclear has become it:

"Can you see your mother figuring about it?"

And whether the preclear can or not:

"Give me another problem you could be to your mother,"

"Can you be that problem?" etc., until the communication lag is flattened.

Then one asks the same question about father (and about other people in the preclear's life), asking the preclear each time for the problem, then asking him to be the problem, and then asking if it makes other people worry and think about it. Finally, one asks:

"Now what kind of a problem can you be to _____ (preclear's name)?"

And when this has finally been flattened to a communication lag constant, one can assume that he has more or less handled this situation for the moment and he uses exactly the same process on solutions. The same wording as above is used, with the exception that "solution" is substituted for "problem."

When the preclear cannot be a problem, the auditor should find some things that the preclear *can* be with great certainty, have the preclear be those things, then have the preclear be a problem.

When processing an auditor, have him be an auditor and a preclear alternately (physically assuming the proper position for each) until all auditing has been run out and the preclear is no longer waiting to find out what is going to happen.

The auditor should keep in mind the fact that a preclear can be a "no-solution," also that the preclear can be a "no-problem," also that the preclear can be a "solution that needs problems." Many various and strange manifestations take place, but this process very severely uses only the above commands. The process can be continued, and should be, into the commands of R1–11 which take up problems in havingness.

It may occur, if the preclear is a mystic or is interested in the occult, that he offers a peculiar problem in problems. Such a preclear may be looking for the solution to all problems, assuming that only one solution is possible for all problems. If he were to discover this solution, he would of course find himself completely out of problems. Thus his havingness, in terms of problems, would be so enormously reduced that he would discover himself without any interest of any kind. But even if the preclear is not in this category, the process which is given in the following paragraph is definitely indicated in the field of problems. Actually, it is a combination of running significances and handling problems and it is useful for any state of case, except of course those upon whom only Opening Procedure of 8-C may be run.

The complete remedy of problems, of course, takes place when the preclear is convinced that he can create problems at will. Until he is so convinced, he is going to hold on to old problems.

The way to convince him that he can create problems is to have him pick out or pick up an object, have him examine this object until he is sure it is real, then ask him the question:

"What problems could this object be to you?"

Have him begin to name off various problems. It will be discovered at first, as always in the handling of significances, that he begins to drain the object itself of the problems which are inherent in the object. And then, he will eventually begin to invent problems. The problem should be run until the preclear is convinced that he can create problems at will. Many objects can be used, rather than just one, if it is discovered that the preclear's attention is fixing too strongly upon the object.

R 2-21:
Granting of Beingness
(Reference: Axiom 28)

Granting of Beingness (life) to something.

The preclear is as well as he can grant life to things, an action which involves the creation of energy. The basic granting of beingness is the thetan duplicating himself as another thinking being.

In the mechanics of the Granting of Beingness, we have "orientation-point" and the "symbol."

An "orientation-point" is that point in relation to which others have location. It is also that point from which the space containing the locations is being created. In the orientation-point we have our basic definition of space: "Space is a viewpoint of dimension."

Dependent upon the orientation-point for its location, and to some degree for its life, is the "symbol." A symbol is an object which has mass, meaning and mobility. A symbol locates itself, if it does so at all, by the orientation-point. It regards the orientation-point as a *continual* source-point and itself as a *continual* receipt-point of that source-point.

So long as one can create life, he more or less considers himself an orientation-point. And as soon as he is convinced he cannot create life in any degree, he becomes to that degree a symbol.

The Granting of Beingness is a complexity of the Communication Formula. In that we have broadly added *space*, rather than linear *distance*, and have introduced the idea of a *continuing* orientation-point and a *continuing* symbol, the *velocity* of the Communication Formula is expanded to *continuing velocities* and we have entered directly from the Communication Formula into our first understanding of *time* and, therefore, *Survival*. It is the symbol which is surviving in minute gradients of time and the orientation-point which is timeless, but which determines the time frame of that space.

As a practical example, most preclears consider the childhood home an orientation-point and themselves a symbol of that orientation-point. Where a preclear has lost too many orientation-points successively, he begins to consider himself a symbol of a symbol. The concept in some religions of God being everywhere and every place at the same time is a direct and overt effort to loose the worshipper by taking from him a finite position for his orientation-point.

The processing of the Granting of Beingness is more complex and therefore less effective than using the Communication Formula in its simpler form. It is well within the attention of an auditor and the problems involving it should to some degree be resolved with the preclear. The preclear has many times sought to give life to something, such as a dying ally or pet or enterprise, and has failed to bring it to life. Resultingly, he has become convinced that he cannot grant life. But senior to this granting of life is the mechanical matter of orientation-point and symbol. A multitude of processes can be applied with profit to this subject.

One of the simplest would be to demand of the preclear:

"Where are you from?"

And then, continue to repeat this question on and on and on, no matter what answer the preclear gave, until the preclear replies that he is from right where he is.

At which time, the auditor changes the question to:

"Where is that?"

And to any answer the preclear gives, again asks:

"Where is that?" until the preclear ceases to locate himself by his environment, and then ceases to locate himself by his body and by himself, and comes to the realization that he is exactly where he says he is and no other place. The Other-determinism to Self-determinism course is marked by the fact that he is first nowhere, then where old orientation-points and present locations tell him he is, and then where his body tells him he is, and then where he seems to be because he can see certain things, to the final realization that he is where he is by postulate and by that alone. This will exteriorize a preclear if continued long enough.

All other processes are only a covert level of this process. He can be made to spot spots which he has considered orientation-points, such as the childhood home, and then remedy havingness. He can be asked, *"Why* (the environment) *is there?"* and for every answer, simply ask again, *"Why* (what he is looking at) *is there?"* Or this can be run as the third step of Procedure 30, which is what it is.

As the third step of Procedure 30, Granting of Beingness is run in this fashion:

"Who would grant beingness to _____?" and in the blank may be placed psychosomatics, letters, cats, dogs, kings and coal heavers, or anything the auditor might think of, each time until the preclear replies without communication lag.

The key question would be:

"Who would it be all right to have grant some beingness?"

The person the preclear will name will be the person the preclear has most recently depended upon thoroughly as a symbol in lieu of an orientation-point.

This is continued with:

"What else would it be all right for _____ (the person he has named) *to grant beingness to?"*

With this last question we are resolving the "only one" complex. The preclear has gotten into a state, ordinarily, where he is the only one who can grant beingness. But he has so long restrained other people from granting life to things that he himself will no longer grant any life to things. The preclear is engaged in some kind of a giddy contest whereby nobody *else* can grant beingness to things, but he can grant beingness to *them*. The resolution of this will mean a considerable increase in case.

There is an additional question:

"Who are you eating for?" and

"Who are you (doing other things) *for?"* item by item, which processed continuously will eventually bring the preclear into certain changes of consideration.

(This last technique is a part of one called "Swizzle-Stick.")

An additional process is to simply have the preclear say to himself:

"I am here," and each time establish for himself the fact that he is.

This is done over and over without further variation.

A part of the Granting of Beingness is having symbols *"out there moving around for you."* An individual who cannot be an orientation-point and who cannot therefore grant beingness, does not have symbols. Thus he cannot predict objects even in the immediate environment. A variation is to have him look at various objects and the walls of the room and *"predict that they will be there in ten seconds,"* then to have him count off the ten seconds and find out whether or not they are there.

Notes

A basic difficulty in auditing and in the case of any preclear lies in the preclear's unwillingness to permit anyone else to grant beingness, particularly the auditor. Where a preclear is making no progress, he is proving that *"they* could grant only death." This is far below even *"I* grant death." This condition can be remedied in R2–21 by improving the preclear's considerations of the giving of life and death, as follows:

"Name some beings you would permit to grant life,"
"Name some beings you would permit to grant death."

"Name some things to which you could grant life,"
"Name some things to which you could grant death."

This should be run until all communication lag is flattened. Then the preclear will improve further.

Many a preclear does something, then sits back to see if anything happened. This, when a severe condition (the "observer," where the preclear cannot *be* anything, cannot occupy a source-point or receipt-point), can be remedied by having the preclear touch a part of his body or the room with his finger and then stand back to see if anything happened. His communication lags can be long on this.

The commands are:

"Touch your nose,"
"Now let go and see if anything happens."

This must be done, to be effective, for some time. Its goal as a process is to wipe out fear of consequences.

For a preclear who has suffered much loss, the auditor can have the preclear place an object (matches, a handkerchief or anything *the preclear owns*) out in front of the preclear, then have the preclear let go of it, sit back and wait for it to come to him (which it won't, of course, without volition on the part of the preclear). Then he repeats the action, waiting for the object to go away from him. The communication lag (of recognition of the process) and the somatics can be severe. The waiting should be in terms of many minutes each time.

R 2-22:
Spanning Attention

Scarcity of attention is manifested on a gradient scale from the top to the bottom on the Chart of Human Evaluation. An individual has so many times excused his failure to direct attention when it was required, by saying that he had not enough attention, that eventually things which sought to seize his attention "distract him." This brings on a certain franticness. Scarcity of attention is the reason why a preclear cannot look at past engrams and present time, at the same time, and be in present time. His attention gets caught or trapped in the past.

The scarcity of attention can be directly remedied by having the preclear put his attention on one object until it is thoroughly real to him, then on another object until it is thoroughly real to him, and then put his attention on both objects until they are thoroughly real to him, then his attention on a third object until it is thoroughly real to him, and then his attention on all three objects until they are completely real to him.

The caution which must be taken is that one does not fixate his attention *on* the objects, but keeps him answering questions *concerning* the objects.

In all Attention processes, a hypnotic condition takes place only when the preclear is unable to comment or respond while his attention is closely fixed upon one object. The body gives the thetan scarcity of attention, and therefore a sort of hypnotic trance, by having only one direction of attention, i.e., through the eyes. A thetan, seeing on a 360-degree periphery, when interiorizing into the head finds himself looking in only one direction. This is sufficient to fixate him.

Exteriorization by Attention is possible simply by directing the preclear's attention to wider and wider spheres. The technique Spanning of Attention is done with the following commands.

The auditor puts a match down in front of the preclear:

"Now look at that match,"
"Is it real to you?"

The auditor puts down another match close to the first match:

"Now look at the second match,"
"Is that real to you?" and then works with such questions until both the first and second match are real.

The auditor then has him put his attention on both matches at once to establish whether or not they are both real at once. Then he has him look at the first match, the second match and then both matches, in that order, until the preclear can see both matches as entirely real.

A third match is now put down, the auditor saying:

"Now put your attention on this third match,"
"Is it real to you?"

When reality on the third match is established, the auditor has the preclear see the first two matches at once, then the second and third match at once, until these two groups (as groups) are real, and then has the preclear look at all three matches until they are real.

WITH THIS PROCESS THE PRECLEAR'S ATTENTION IS NOT PERMITTED TO LINGER ON ANY ONE OBJECT FOR MORE THAN A FEW SECONDS. CONTINUOUS STARING AT THE OBJECT WILL NOT PRODUCE ANY FURTHER RESULT THAN BOIL-OFF.

CHAPTER FIVE
INTENSIVE PROCEDURE: ROUTE 2

This process is continued until the preclear can do this: See with entire reality ten matches simultaneously laid out in front of him.

Now the auditor begins by taking an object in the room, such as a chair, has the preclear examine that until it is entirely real. Then takes another chair in the room and establishes its reality with the preclear. Then he works on the first and second chairs and on both, until the preclear can see both chairs with complete reality. Then a third chair is picked out and reality is established on this. And then reality is established on the first and second chair. And the second and third chair. And then on all three chairs.

This is done until all the objects in the room are included in the reality of the preclear, at which time he will very probably be exteriorized.

R 2-23:
Attention by Duplication

Two similar objects, preferably black and not shiny, are placed before the preclear in such a way that they are more or less even with his level gaze and making, with each other and the preclear's space, a 90-degree angle so that the preclear has to turn at least 45 degrees out of his normal line of sight in order to put his attention on either one of them.

The preclear's attention is directed to Object One, on the right. And then he is asked to put his attention on Object Two, on the left:

"Put your attention on the right-hand object,"
"Put your attention on the left-hand object."

These two commands are then given consecutively many, many times, each time the auditor waiting for the preclear's execution of the command before giving the next command. The process can be done with only these two commands – for the preclear is not asked to fix his attention on either object, he is only asked to look at these two objects. If there is any question about the preclear's general reality, this should be remedied by Opening Procedure of 8-C (R2-16). Further, the preclear, prior to the process, no matter what his reality may be, should be put into communication with the two objects.

This process is often found to be more workable by having the preclear describe the objects he is looking at each time he looks at them. This keeps the preclear outflowing. And where the preclear begins to demonstrate hypnotic manifestations, the step of making him describe each object should be used.

The commands would be:

"Now put your attention on Object One."

The preclear executes.

"Tell me about it."

The preclear does so.

"Now put your attention on Object Two."

The preclear does so.

"Tell me about it."

"Put your attention on Object One," and so forth, over and over.

This process should be run as long as it produces perception changes in the preclear. Attention by Duplication can be applied to any sense perception. Here we have the example of it applied to *sight*. This step should also apply to Attention by Duplication by *hearing*. If there is a noise in the room, preferably a monotonous one such as a motor or fan or even a record of a monotonous voice (but not the radio), the auditor commands the preclear:

"Listen to that _____," naming the source of sound.

And when the preclear has done so for a moment:

"Now put your attention on the silence present in the room."

"Now on the _____," again naming the source of sound.
"Now on the silence," back and forth, for a considerable length of time.

A second step, both in Attention by Duplication for sight and Attention by Duplication for hearing, is accomplished by adding in the command:

"Now take your attention off _____," before the next command, to put his attention *on* something, is given.

In this wise the commands would be (for Attention by sight):

"Put your attention on Object One."

And when the preclear has complied:

"Now take your attention off of Object One."

And when the preclear has complied:

"Now put your attention on Object Two."

And when the preclear has complied:

"Now take your attention off of Object Two," and so on, back and forth between the two objects.

An additional step can be run, having the preclear *decide* when to take his attention off the objects. This is similar to the pattern of Opening Procedure of 8-C, with the addition that it is run by monotonous duplication of the process and the objects.

R2-24:
Exteriorization by Distance, extroverted and introverted alternately

The simplest form of Exteriorization by Distance is accomplished simply by having the preclear sit still and spot various objects in the room without calling his attention to any distance involved. This would be done with this one command and with no further qualification as to what the preclear puts his attention on:

"Find another spot in this room."

This can be run for hours with benefit. All other Exteriorization by Distance processes are simply complications of this basic process.

The next most used Exteriorization by Distance process uses three spots in the body alternately with three spots in the room, on these commands:

"Find three spots in your body."

And when the preclear signifies that he has:

"Now find three spots in the room."

And when the preclear signifies that he has:

"Find three spots in your body."

And when the preclear signifies that he has:

"Now find three spots in the room."

This is done over and over without any change of command.

This process is commonly run on groups. Spotting one spot at a time, not designating whether it is in space or on objects, may also be run on groups as above. When a preclear's reality on Exteriorization by Distance is very poor, the simpler forms of this process as above should be used.

The commands of Exteriorization by Distance are as follows:

"What distance could you tolerate to your right foot?"

"What distance could you tolerate to your left foot?"

"What distance could you tolerate to your genitals?"

"What distance could you tolerate to your stomach?"

"What distance could you tolerate to your rectum?"

"What distance could you tolerate to your back?"

"What distance could you tolerate to your right hand?"

"What distance could you tolerate to your left hand?"

"What distance could you tolerate to your right eye?"

"What distance could you tolerate to your left eye?"

"What distance could you tolerate to your mouth?"

And then consecutively:

"What distance could your right foot tolerate to a thetan?"

"What distance could your left foot tolerate to a thetan?"

"What distance could your genitals tolerate to a thetan?"

"What distance could your stomach tolerate to a thetan?"

"What distance could your rectum tolerate to a thetan?"

"What distance could your right hand tolerate to a thetan?"

"What distance could your left hand tolerate to a thetan?"

"What distance could your right eye tolerate to a thetan?"

"What distance could your left eye tolerate to a thetan?"

"What distance could your mouth tolerate to a thetan?"

"What distance could your back tolerate to a thetan?"

This complete series on the body is called the "introverted" part of the process and is immediately followed by these commands:

"What distance could you tolerate to the front wall?"

"What distance could you tolerate to the right wall?"

"What distance could you tolerate to the left wall?"

"What distance could you tolerate to the back wall?"

"What distance could you tolerate to the floor?"

"What distance could you tolerate to the ceiling?"

"What distance could you tolerate to your chair?"

And this is followed by:

"What distance could the front wall tolerate to a thetan?"

"What distance could the right wall tolerate to a thetan?"

"What distance could the left wall tolerate to a thetan?"

"What distance could the back wall tolerate to a thetan?"

"What distance could the floor tolerate to a thetan?"

"What distance could the ceiling tolerate to a thetan?"

"What distance could your chair tolerate to a thetan?"

And this is followed by the first of the series on the body:

"What distance could you tolerate to your right foot?" and so forth, around and around on these commands.

Important

THE PRECLEAR MUST NOT BE PERMITTED TO USE MOCK-UPS IN THE MATTER OF WHAT DISTANCE THE PARTS OF THE BODY OR THE ROOM COULD TOLERATE TO A THETAN. THE AUDITOR WANTS THE ACTUAL PARTS OF THE BODY RIGHT WHERE THEY ARE AND THEIR TOLERANCE TO THE THETAN IN EACH CASE. AND HE WANTS THE PARTS OF THE ROOM RIGHT WHERE THEY ARE AND THEIR DISTANCE TO THE THETAN. THIS PROCESS IS NOT TO BE DONE BY MOCK-UPS. BUT IF MOCK-UPS APPEAR IN THE MATTER OF WHAT DISTANCE THE THETAN CAN TOLERATE TO THE PARTS OF THE BODY OR ROOM, THEY ARE ALLOWABLE (BUT ARE *NOT* ENCOURAGED). IF MOCK-UPS ARE USED IN THE MATTER OF DISTANCE OF THE OBJECTS TO THE THETAN, THE REALITY OF THE PRECLEAR WILL DECREASE MARKEDLY. THE PRECLEAR IS NOT BEING EXTERIORIZED FROM MOCK-UPS, HE IS BEING EXTERIORIZED FROM ACTUAL PHYSICAL UNIVERSE OBJECTS.

R 2-25:
Viewpoint and Viewpoint ARC Straightwire

Viewpoint and Viewpoint ARC Straightwire, in a brief form, has the following commands:

"Give me some things which it would be comfortable for you to look at."

And when the communication lag on this is flattened:

"Give me some emotions it would be all right for you to look at."
"Give me some efforts it would be all right for you to look at."

These are the chief concerns of the auditor in this process. The auditor must make sure that the preclear is absolutely certain he is *comfortable* in viewing such objects. The process fails when the auditor is incapable of pressing the preclear until this certainty is attained.

Viewpoint ARC Straightwire then follows:

"Who would it be all right for you to like?"

And, as in any of these questions, when the communication lag has been flattened by repeated use of the first question:

"Who would it be all right for you to agree with?"

"Who would it be all right for you to communicate with?"

"Who would it be all right to have like you?"

"Who would it be all right to have agree with you?"

"Who would it be all right to have communicate with you?"

The basic formula and goal of this process is to increase the preclear's ability to tolerate views. The auditor is trying to do two things: He is trying to improve the *tolerance* and *comfort* of the preclear in viewing and experiencing Knowingness, Lookingness, Emotingness, Effortingness, Thinkingness, Symbolizingness, Eatingness, Sexingness and Mystery.

R 2-26:
Remedy of Laughter

The earliest known psychotherapy consisted of getting a patient to laugh. Laughter is rejection. A preclear being continually inflowed upon by the physical universe, at length may find it difficult to reject anything. Getting him to reject something could be made an auditing goal. The best manifestation of this is laughter. Laughter includes both surprise and rejection. The individual is surprised into rejecting. In order to laugh, he must have laid aside some of his ability to predict. An individual who is serious has laid aside so much of his ability to predict that he now cannot be surprised into rejection. The anatomy of mystery consists of, in this order, unpredictability, confusion and chaos – covered up because it cannot be tolerated. Therefore, this is also the anatomy of problems. Problems always begin with an unpredictability, deteriorate into a confusion and then, if still unsolved, become a mystery which is massed confusion. It will be observed that as a person falls further and further away from the ability to laugh, he becomes more and more confused until at last he sees no points in any jokes. He sees only embarrassment when confronted by laughter and the whole action of laughter itself escapes him. The ability to laugh is rehabilitated in general by Scientology, as it advances the ability of the preclear to know – which is to say, *predict.*

The Remedy of Laughter could be entered simply by having the individual predict that a wall would be there in ten seconds, count off ten seconds on his watch and then ascertain with thoroughness that the wall is still there, to establish if the wall is there, then to predict that it will be there in ten seconds, then to count off ten seconds on his watch and ascertain if the wall is still there.

By thus bringing solid objects into the realm of prediction, an individual at length comes to a point where he can predict very slowly moving objects. A cheap train and track could be set up for this purpose and the preclear could be led to predict with accuracy the position of engines on the small circular track. However, the preclear can be made to watch automobiles on the street—a process which serves just as well with no such equipment.

The preclear would then be led to predict the positions of his own body, first by predicting that it was going to be in a certain spot, then moving it there and seeing whether or not it had arrived at that spot. He would then be brought to swing his arm in a circle, predict that it would swing faster and swing it faster.

And thus, being led to predict the motion of his body with these simplicities, he could be exercised in making his body go tense and go limp by his command, until he was thoroughly certain that he could both predict the tension or relaxation by doing it.

Then he could be led to predict the positions of people walking on the street, until he felt some security in predicting without exercising physical control.

By thus remedying his ability to predict, one brings the preclear up into a tolerance of motion. He is then led to put his attention on one moving object, then on two moving objects at once, and so forth, using the processes of Spanning Attention on moving objects.

A direct mock-up process can be applied to the Remedy of Laughter by having the preclear mock-up, alternately, himself and others laughing. Or, by having him mock-up an acceptable level of amusement and remedy his havingness with it, until he can have people laughing very broadly in his mock-ups.

EXTERIOR OT ABILITY

here is the panoramic view of Scientology complete. Having codified the subject of Scientology in *The Creation of Human Ability*, Ron then delivered a series of half-hour lectures to specifically accompany a full study of the book.

From the *essentials* that underlie the technology: *The Axioms, Conditions of Existence* and *Considerations and Mechanics*, to the processes of *Intensive Procedure*, including twelve lectures describing one-by-one the thetan exterior processes of *Route 1*—it's all covered in full, providing a conceptual understanding of the *science of knowledge* and *native state OT ability.*

Listened to in conjunction with study of the book, provides a depth of understanding not previously possible.

Here then are the bedrock principles upon which everything in Scientology rests, including the embracive statement of the religion and its heritage—*Scientology, Its General Background*. Hence, this is the watershed lecture series on Scientology itself, and the axiomatic foundation for all future research.

On compact disc, complete with transcripts, glossary, index and guide.

THE
Phoenix Lectures
BY
L. Ron Hubbard

BUSINESS REPLY MAIL

FIRST CLASS MAIL   PERMIT NO. 62688   LOS ANGELES, CA

POSTAGE WILL BE PAID BY ADDRESSEE

Bridge

PUBLICATIONS, INC.

4751 Fountain Avenue
Los Angeles CA 90029

The preclear can also be made simply to stand up and start laughing. He at first will demand to have something to laugh at, but at length will be able to laugh without reason. The goal of the process is contained in the last line—to regain the ability to laugh without reason.

In this Intensive Procedure, only two steps are employed to Remedy Laughter. The first consists of these commands:

"Be completely certain that that wall is there."

And when the preclear has become, with considerable conversation, completely certain that the wall is there, touching it, pushing against it and so forth, the auditor then says:

"Sit down,"
"Take this (your) watch,"
"Now predict that the wall will be there ten seconds from now,"
"Have you done so?"
"All right. Wait ten seconds by your watch."

And when this is done:

"Is the wall still there?"

And when the preclear has answered:

"Now make absolutely certain the wall is there."

And the preclear does so by touching it, pushing at it, kicking it:

"Now make very sure that the wall is there."

And when the preclear very vigorously has done so:

"Now predict that it will be there in ten seconds."

And when the preclear has done so, the remainder of the commands are given and this is repeated over and over.

Then, the second part of Intensive Procedure's process of Laughter, but only after the preclear has experienced considerable relief and is absolutely sure that he can predict that all parts of the room will be there, not only in ten seconds, but in an hour (although no such timing is used and only ten seconds of time is employed):

"Start laughing."

And no matter what the preclear says thereafter, or what arguments he advances, or how many things he asks about, or how many reasons he wants or gives, the auditor merely says (adding words that urge the preclear):

"Start laughing."

And when the preclear at length does so, no matter how halfheartedly:

"Keep on laughing."

The two commands which are used, in addition to words necessary to urge the preclear without giving the preclear any reason whatsoever, are:

"Start laughing," and
"Keep on laughing."

This process is then done until the preclear can actually enjoy a laugh without any reason whatsoever, without believing that laughing without reason is insane, without feeling self-conscious about laughing and without needing any boost from the auditor. The auditor, in this second part, need take no pains to agree with the preclear by laughing, he need not chuckle or smile, nor need he even particularly act seriously. His laughter is not needed or used in the process. An auditor can be as serious as he pleases and, indeed, if he wishes to do so, can be even more serious than is usual when running this second step of R2-26.

In earlier Scientology, it was learned that serious preclears would often recover considerable ground simply when they were made to do things without any reason whatsoever. This achievement is much greater when they are made to laugh without any reason.

R 2-27:
Resolve Dangerousness of Environment, Cause and Effect

Resolving the dangerousness of the environment could be done in many ways, but by experience it should not be done by deleting various things which could be dangerous (by the use of mock-ups). If there is any trouble with the preclear, it is that the environment is insufficiently dangerous and so does not produce sufficient amusement.

The physical body was built in the time when escapes from death by wild animals, by falling, were routine. It was built in an operating climate of great hazard over a period of many millions of years. It requires about three escapes from sudden death, daily, to stay in present time. Many of the preclears being audited in Scientology are being audited simply to experience a new adventure. However, it can be said with some truth, and was said in *Excalibur* in 1938, that a man is as sane as he is dangerous to the environment. What occurs is that the environment becomes dangerous to the man and the man cannot be dangerous to the environment. And his answer to this is immobility and general deterioration.

The basic remedy of this condition consists of getting a living thing (a pet, a child, a sick person) to reach out toward one's hand. At that moment, without moving so suddenly that the living being will be startled, the person doing the process would withdraw his hand. The auditor would then advance, again to be driven away, over and over. And it would be observed that the living being would strike out with more and more enthusiasm and would recover considerable sanity. This, of course, is done on a gradient scale.

118

CHAPTER FIVE
INTENSIVE PROCEDURE: ROUTE 2

While an auditor should know and use this basic process in assists (or when processing animals, very small children or people who are extremely ill), the remedy which is used in Intensive Procedure is Cause and Effect. Parts of the body can be used in this process, the whole body or the thetan. But the auditor must be specific about what he is addressing.

The basic commands are:

"What are you willing to cause?"

And when the preclear has answered this and the communication lag on the question has been flattened:

"What are you willing to be the effect of?"

And when the communication lag has been flattened by the repeated use of this question:

"What are you willing to cause?"

And so forth, using just these commands.

One can additionally apply this, particularly when the preclear has a psychosomatic illness, to a limb or organ of the body as an assist. But in Intensive Procedure, the most permissive of these questions (as given) is used.

R 2-28:
Nothing-Something

Nothing-Something is run by asking:

"What distance wouldn't you mind making nothing of?"

And when there is no communication lag on this:

"What distance wouldn't you mind making something of (making longer)?"

The process is completed by making certain the preclear can tolerate many nothingnesses and many somethingnesses with complete comfort.

If the preclear found R2-24 (Exteriorization by Distance) unreal or did it peculiarly, use R2-28 immediately, then R1-10 (Occupying the Same Space), then R2-24.

The goal of this process is the toleration of nothingnesses and somethingnesses by the thetan.

R 2-29:
Time Tolerance

This uses the *velocity* factor of the Communication Formula.

a. Ask the preclear:

"How much time can you tolerate between yourself and (the door), (the window), (etc.)*?"*

Then make him "walk it out" in the interval of time he named. Have him do this until, without coaching, he can tolerate a *very, very* slow velocity or a very fast one.

b. Then use this command:

"Start lying about your past."

And when he finally does:

"Keep on lying about your past," until he can lie with complete comfort about all phases of his past.

This is a ten-star process.

c. Then use this:

"What is the significance of your past?"

And keep on asking the question, no matter what the preclear says, until his past is not important.

Then:

"What is the significance of your future?" (or *goals*, if that communicates better, *"What are your goals in your future?"*) and keep on asking it until the preclear feels free to live an unplanned life.

Note

The present time problem is best resolved by remedying the havingness of the preclear on the subject or people involved in the problem. Have him mock these up in acceptable form and accept many, then in rejectable form and reject many, until his "acceptance level" and "rejection level" are the same.

R2-30:
Position by Security (SOP 8-D)

Used in Intensive Procedure for only two purposes – to resolve a present time association with a person (PT problem) or to resolve "Body Recruitment" of the thetan by some part of the body, such as teeth, eyes, stomach, etc.

In the matter of a present time problem, using the name of the person involved with the preclear:

"Where would _____ be safe?" and
"Where would _____ find you safe?" as the sole commands, actually having the preclear spot the locations in the MEST universe.

In the matter of fixation on teeth, etc.:

"Where would _____ be safe?"
"Where would _____ find you safe?"

Body Recruitment is suspected whenever a preclear cannot exteriorize after a few hours of processing. The part of the body he is most anxious about is then run as responsible for dragging "in" the thetan.

Another method of running this problem is a variation of Description Processing (R2-34). The command is:

"How close does your _____ seem to you now?"

This is the only command employed. Body parts such as head, genitals, teeth or the body itself are used in the place of the blank.

R 2-31:
Beingness Processing

The cardinal rule where mental or physical compulsions are concerned follows:

WHATEVER THE THETAN IS DOING OBSESSIVELY OR COMPULSIVELY, HAVE HIM DO IT ON A SELF-DETERMINED BASIS.

This applies to machines, habits, twitches, etc.

There is a Gradient Scale of Exteriorization which could be described as follows:

First, the thetan without contact with a universe;

Then, a thetan in full contact with a universe;

Then, a thetan in contact with part of a universe, who considers the remainder of the universe barred to him;

Then, a thetan in a universe without any contact with any part of the universe;

Then, a thetan unknowingly in contact with a large part of a universe.

The first condition would be a true static. The last condition is called, colloquially, in Scientology "buttered all over the universe."

As it is with a universe, such as the physical universe, so it is with physical bodies. The thetan, who has already gone through the cycle on the universe itself, may be in contact with a physical body in the same order:

At first, he would be without association with a physical body;

Then, with occasional contact with bodies;

Then, with a fixed contact on one body but exteriorized;

Then, interiorized into a body but easy to exteriorize;

Then, in contact with and interiorized into a body, but withdrawn from the various parts of the body;

Then, obsessively "buttered all through the body";

Then, obsessively and unknowingly drawn down to some small portion of the body, and so forth.

This is the gradient scale which includes inversion and then inversion of the inversion. The auditor will discover preclears are very variable in the matter of exteriorization. Some preclears, even when they have a dark field, exteriorize rather easily. Others, after a great deal of work, are still found to be difficult to exteriorize. The matter of exteriorization is the matter of which level of inversion the preclear is in.

One of the more difficult levels to work is so inverted that he thinks that a thetan is running him. In other words, here is a thetan functioning in a body, and actually running it through various covert communication lines, who yet believes he is a body to such an extent that he considers himself or any life around him to be some other being. When discussing the matter of a thetan, this preclear is likely to tell the auditor, "I'm over there." This is about the only signal the auditor gets from such a case which tells him that the preclear is being a body and considers that he is being run by another thetan.

Very often an auditor will "exteriorize" such a person, he thinks, only to have the preclear say, "I'm over there." A thetan who knows he is a thetan is always "here" and never "there."

The diagnostic manifestation, however, which the auditor first encounters in any case where he is having difficulty with exteriorization, is contained in *beingness*. Those on lower levels of inversion are having a great deal of difficulty being anything. Such people are below the level of being a body. Therefore it would be far upscale for this person to be able to be a body with certainty. A person who cannot exteriorize easily must be brought up to the level where he can *be* a body before he can then be exteriorized *from* the body. In other words, an auditor exteriorizing anyone has to follow this gradient scale of contact. One of the easy ways to follow such a scale is Beingness Processing. Oddly enough, Beingness Processing is an excellent exteriorization tool. And I say "oddly enough" because, in one sense, Beingness Processing is an Alter-isness process. When a case is extremely inverted, it is necessary to get the case up to a level where it can identify itself with *something*. Beingness is essentially an identification of self with an object. The commands used in Beingness Processing should begin with the environment and the vicinity of the preclear. One has the preclear look around the auditing room and select an object, let us say a chair.

The auditor does this by saying:

"Look around the room and discover some object which you don't mind being present."

Remember, always, that when an auditor asks a question, that question has to be answered by the preclear. It is the auditor's bad luck if he asks a question which introduces an enormously long communication lag in the preclear. The preclear must still answer the question.

At this question, then:

"Discover something you don't mind being present," it is necessary that the preclear actually locate something, even if a dust mote.

The auditor then asks the preclear to:

"Locate something else you don't mind being present."

And when all communication lag is gone from this level of process, the auditor then picks out an object which the preclear was comfortable about and says:

"Now see this (chair) *here?"*

"All right. What else wouldn't you mind this (chair) *being?"*

And then, as the preclear answers this and using this same object, the auditor continues to ask the same question until all communication lag is gone from the question:

"What else wouldn't you mind this (chair) *being?"*

The auditor then selects other objects in the area and uses the same question on them:

"What wouldn't you mind this (couch) *being?"*

"What else wouldn't you mind this (couch) *being?"*

When the preclear is perfectly willing to have anything in the room be a large number of things, including the walls, the ceiling and the floor, the auditor asks:

"Now what wouldn't you mind your body being?"

And whatever the preclear answers:

"And now what else wouldn't you mind your body being?"

Finally, when the preclear is able to do all the foregoing in Beingness Processing, the auditor commands him:

"Now let's find something you wouldn't mind being."

And as this is the question for which the auditor has been working, he uses this question for a very long period of time, asking over and over:

"What else wouldn't you mind being?"

It will be discovered in working Beingness Processing that the entire mechanism of "winning valences" occurs. Here, for instance, is a thetan who is caught in a theta trap. After a while, he will consider that the trap itself is surviving–which is to say, that the motions of the trap have themselves set the thetan into motion so that he now thinks of himself totally as a trap. (This is how anybody gets to be anything–by getting set into motion by the vibrations in his vicinity.) At first the thetan is willing to be the trap. But after a while, if asked to be the trap and then asked to be the thetan (and this is *not* a process), the most terrible Apathy will be found to intervene between the two steps. The thetan, while fairly comfortable being the trap, on beginning to recover some of his own identity will be found to be at a point on the Tone Scale so low as to contain an unbearable and agonizing Apathy. Beingness Processing recovers the various valences which the thetan is trying to avoid.

As a practical example in life, we find a housewife who is incapable of keeping house. Although intelligent and able in most things, we find she cannot sweep, make beds or even shop for the house. We discover that her mother was an excellent housekeeper, an excellent cook and could shop very well. If this is the case, then we would also discover that the one person in this world our preclear does not want to be is her mother.

In other words, by being unable to be her mother, she is also unable to be all those things which her mother could do or be. In other words, the matter of valences is also a matter of "packages of abilities," and where an individual is unable to be something which has certain definite abilities, he also cannot achieve those abilities. And this, in itself, is the heart of disability.

In running Beingness Processing, it will be discovered that the imagination of the preclear revives to a marked extent. This is a process which requires a skilled auditor, a patient auditor, and one who is willing to level every communication lag he encounters by repeating the same question over and over, each time waiting to receive a definite answer. It is not a process which one starts and leaves uncompleted.

R 2-32:
Assignment of Attributes

The forerunner of this process was Significance Processing. Significance Processing was done as follows: One had the preclear take some picture or object and assign innumerable significances to it.

This is an excellent process, even now, for those who are always looking for deeper significances in everything. It will be discovered that the preclear with whom one is having difficulty cannot duplicate. He cannot duplicate because he has to make everything more complicated. Everything which is given to him has to be given a deeper significance.

However, Significance Processing is quite limited in its effects upon the preclear and it is not to be compared with Opening Procedure of 8-C. Where one has a case who is introducing deep significances into everything, who is pondering and philosophizing during processing, one will discover that Significance Processing is far too heavy for the case. Opening Procedure of 8-C is all that is indicated for this case, for many hours. And this should be followed by Opening Procedure by Duplication, for many more hours.

The Assignment of Attributes is a process which uses the principle:

WHATEVER THE THETAN IS DOING OBSESSIVELY OR COMPULSIVELY, HAVE HIM DO IT ON A SELF-DETERMINED BASIS.

Here we have the entire environment assigning meanings and attributes to the preclear. It seldom occurs to the preclear to assign attributes to himself. Throughout life he has been insulted, made nothing of or complimented, and he has begun to depend upon Other-determined assignment of attributes.

The commands of this process are as follows:

"Assign some attributes to other people."

Now, if at this stage the preclear wants to know what an attribute is, the auditor can tell him, "a quality, characteristic or ability, factual, insulting or flattering." The auditor continues with this command for some time and then asks:

"Now have some people assign some attributes to you," and *"Have them assign you some more attributes."*

Then:

"Have them assign you some more attributes," and *"Have them assign you some more attributes."*

One then returns to the first command:

"Assign some attributes to other people," and so forth.

Finally, when the preclear is able to do this easily, the auditor goes to this step of the process:

"Now assign your body some attributes," and continues to have the preclear assign to his body attributes.

Preclears have exteriorized on this process.

The preclear uses insults, compliments, abilities, skills and various states of beingness, and will be found to be coming up the Tone Scale with the attributes he is assigning on each stage of this process.

The auditor should not overlook the fact that this process can be very widely used with the same type of command on any of the dynamics or on the Know to Mystery Scale, such as:

"Assign some attributes to mystery,"

"Assign some attributes to sex,"

"Assign some attributes to women,"

"Assign some attributes to spirits," using each question repetitively, until such time as all communication lag is gone in the preclear on this process.

R 2-33:
Perfect Duplication

Had this process existed in 1950, there would have been no difficulty in Dianetics. For in the *perfect duplicate,* we find how to vanquish an engram. All one needs to do is to make a perfect duplicate of the engram and then make a perfect duplicate of having perfectly duplicated the engram in present time, and the engram is gone. This would also apply to ridges or any other energy manifestation. It is not the purpose of the Scientologist, today, to process engrams or to use this particular process. And it is only called to his attention that by making a perfect duplicate of an engram, the engram disappears entirely except for the action of making the perfect duplicate in present time. But when this is perfectly duplicated, then the engram really is gone. Engrams, or whole chains of engrams, can be vanquished in a few seconds by Perfect Duplication. Thus it may be seen that the theory of a perfect duplicate is a very valuable one.

There are two kinds of duplicates. The word "duplicate" is used, rather sloppily, to indicate a *copy.* However, a copy is not a complete duplicate. A copy is a facsimile and will remain in suspension as such.

A PERFECT DUPLICATE IS ONE WHICH IS MADE IN THE SAME TIME, IN THE SAME SPACE, WITH THE SAME ENERGIES AS THE ORIGINAL.

Now, if you have not had this explained thoroughly in class, you may discover it eluding you slightly. So let us take a good solid look at this, for it means exactly what it says: A perfect duplicate is one which exists in the same instant of time, in the same place and has the same mass (or particles) as the original.

A thetan placing a perfect duplicate does not do it alongside of the original, nor does he put another image inside the original, nor does he mock-up more particles. He makes a perfect duplicate by simply duplicating the original with itself, with its own time, mass (particles), space and motion.

There is something else he can do with an original object. He can simply look at one and claim that it is his duplicate. Now this, again, is not making a perfect duplicate.

The perfect duplicate violates the law of universes which keeps space stretched and causes things to come into existence in the first place. And this law of universes is that "two things cannot occupy the same space at the same time."

We then discover that a universe will vanish, or any part of that universe will vanish, the moment this law is violated. A perfect duplicate restores the As-isness of an object. A perfect duplicate may also have to contain in it the persistence of the object. It is simply made by postulate. And because the body itself is making *im*perfect duplicates continually–which is to say, is copying and making facsimiles continually–it may be that the thetan has fallen into this. And the making of *perfect* duplicates is a necessary part of his ability.

The auditor should, then, take an object right in the room with the preclear and have the preclear make a perfect duplicate of the object, then consider it is there again, then make another perfect duplicate of it, then consider it is there again. With some preclears who are having a difficult time, it will be found that the object will become more pronounced and more real for a short time and only then will begin to vanish. With thetans who are in fairly good condition, the object dims. With the thetan in excellent condition, the object vanishes.

The commands are as follows:

"Do you see this ashtray?"

"Now make a perfect duplicate of it. A duplicate in the same time, in the same place, with the same energy as the ashtray."

The preclear may have some difficulty getting this. The auditor should be very watchful and should coax the preclear using any language necessary to bring about the preclear's making a perfect duplicate. However, the auditor should not tell the preclear that the object "will vanish" or that it "will seem to vanish" for the preclear. The auditor should simply insist that the preclear make a perfect duplicate of the object, in its same time and same space, with its same mass or energy.

When the preclear finally has this, the auditor then says:

"Now consider that it is there again."

When the preclear has done so, the auditor says:

"Now make a perfect duplicate of it."

And when the preclear has done so:

"Now consider that it is there again."

"Make a perfect duplicate of it."

The preclear should be drilled in this until the object appears to vanish very thoroughly for him. If the preclear is actually in very good condition, the object simply will vanish.

THIS SKILL AND UNDERSTANDING SHOULD BE THOROUGHLY MASTERED BY THE PRECLEAR BEFORE HE IS TAKEN ON THROUGH TO DESCRIPTION PROCESSING (R2-34).

Making perfect duplicates of the whole track–which is to say, returning to incidents and making duplicates of them at that moment, or sending a remote viewpoint "down the track" and having it make a perfect duplicate of incidents, and then making a perfect duplicate of having done so in present time to vanish the present time picture–is the process of vanquishing engrams. However, if the process is done to wipe out engrams, remember to remedy the preclear's havingness as in the last sentences of R2-18.

This practice of As-isness, by the way, is the reason why people do not consider it polite for other people to stare. People have a hangover in that they know, instinctively, that if they are completely looked at they would disappear.

Having had the preclear learn how to make perfect duplicates, now ask him this question:

"Give me some things which are not making perfect duplicates of you," many times.

"Give me some people who are not making perfect duplicates of you."

"Give me some things of which you are not making perfect duplicates."

"Give me some people of whom you are not making perfect duplicates."

Healing at a glance is done by a thetan, not interiorized, making perfect duplicates of the illness of a body without perfectly duplicating the body itself. It is *not* done with energy.

Notes

THE FIRST AND MOST BASIC DEFINITION OF ANY PART OF COMMUNICATION IS THAT COMMUNICATION OR ANY PART THEREOF IS A *CONSIDERATION*.

If this were not so, communication in this universe would be impossible as a perfect communication requires an exact duplication of source-point at receipt-point. A duplication, to be perfect, would mean a "copy" in the same time, same space, with the same mass. The law that two objects cannot occupy the same space is peculiar to the MEST universe and is the law which keeps its space stretched. Thus a *perfect duplication* defies the basic law of the universe. But as duplication is a consideration, communication is possible to the degree that the preclear can freely make considerations. Any process which improves the ability to duplicate, by removing the fear of it or improving the ability of the preclear to consider freely without large reasons, improves as well communication.

"Things you are not duplicating,"
"Things which are not duplicating you," is one of a variety of processes.

The game of the preclear is to set up things which cannot be duplicated and to duplicate anything set up. He can play it as well as he can consider freely or as well as he can duplicate.

Considerations are bettered by having the preclear put considerations into any object for a long time, then having the preclear make the object have considerations about him. The commands are:

"Put some considerations into that _____,"
"Have the_____ have some considerations about you."

All communication lag, as in all other processes, must be reduced. Havingness may have to be remedied.

R 2-34: Description Processing

Before engaging in Description Processing, it will be necessary for the auditor to perform R2-33 with the preclear. It is not that the preclear is going to make perfect duplicates with this Description Processing, but that the preclear has some understanding of what he is confronting. Description Processing is the single most powerful process in Scientology. It uses As-isness in present time to remedy the restimulations beheld by the thetan. The total command content of Description Processing is the phrase:

"How does _____ seem to you now?"

This is used over and over and over by the auditor. In the blank, he puts any difficulty the preclear is having.

For an old-time auditor, for instance, who has become rather laggardly about auditing, the single question, *"How does auditing seem to you now?"* asked over and over, for about three hours, would most probably bring about a complete rehabilitation of the auditor as such.

Here, all we are asking the preclear to do is to view the situation. We do not care whether he makes a perfect duplicate of it or not. We merely want him to observe the situation. His observance of the situation determines its As-isness and his health depends upon his ability to accept things as they are. As we run this process, we will find that a considerable amount of change takes place in a case. Energy masses move, alter, shift, and the environment takes on different aspects. This is not particularly a good manifestation, it is the manifestation of time or persistence.

We are running an As-isness of Alter-isness. Thus, the occasional interjection of, *"Does it seem to be persisting?"* on the part of the auditor, calls the attention of the preclear to the persistence of the manifestations and clears up hang-ups.

Now, here in this process we view the entire philosophy of life. We see quite adequately here that an individual still retains anything which he has never accepted As-is. In other words, if a man has fought evil for years, he has never viewed evil As-is. Thus evil will remain with him. If he has fought ugliness for years, ugliness will remain with him. Terribly enough, because he has accepted As-is the goodness of life and the beauty of life, these things are continually being unmocked. We eat good food, we leave bad food alone. When something smells bad, we turn our face away from it. Here we have the entire anatomy of the "dwindling spiral." We see that individuals continually take the upper cream off life and leave the skimmed milk, and then take skimmed milk and leave the drowned flies, until they are trying to go all the way to the bottom to close with the basic As-isness of existence. And this basic As-isness is mystery and stupidity.

This works in other ways. An individual walking through life and seeing, for instance, beautiful people, comes at length into a condition where he does not believe beautiful people exist. For he has taken their As-isness so long that the only thing which can make any effect upon him is less beautiful people. These he has not unmocked. Thus we get the entire engram bank backing up those things which were never directly observed. One can understand, then, that ten thousand years ago in the civilizations of Earth, there might have been incredible beauty. And one can easily see that these would have no background in the bank of the preclear. However, the ugly spots of ten thousand years ago would still be there and so would bring up the humdrum, routine present time, existing without valor, gallantry or beauty.

This is the anatomy of what Krishna might have meant when he inferred that the bad must be taken with the good. Here we see, then, the explanation of why some men can tolerate only disease and dirt, why some can tolerate only poverty. And we behold, in short, the entire mechanism behind "acceptance level."

Acceptance Level Processing, as contained in the PABs, was one method of reaching a betterment of conditions. Description Processing is a far better method of reaching that condition.

Now let us take, more or less in their order of importance, the various things with which we fill in:

"How does _____ seem to you now?"

The auditor should be cautioned that he must never start in on one of these subjects without flattening the communication lag resulting. Any one of these items which is mentioned here might very well take ten hours of questioning before it could be run entirely flat, for these are very powerful items. An auditor might as well poison his preclear as to run this list one item after another without a repetition of the question.

The keynote of this entire process is that the auditor asks his question:

"How does _____ seem to you now?" over and over and over and over, interjecting only:

"Does it seem to be persisting?"

The auditor can add dunnage (irrelevant remarks aimed solely to stay in communication with the preclear) only so long as he does not distract the preclear from this process.

The items used follow:

Time
Change
Motionlessness
Creation
Survival
Persistence
Destruction
Distance
Agreement
Disagreement
Stupidity
Copying
Beauty
Ugliness
People
You
Seriousness
Resistance
Restraint
Objection
Nothingness
Any one of the dynamics
Any part of the fundamentals of Scientology

In the matter of Time, the preclear must necessarily have been run at least on Opening Procedure of 8-C (R2-16) and Opening Procedure by Duplication (R2-17) before the process is attempted. Additionally, he must have been run on Perfect Duplicates (R2-33) so as to gain some stability for him in present time on the subject of looking at things. The question, once posed, is used over and over and over again. Remember that the process (which is to say, the *phrase*) which turns on a somatic, if repeated many times, will turn it off.

Now we have special cases of preclears who seem to be having peculiar difficulties. The first of these is the preclear with the black field. On such a preclear, before anything else except R2-16 and R2-17 are run, blackness should be run:

"How does blackness seem to you now?"

Obviously, a thetan has always looked toward the light, the brightness, the form, the object, and has ever neglected the dark areas. This can be run objectively by having the preclear sit in a dark room and simply have him look at the darkness (which is the poorer of the methods, by test) or the auditor can have the preclear close his eyes and run the process.

If an auditor *must* address a psychosomatic illness, it is only necessary for him to ask:

"How do your (legs, hands, eyes) *seem to you now?"* using one of them at a time.

The lame can walk simply if asked *"How do your legs seem to you now?"* enough times.

Another version of this was developed by combining Problems and Solutions (R2-20) with Description Processing, with these commands:

"Can you recall a problem which concerned you?"

When the preclear does:

"How did it seem to you then?"

When he describes this:

"How does it seem to you now?"

He is then asked for another problem using the same commands.

Important

DO NOT FORGET TO REMEDY HAVINGNESS ON A PRECLEAR
WHEN YOU RUN ANY AS-ISNESS PROCESS SUCH AS R2-34.

R 2-35:
Location Processes

This is an entire class of processes which depends upon the utterance of one challenging question, as to location, and repeats that question over and over many times. The simplest phrasing of this is:

"Where are you now?"

The auditor, no matter how maddening it may seem to the preclear, simply continues to ask this question. This question, asked for an hour, produces singular results in a preclear.

But a word of warning: This question should not be asked of some preclear who is still struggling on Opening Procedure of 8-C (R2-16) or who is definitely out of contact with present time, for the process is butchery.

A very effective use of this process is contained in the phrase:

"Where is your face?"

This applies very specifically to people who are exteriorized. It does not occur to them sometimes for an hour of *"Where is your face?"* that they themselves have no face and that they are still locating the body's face. They have to understand this on their own.

R 2-36:
Self-determinism

As an up-to-date Scientologist knows, "Self-determinism," as an ideal state, went out the window with Dianetics. As long as you consider yourself intimately one thing confronting another thing, which is not yourself, you are not balanced in your environment. Self-determinism is a much higher peak than that attained by Homo sapiens previously. But in Scientology, there is a much better concept–that of "Pan-determinism."

There are all manner of traps and social twists to keep a person located and identified with one object. The society insists that one have a label. It should be called to the attention of anyone interested in auditing that a symbol has "three M's": Mass, Meaning and Mobility. As soon as one accepts entirely *meaning* (such as a name) and accepts intimately *mass* and is made to be *mobile*, one is then dependent to some degree upon some orientation-point in order to have *space*. One is inhibited in constructing space. Therefore, the goal of processing in Scientology is not Self-determinism. The goal of processing is Pan-determinism. Spanning of Attention (R2-22) and other processes go in this direction.

The practicality of Pan-determinism is immediately seen in an elementary, if uncommon situation where one is being robbed. If one continues to be solely one's self, the determinism of the robber is left entirely free. The way to combat a robber is, while one is being robbed, be the robber and go away.

Here, immediately, we cross the bridge into a complete First Dynamic. A complete First Dynamic is a Pan-determined Dynamic. All earlier processes of Dianetics and Scientology audit mainly the Third Dynamic.

The subject of Pan-determinism is a very touchy subject on a social line. For it becomes apparent immediately that "bravery in the face of odds," while dramatic, is less than optimum. One should simply be the target and the odds at the same time. Here we have the whole question of randomity. Randomity comes about when one selects out and gives determinism to another entity or object. This tells you immediately that the problem of healing at a distance could be looked upon with some favor. And this would be true if the concept of Nirvana were true, where all life comes about as a fragmentation of life. But this is no essay or determination of whether it is bad or good to heal at a distance, or to do healing of the kind which Christ did. The only thing I would care to say on the subject, at this time, is that if one does healing of this character, simply, that he should do it well and thoroughly. Such healing does not happen to make Self-determined individuals out of those so healed. But this, again, is a matter of ethic and not a matter of practicality.

An auditor, by applying processing skills, is actually making somebody well. But he is also bringing that person up the line toward a higher goal of Self-determinism and, if he wishes, up to a higher goal of Pan-determinism. There could be billions of Pan-determining individuals, since a universe is composed of time-continua of particles in common. As long as one does not cross particles into other time-continua and so get two time-continua, one would not get a mergence of universes.

While there are many processes yet to be delineated on the subject of Self-determinism and Pan-determinism, one can expect people to confuse the condition of "buttered all over the universe," "clairvoyance," "telepathy" (and other half-felt, half-experienced things) to be taken up in lieu of clear-sighted, knowing Pan-determinism.

The first goal of the auditor is to get somebody up into the Self-determined category. And then to remember afterward that a person can be in a Pan-determining category. All a thetan has to do to be Pan-determining is simply move in back of somebody else's head. It is as simple as this. A thetan should also be able to make perfect duplicates of himself.

The recovery of Pan-determinism is necessary to get somebody out of the rut of obsessive Self-determinism. Beingness Processing (R2–31) directly processes obsessive Self-determinism. Under the heading of Self-determinism and Pan-determinism, we have also the subject of "control." The necessity to predict, with actual force or energy, the future course of an object is a refusal to have something As-is. Thus, with *control* we get *persistence*. And that individual whose case will not change is in such a level of persistence and obsessive "Self-determinism" that he must control everything.

The easiest process with which to approach this problem is contained in the command phrase:

"Indicate something which is not making space for you."

And when the preclear has:

"Indicate something else which is not making space for you," and so forth, until we have recovered certainty and clarity on the viewpoint of dimension.

It will be discovered very rapidly that there are many people making space for the preclear and that he is to some degree contained in the universe of each one of these people and has many particles in common with them.

R 2-37:
Yelling

In that Man has for a long time used words to make space and as any barbaric people uses noise to make itself big, it will be found that an inhibition of making noise is a major difficulty on the case of any preclear. When this process is done, the auditor should be very careful that the preclear will not be suppressed by his environment. It is more than the auditor's simply being careful of the neighbors. It is the auditor being careful of the preclear, for the preclear will be careful of the neighbors. The auditor should take the preclear to some place where the preclear would be free to yell.

The auditing commands are:

"Start yelling," and
"Keep yelling."

The preclear can be sent off by himself to yell.

If a group is being processed, where its noise will not disturb others, a back and forth interchange between the auditor and the group will be found beneficial.

This process is very limited and has a tendency simply to make people cheerful. But, occasionally, some cases are so inhibited on the making of noise that they are having difficulty with their vocal cords or with their mouths. Tooth trouble can be traced to the inhibition of making noise. Distaste for singing is equally traced to the making of noise.

This process can also be done by Creative Processing (the making of mock-ups).

This is, at first glance, a body process. But it will be discovered in processing a thetan, who is exteriorized, that he is very afraid to make noise. In such a case, the auditor should exteriorize him into some place far from the auditor and far from the body. And the auditor should use Description Processing for a while on the thetan:

"How does making noise seem to you now?"

And then:

"Start yelling,"
"Keep on yelling."

This is an exteriorized process.

R 2-38:
Holding Anchor Points

There are innumerable drills concerning space. In that a thetan, to have vision, must be able to tolerate or make space, and in that three-dimensional space requires four points, one sees that a thetan must be able to view three separate anchor points at once to have the illusion of space.

The hypnotic effect of the body on a thetan is created by narrowing the thetan's view to two eyes, one point. The optical trick of seeing depth with two eyes is not seeing three points at once.

The remedy of the "hypnotic trance" of the thetan, which makes him believe he *is* a body, is the remedy of his looking through eyes at one point.

The simplest and most workable remedy, which results in exteriorization most often, if then after some time, is "holding corners." The preclear is seated in a chair (preclears are audited while seated or standing or walking these days, *never* lying down) and is asked to close his eyes.

The commands then are:

"Close your eyes."
"Locate an upper corner of the room behind you."

When he has done so:

"Now locate the other upper corner behind you."
"All right, hold on to these two corners and don't think."

The preclear is quietly enjoined, from time to time, to continue his attention on the corners and not to think. At the end of fifteen minutes, the auditor says:

"Now find the third corner behind you" (meaning a lower corner).

When the auditor is assured the preclear has done this, he says:

"Now hold on to the same two you had before and the new one."

When the preclear has all three corners at once, the auditor says:

"Now hold on to those three corners and don't think."

The auditor has the preclear continue to do this last for at least fifteen minutes. Then:

"Now find the fourth back corner."
"Now hold all four corners, sit back and don't think."

This is done for at least fifteen minutes. The auditor then has the preclear locate all eight corners of the room and says:

"Now hold on to all eight corners of the room, sit back and don't think."

Occasionally and quietly checking to see that the preclear is following the command, the auditor has the preclear do this for at least fifteen minutes.

If this process is to be done longer than this total time of one hour, as indicated in the above commands, go through the above sequence of commands again as a process for another hour. Do not simply have the preclear hold eight corners for another hour. Put him through two corners, three, four and eight again, as given. In other words, use this sequence every time you use the process.

R 2-39:
Conceiving Something Interesting

Interest is a keynote of interiorization.

A preclear, difficult to exteriorize, has become so deeply interested in his body that he has become involved with it.

Experimental proof of this exists. When the preclear who won't exteriorize becomes so ill that he cannot envision any future for his body, he will exteriorize. Indeed, this is the mechanism at death. The body will not be useful, has reached past interest to finality and so the thetan exteriorizes. It is remarkable with what ease. In testing, I have purposely brought experimental preclears (who were as resistive to exteriorization as any to be found) to a point where they believed it was "all up" with the body. They left the body then.

Interest is the consideration above the mechanical action of control. Controlling is starting, changing, stopping. Deepening of interest is manifested by a passage from watching to participating. As the thetan watches several particles or bodies in motion, he may become prejudiced in favor of one. He sinks from Pan-determinism to "Self-determinism," where "self" is the one in which he became interested to the exclusion of others or counter to these others. Now, having become the object, *his* interest is *its* interest. It against its environment is a problem the thetan involves himself in solving. He may do this with something he creates or something he finds already created. His interest led him to seek to predict its actions in favor of its survival. When he fails to predict, he may enter a confusion of motion for he "does not know" the next movement of the object. Confusion then leads to mystery.

Thus the anatomy of mystery begins with interest, leads to "Self-determinism," leads to prediction of starting, changing and stopping (control), leads to a shortening of communication lines, may become at length confusion and end with mystery.

Interest is not *bad* simply because it leads to interiorization. For interiorization ceases, by test, when the thetan can no longer feel there is anything more in which to be interested. A thetan is indestructible.

There are several stages of interest. The qualities of these are represented by the Know-Sex-Mystery Scale. Most notable are those used in the Chart of Human Evaluation. Interest is at first without particles. Then, as "Self-determinism" (effort to determine the future of a "self") enters, postulates dedicated to control are used. As misprediction occurs, particles are employed to guide and these are of many qualities and solidities such as Enthusiasm or Anger, play or work. (See scales.) Inversions take place at those points where the thetan uses the "self" to acquire, notably Eating and Sex.

When the thetan becomes doubtful of the continued "interest quality" of the self, either for other selves or himself, there ensues an undecided period where he is disinterested.

When interest is withdrawn while attention yet remains, we have a solid. This is a ridge, it is mass. One "As-ises" the interest from a bank. When he ceases to create interest, he takes interest from the bank thus leaving the solid deposits of "disinterest." Searching for more interest, he becomes less interested and so becomes involved and interiorized.

The auditor is attempting to exteriorize the preclear so that the preclear can assume a higher Pan-determinism on the dynamics and, usually, so that the preclear can again "run a body" from outside.

Where the auditor so fails, the preclear is under the impression that the auditor is trying to get him to abandon the body–thus a sort of grief ensues. (See R2–40.)

When interest becomes fixed, we have attention. When attention becomes fixed, we have an unawareness of little else but the object of fixation and a decrease of Pan-determinism down to Self-determinism. When this fixity of attention goes to an extreme, we have a lessening of Self-determinism to a point of Other-determinism. As Self-determinism lessens, we find a hypnotic state of "total" Other-determinism which becomes, then, "Self-determinism" (dramatization). We discover, in this last, all the mechanisms of the engram and, as well, the mechanism of shifting valences. For the preclear assumes the valence of greatest determinism (winning valence) as being the valence of greatest interest.

The process used to remedy a fixation of interest to the exclusion of self consists of broadening interest. By the broadening of interest we *do not* achieve a liability which will again collapse, but a greater freedom. Broaden, do not contract a preclear's width of interest.

The spheres of interest *are* the eight dynamics. A series of concentric spheres (each one larger than the last) with the First Dynamic at center and the Eighth Dynamic at the extreme of any universe gives a spatial picture of interest. When a retreat or inversion occurs, the Eighth (the extreme outside sphere) becomes the inverted First Dynamic, the Seventh becomes the inverted Second, the Sixth the inverted Third, the Fifth the inverted Fourth, the Fourth the inverted Fifth, the Third the inverted Sixth, the Second the inverted Seventh, the First the inverted Eighth. Then they progress, in interest and Alter-isness, outward again. The inverted Eighth becomes the reinverted First, the inverted Seventh becomes the reinverted Second and so forth.

Each inversion is occasioned by a falling back of interest while yet retaining contact with the area from which one fell back. Hence, we get such manifestations as "buttered all over the universe" and "my thetan is over there" and other such ridiculous manifestations.

The processes of Spanning Attention (R2–22), etc., resolve this sort of thing.

Here is the process specifically aimed at interest, for a Homo sapiens badly interiorized:

"Mock-up (get an imaginary picture of) the most interesting body form other people would conceive."

The preclear may not be able to get visible (to him) mock-ups. But he will mock-up something, black or invisible. And this *will be* the most interesting body form he can conceive. He is so fixed on it he cannot do otherwise than mock it up.

Then have him mock-up another by saying:

"Do it again,"
"And another,"
"And another."

Have him pull these (visible or not) in upon him to remedy havingness by saying:

"All right. Now pull those in upon you."

Then:

"Mock-up the most interesting body form you can conceive,"
"And now another,"
"And another,"
"And another,"
"Now pull those in upon you."

Now repeat the first command (other people), have him remedy havingness with what he got. Then the second phase (his most interesting body), back and forth, time after time. He will learn exactly what he conceives to be interesting and what he believes others would find interesting.

Do this for at least half an hour. Four hours would be better.

His ability to mock-up, his acceptance levels will change.

The second part of the process consists of a more objective (and better) process. As the preclear is a man, we can suppose that he is interested in his species. But we may have learned in part one of this process that he is more interested in other forms than Man. The auditor either assumes that a thetan interiorized into a man would be interested in men or, with an earlier clue, substitutes another form.

The auditing command is:

"What other person could you be interested in?"
"And now another one,"
"And another one," until a broad array of people are disclosed.

Getting the preclear to pretend he is various objects with various viewpoints also resolves this.

A fundamental way of looking at interest is to qualify its two major divisions as "interested" and "interesting."

A thetan in good condition is *interested.* When he has become a "self," he feels he must have energy from exterior sources and so he becomes *interesting.*

Interest*ed* could be said to be an *outflow.* Interest*ing* could be said to be an *inflow.* Being interest*ed* yet leaves one considerable freedom. Being interest*ing* pulls in particles upon one and so restricts him.

An interest*ed* thetan is the solver of problems.

An interest*ing* self is a problem.

More broadly, a thetan is interest*ed* in problems. MEST *is* a problem.

The passage from interest*ed* to interest*ing* has many phases. When one is no longer interested, but is only interesting, he has lost his principal quality as a thetan—freedom and the ability to change at will.

Having the preclear mock-up interest*ing* bodies, forms, machines and universes discharges much of his interiorized condition and fixation. Then having him look at actual people and objects and "get the idea" of how it would be to be them and move them about brings him again toward Pan-determinism.

"Let's find something in which you could be interested."

And when the preclear does:

"Find some more things in which you could be interested."

And when he has:

"Find some more things in which you could be interested."

And so on, with these commands, for at least an hour.

Do not use "interest*ing*." Use only "interest*ed*." In other words, process the preclear toward theta (interested), not toward MEST (interesting).

You can see that the preclear is "As-ising" situations, that he is also broadening attention and unfixing from the body.

The only thing you can do wrong with this process is not to run it long enough.

The process works subjectively or objectively. But it is well, if the preclear reaches an impasse, to have him find things in the present time environment in which he can be interested.

Without directing the preclear's attention to specific things, just by running the command *"Find some things in which you could be interested,"* exteriorization takes place.

THIS IS A DANGEROUS PROCESS UNLESS IT IS RUN LONG ENOUGH TO MAKE THE PRECLEAR CREATE AND ABANDON INTERESTS. IF RUN A SHORT TIME, IT WILL SIMPLY DRAIN THE BANK OF OLD INTERESTS LEAVING THE PRECLEAR EXTREMELY BORED.

The factors which make R2-39 Interest a very important process is the fact that interest is the entrance point to havingness. Heretofore we have used attention, but have used it very sparingly in processing. The reason for this is that attention is into the field of mechanics. It has, however, become evident that interest is more consideration than attention and is, therefore, attention with *intention*. Interest, therefore, could be defined as this: "Attention with an intention to give or attract attention."

If you will have the preclear look around his environment and point out things which have the intention to alter things, and other things which have the intention to keep them from altering things, we will discover that we are running time. The intention to alter and the intention to keep things from altering are, together, the two factors of change. Interest added to this gives us the determinism of attention. The auditing commands for this would be:

"Look around the environment and find some things which have the intention of altering things,"
"Now look at them again and get interested in them," and so forth.

"Look around the environment now and find some things which have the intention to keep things from altering,"

"Now get interested in these items one after another," thus directing the preclear's attention and inviting him to mock-up interest.

It will be readily discovered that he will shift on the time track and that he will consider himself detached from time.

The keynote of a preclear who is having a difficult time is that he has no interest in outside things. One who is having a less difficult time would be interested only in things in his immediate vicinity. A preclear who is fairly well-off has an interest in altering things or in keeping them from altering. But unless interest can be given on a postulated basis, it is obsessive. The only reason a preclear keeps a psychosomatic illness around is that a great deal of residual interest has accumulated in that illness.

A preclear will have discovered roles up and down the time track which interested people and he will be trying to occupy these roles in order to increase his own havingness. If you were to ask a preclear:

"What were your parents interested in?" he would eventually recover from the very things from which he is suffering.

Quite normally the whole career of a child is established by the things in which his mother is interested. And the child will try to be those things in which his mother was interested if his mother's attention and interest in him has been slight. Here is the complete backbone of orientation-points and symbols. If the orientation-point is interested, the symbols are interesting. When one can no longer be an orientation-point, he of course becomes a symbol and tries to get interest from the orientation-point. The basic orientation-points in a family are the parents or grandparents and the symbol is the child.

Usually the preclear has come to the auditor because he feels that the auditor will at least be interested in him. And when the auditor's interest in the preclear is not demonstrated in such ways as not keeping appointments or in failing to let the preclear communicate, the preclear will worsen in the process. However, such an omission can be remedied, although it shouldn't have happened in the first place, by running Interest Processing.

A much later process, Other People (R2–46), can be run by picking out in the preclear some obvious difficulty, such as a bad eye or a bad leg, and have him get interested in the bad eyes and bad legs which he postulates at people in his vicinity. This puts the preclear into the role of an orientation-point and takes him out of the role of a symbol by making him the one who is interested and making other people in his vicinity the ones who are interesting.

A great many significances can of course be entered into this process. One can have the preclear be interested in things under attack, interested in things not under attack, picking them out one after another in the environment. The auditor can have the preclear be interested in the weakness of MEST, the forgetfulness of MEST, the non-determinism of MEST and other factors.

The Mystery to Know Scale, with the addition of Inhibited, Enforced and Desired, can be run (adding the factor of interest) with the following commands:

"Pick out some things which are inhibiting mystery,"
"Now, one after the other, get interested in them."

"Now pick out some things which are enforcing mystery,"
"Now get interested in them one after the other."

"Now pick out some things which desire mystery,"
"Now get interested in them."

This can be run straight on through the Mystery to Know Scale, which is (to give it in its most complete form):

Mystery

Sex

Eatingness

Symbols

Thinkingness

Effort

Emotion

Lookingness

Knowingness

R 2-40:
Conceiving a Static

THIS IS A HEAVY PROCESS. IT IS NOT RECOMMENDED FOR
CASES HAVING ANY REAL DIFFICULTY.

Here we use the discovery and principle of Ultimate Truth
(see *A Summary of Scientology*, Chapter Four).

If one has no prior postulate and makes a postulate, then that
postulate cannot be a lie.

If one then makes a denying postulate second to this primary
postulate, he then has accomplished a lie.

A prime postulate on any subject cannot be a lie.

A second postulate can be a lie.

In such a case, the second postulate permits the prime postulate
to exist. *But* in such a case it is the second postulate, the lie, which
persists.

All second postulates depend on prime postulates for their
force.

Examples:

1. All evil depends upon a prime postulate of goodness if the
   evil is to persist.

2. The Satanists claim that Satan is God *after* He made the
   Universe.

3. A hatred of a person depends for its only strength upon a love
   for that person prior to the hatred. The hatred persists, but
   only has strength from the love.

4. A man considers himself to be worthless. This state of mind, persisting, denotes that he must have had a considerable opinion of himself before he felt worthless.

But beware of thinking that "all is good" or "all is evil." The force comes from prime postulate, the state persisting from the second postulate.

Example:

A doctor considers himself a *good charitable* man, a wholly unselfish healer. On examination, we see the second postulate persists so his goodness must be the second postulate. It must have force from a prime postulate it denies and so we find this doctor entered medicine because it had more chance of easy sex. Then he denied this to himself and argued he did it from humanity. His pious mien ceases to persist and he is freed from this pose by straightwiring the prime postulate.

Rules

RULE: ALWAYS STRAIGHTWIRE OUT A CONDITION CONTRADICTING THE CONDITION WHICH EXISTS.

Examples:

1. We have a preclear with bad legs. We see that bad legs are persisting. Thus we know that the forceful postulate is prior and opposite so we Straightwire out *good* legs.

2. A man is sick because of a jilt in love. We Straightwire out *not* the jilt, but the times he loved the girl.

3. Our interiorized preclear is stuck, won't exteriorize. We Straightwire the times he was free and so discharge the stuck (the second) postulate and thus exteriorize him.

RULE: THAT WHICH IS CLOSER TO AN ULTIMATE TRUTH (THE STATIC) GIVES POWER TO THAT WHICH CONTRADICTS IT.

The process, and a vicious one it is, contains only the command, repeated over and over:

"Conceive a thetan."

Caution

This is a long process. The auditor may have to remedy the havingness of the preclear. (Do not forget R2–16, Opening Procedure of 8-C, if preclear bogs.)

Notes

The "top buttons" of the Chart of Attitudes (see *Scientology 8-8008*) are the main qualities of a static. A static has no quantity. It does have quality and consideration.

FREEDOM CANNOT BE ERASED. A STATIC CANNOT BE AS-ISED.

R 2-41:
Via

VIA is the curse word of existence. *Via* means a relay point in a communication line. To talk *via* a body, to get energy *via* eating alike are communication by-routes.

We are trying to string in a preclear a straight line from Cause to Effect. The reasons we cannot are all vias or complete stops. Enough vias make a stop. A stop is made out of vias.

There is no real reason one should go into the past to straighten the present. There is no time but postulated time. Thus it is all present. Why not, then, postulate the desired condition in the present?

It is painful to do so. For the moment one does, he tends to slip from the ideal to the first lie. One slips because the first lie was *time*. Time persists because it is a lie deriving its force from the absence of time in the static. Then, forthright postulation of the static at first restimulates time. When the time postulate restimulates, the literal blackness of lies, somatics, etc., come into view. All one has to do is endure these and repostulate the static. The reason earlier efforts along this line failed lay in their restimulating the *second* postulate each time, the lie. And then, not repostulating the static, mooning over the lie or the sign.

Recent efforts, such as Couéism, do not postulate the static, but validate time ("Every day in every way I am getting better and better"). Don't postulate to *become* beautiful, postulate current beauty ("I am beautiful"). Thus postulating the static at first swings one into *time* and the *second* postulate, then finally the static itself occurs.

Remember: A static has no mass, wavelength, energy, location or time. *But* it can consider. And it *has* qualities. Those qualities are its basic definition *plus* the top buttons of the Chart of Attitudes plus beauty.

A solution would be something which solves the problem. Thus the As-isness of the problem *is* the solution for it would vanish the problem. Thus, in Scientology we have attained an Ultimate Solution–the Static. And an Ultimate Truth–the Static.

To work this clearly, the auditor commands:

"Get the idea of having infinite leisure."

When the preclear does:

"Now get it again,"
"Get it again and better,"
"Again," and so forth, regardless of what somatics or locks appear. He does this for at least fifteen minutes.

Then:

"Now get the idea of complete freedom,"
"Again,"
"Again," for at least fifteen minutes.

Then:

"Get the idea of having total ability," for at least half an hour.

Now use this command, but include in it the Chart of Attitudes and beauty:

"Assume complete _____,"
"Again,"
"Assume complete _____ again,"
"Again."

The Chart of Attitudes buttons are Survives, Right, Fully Responsible, Owns All, Everyone, Always, Motion Source, Truth, Faith (Trust), I Know, Cause, I Am, Win, Start, Differences, Being, plus beauty. Do not do these briefly.

LET THE PRECLEAR EXPLAIN HOW THESE SEEM TO HIM BUT DON'T MIX THIS WITH DESCRIPTION PROCESSING.

R 2-42:
Pan-determinism

(R2-42, R2-43 and R2-44 are a processing group.)

Pan-determinism is a new idea in Scientology. Its validity is demonstrated by the fact that it is a five-star process.

Pan-determinism is the ability to regulate the considerations of two or more identities, whether or not opposed. Previously our goal was the relatively limited goal of Self-determinism. It was for some time realized that this did not embrace the total concept, since Self-determinism expressed in the main the First Dynamic. But the moment one begins to consider the fact that the thetan is controlling the body, one sees that he is not dealing with a "person" or "identity" with the First Dynamic, but is dealing with the Third Dynamic. Thus we have "Self-determinism" as a misnomer. We see that Survival is as successful as determinism is stretched across the environment. In other words, up the dynamics. Certainly where Man is concerned, it is never a problem, then, of Self-determinism. It is a problem of Pan-determinism. For here we have in one individual several items, each distinct, under control. When a thetan came into full control of himself and his activities, we would have, and only then have, Self-determinism. But a thetan in his playing of the game is attempting Pan-determinism and is assuming Self-determinism. His first goal might be said to be Pan-determinism.

Under Pan-determinism, we have of course the problem of "control." The component parts of control are *start, change* and *stop*. Thus a person controlling something is trying to start, change and stop that thing. Where he loses his ability to start and stop it, he only retains his ability to change it.

And thus we have a low-level case trying desperately to change, being unable to change and very certainly being unable completely to start and stop. His last effort is to change.

Any time you are addressing a preclear, you are addressing something which is attempting Pan-determinism. Here is a thetan trying to control a body, an engram bank and the various symbiotes of the body, such as its possessions, vehicles and servicing items. In Pan-determinism we are not concerned with either "bad" or "good." We are only concerned with the fact that a thetan is trying to control many identities, some of them opposed to others, and that his inabilities in the past to control certain beingnesses have brought him to a level of belief where he does not feel that he can control anything. And as a result, we discover him unable to be Cause, thus unable to find himself or be at the source-end of a communication line. Pan-determinism is the direct reason why one becomes "buttered all over the universe."

This effort toward Pan-determinism is the monitoring point in all processing. The discovery of Pan-determinism was the difference between success and failure in many cases.

Under the heading of Pan-determinism, we discover such things as Owning, Protecting and Hiding bodies. One declares the ownership of something so that he will be given the right to control it. One protects something because he considers that something else is trying to control it. One hides something because he is afraid something else may appear to control it.

An enormous variety of processes stem from Pan-determinism. Here, any and all of the training of an auditor can exert itself. This is the common denominator and the one fast line through to the upper ranges of the Tone Scale. There is a second line, that which is described in R2–43 Fighting. Pan-determinism is what one is fighting for. It is the "reason why" behind existence.

The auditing commands for the running of Pan-determinism are as follows:

"What do you feel you could control?" and
"Give me some more things you feel you could control," and
"Give me some more things you feel you could control."

One runs this so as to improve the considerations of the preclear. He can fully expect the preclear to drop into very deep Apathy on occasion. But the process carried forward determinedly by the auditor (and not "patty-caked" or left off simply because the preclear is having difficulty) will produce, all by itself, a considerable resurgence of case. R2-43 takes care of most of the factors which are encountered as the reason why one does not feel one can determine the course of something.

Note

PAN-DETERMINISM APPROACHES THE PERSONAL SOUL TOWARD THE INFINITE MIND.

R2-43: fighting

Basically this universe is a game. The MEST universe pretends to be a universe of peace. In order to become a universe of peace, it is necessary to stop everything from fighting. In order to have a game, it is necessary to have opponents. If one has opponents, there must be fighting. This universe is organized to immobilize a thetan.

So eager is a thetan to have a game that he will adopt to himself all manner of liabilities in order to have a parity with his opponents. One cannot have a game with people who are too inferior in strength or cleverness. Thus one reduces his own strength and cleverness in order to have a game.

As given in R2-42 Pan-determinism, one uses as his reason why he is fighting "the necessity of controlling something else." The effort to control is the "reason why" for fighting. Fighting, itself, is the game.

R2-42 and R2-43 are very close together in workability and between them, worked one against the other, back and forth, will lift the preclear up through the barriers of force. It could be said that a preclear stops fighting when he considers that other forces, or ideas, or emotions are too much for him. As given in the Philadelphia Lecture Series, one has to go up through force before one can cease to use force. If one does not rise superior to force, then one is the subject and slave of force.

Peace is only to be found at the high levels of the Tone Scale. Any effort to have peace after one has become the victim of force and is afraid of force, simply involves further struggle. There is no peace below the level where one cannot fight.

We are not here concerned with moral values. We are only concerned with the workability of processes. And whereas it might be said of Scientology that it is attempting to sell fighting and war, this would only be said by those who were themselves badly defeated and afraid of force.

Here we have, as well, "automaticity" and "randomity." In order to have more attention to control other things, one sets up the things he is already controlling as automatic. Having done so, he has given to them a determinism of their own. And having so given them their own determinism they can, if he ceases thus to control them, attack him. Thus we have the machines of a thetan. These machines work only so long as they are in control of the individual and then begin to work against the individual. Thus it is with the remainder of the universe. One only fights those things which he has selected out as not under his control. Anything which is not under an individual's control, but which has taken the individual's attention, is likely to be an identity used to fight.

The motto of this universe is "We must have a game." Games consist of "opponents" and "reasons to have a game" and "things to have a game about." Reasons to have a game are summed under "Pan-determinism." Things to have a game about are summed up under "havingness."

The game is the thing. The wins and losses are not the thing. One loses every time one wins, for he then has no game. Any cessation will bring about a change in the status of an individual, for he will then impose upon himself other opponents and liabilities and impose reasons why upon others so as to create a new game. Although it is antipathetic to most preclears, as you will discover by processing them, a game is no more and no less than fighting an opposition.

One falls out of having a game when one begins to believe that the forces being used against him, or the ideas being used against him, or the emotions being used against him are too great to oppose. Once he has this idea, he can then be subjected to other forces.

As all forces, emotions and efforts in general can be categorized under "considerations," to have a consideration about a force has greater actuality than having the force itself. Changing one's mind about force is senior to changing force.

It must be realized that an individual who has drawn away from force has also drawn away from the material of which his engram bank is made. People on whom engrams collapse are people who have become afraid of force. This is best approached not by using work or other factors, but by directly approaching the problem of games and running fighting only.

It will be discovered that most individuals are involved with fighting themselves. After all, an individual is a Third, not a First Dynamic. The body, the engram bank, the thetan, his machines form four items which can be at war one with another. And when an individual has an insufficiency of fighting out in his environment, he will begin to fight with himself. The condition of most preclears who come to an auditor is this. One of the ways to handle this is with the auditing command:

"Point out some things in the environment which are fighting themselves."

This, run for an hour or two out where the preclear can actually see things and point them out, will key-out most of the engram bank with which he is in conflict. He will recognize fully and clearly, very shortly after he has started on this process, that he is fighting himself.

In view of the fact that there is a scarcity of fighting imposed by police, mores, and the motto "Peace! Peace! Peace!" of this universe, you will discover that you have to start and run, for a very long time, the factor of "wasting." Thus, the first entrance to this problem could be *wasting fighting*. One would do this in brackets, with the following auditing commands:

"Waste some fighting."

And when the communication lag is flat on this:

"Have somebody else waste fighting."

"Waste some fighting,"
"Have somebody else waste fighting."

It will be discovered that the preclear will do this for many hours of processing, all with a betterment of his case, before he actually gets up to the point where he can touch the next level of this process, which is "accepting." However, one does not at this stage run *accepting fighting*.

The next part of this process is done with the following auditing commands:

"Waste some opponents,"
"Have somebody else waste some opponents."

After the preclear can handle this without any appreciable communication lag, one then goes to the next part of this process:

"Waste some liabilities,"
"Have somebody else waste some liabilities."

"Waste some liabilities,"
"Have somebody else waste some liabilities."

And this, too, will have to be run for a long time until the individual has flattened his communication lag.

CHAPTER FIVE
INTENSIVE PROCEDURE: ROUTE 2

Having handled the subject of wasting fighting directly, opponents and liabilities, one can then go on to accepting. But one does this *only* when the communication lag on wasting of fighting, opponents and liabilities has been done. One uses accepting, in this case, by remedying havingness:

"Mock-up something you could fight,"
"Pull it into you."

"Mock-up something else you could fight,"
"Pull it into you."

Even though the mock-up is invisible or black, it is still done. If you are having the individual point out things he could fight in the environment itself, do not be surprised at this stage if he simply pulls out of his body (as a thetan) and occupies the area of that which he thinks he could fight. One follows this with:

"Mock-up an opponent,"
"Pull it into you."

"Mock up another opponent,"
"Pull it into you."

One follows this with:

"Mock-up a liability,"
"Pull it into you."

"Mock-up another liability,"
"Pull it into you."

You should run Fighting (R2–43) in conjunction with Pan-determinism (R2–42) and the process Must and Must Not Happen (R2–44). In other words, do not run R2–43 without also running, interspersed with it, R2–42 and R2–44. These three processes work together. Any time a communication lag is fairly flat on any one of these, you should shift to either of the other two.

Remember, R2-42, R2-43 and R2-44 work together interspersed and make, themselves, a process. If you have a preclear out in the open, you can have him point out things in the environment that he could *fight*. Just as, if you have him out in the open, you can have him point out things he wouldn't mind *controlling* and, in the case of R2-44, things that he wouldn't mind *having happen* or *not happen* again.

"What would be safe to fight?" until the communication lag is flat.
"What would others find it safe to fight?"

"What would it be safe to fight?"
"What would others find it safe to fight?" is a continuation of Fighting as a process.

"What thoughts would it be safe for you to fight?"
"What thoughts would it be safe for others to fight?" run back and forth many times until the communication lag is flat.

"What emotions would it be safe for you to fight?"
"What emotions would it be safe for others to fight?" run back and forth until the communication lag is flat.

"What efforts would it be safe to fight?"
"What efforts would others consider it safe to fight?" run back and forth until the communication lag is flat.

"What imaginings would it be safe to fight?"
"What imaginings would others consider it safe to fight?"

"Indicate some things which are fighting."

"Spot all the spots where you had to stop fighting them,"
"Spot all the spots where you won," is excellent, since either a win or a lose is a "stop fighting" and therefore a loss of opponents.

You will find many preclears hung up in past moments of victory. This is only because they lost their opponents at that moment and the loss stuck them on the track by bringing about motionlessness.

"What would you need to fight things?"
"What would others need to fight things?"

If you have the preclear out in the open where there are lots of people (a very good method of processing), have him place into these people, unknown to them, the preclear's own attitudes about fighting. Take one attitude and have him place it in several people, another of the preclear's attitudes about fighting and have him place it in many more people, and you will discover considerable changes take place in the preclear.

"What mechanisms could you use to continue fighting?" is another fine process.

"What changes could you make and still fight?" is yet another interesting process.

"Describe some fighting that would interest you," is another facet of this process.

The key process to alter behavior is:

"Invent some things you could fight,"
"Invent some things that could fight you."

R 2-44:
Must and Must Not Happen

A preclear is stuck on the track where motionlessness occurs. One of the reasons he has used to fight was to "make something happen" or to "keep something from happening." Thus it is of interest in the case to undo these stuck points in the preclear. There are many ways these could be undone, but there is apparently only one way that is actually effective. This is done with the following commands:

> *"Tell me some things you wouldn't want to have happen again,"*
> *"Tell me some things you would like to have happen again."*

The preclear will get, in accordance with these commands, various recalls, incidents, facsimiles, or environmental situations, or future fear or hopes, and may be steered more directly into these.

I first discovered this process by running *concepts*, but in the running of concepts it has a very limited workability. By pointing out live or imaginary situations, great workability is achieved. The auditor must be very careful to do this process long enough so as not to leave the preclear hung up in an incident.

This is the basic key of *time*.

R 2-45:

An enormously effective process for
exteriorization but its use is frowned upon
by this society at this time.

R2-46:
Other People

(R2-46, R2-47 and R2-48 are a processing group.)

Here is one of the more curious and one of the more swiftly workable processes. An auditor may find himself reluctant to use this process, but experiment has demonstrated that it did not bring harm to other people. This is one of the fastest ways of getting rid of a psychosomatic known in Scientology. It is practically the only method known to get rid of the "unknowns" in the bank. It is a direct environmental process, utilizing actual, visible other people.

To run this process, one must be in a heavily populated area where people are on the street, walking about, sitting down or otherwise directly visible to the preclear. The process is not run in mock-ups. This process has been known to get rid of heavy chronic somatics in a few minutes. The auditor takes the preclear into a railroad station or a park, or has him sit in a car on a heavily used street, and says to him:

"What do you think is wrong with you?"

He has the preclear name some specific thing and, having named it, the auditor then says:

"All right. Pick out one of these people and have that thing wrong with that person."

And when the preclear has done so:

"Now pick out another person and have this same thing wrong with that person."

The auditor continues to have the preclear place into these people this thing which is wrong with the preclear, only so long as the item is wrong with the preclear. For this is a very rapid process and a very rapid change takes place.

Any concept or idea of any kind can be utilized in this process. The auditor can pick out obvious things the preclear has and have the preclear find these things wrong with other people around.

This also works if the auditor has the preclear find each person, one after the other, which he actually sees during the process, *perfect*. In other words, the auditor can say:

"Postulate perfection into that person,"
"Now postulate perfection into that one."

This is mixing Other People with Conceiving a Static (R2–40). But, for that matter, almost any process in Scientology can be employed in this fashion.

One of the very effective ways of using this process, Other People, is to have the preclear place into them "lostness," or stupidity, inability to locate themselves and, in short, all the factors making up "unknowns" as covered in R2-52 Unknowns.

Blackness, inability to get mock-ups and other Scientological liabilities can also be placed into people in this fashion.

It is interesting to note that the preclear, being incapable along the lines of energy and postulates, only very rarely gets through to anybody with this postulation. For the preclear is too "weak" to cause such effects. However, he should do this with great sincerity and with full belief that he is doing it. After a preclear has exteriorized, it is interesting to note that he still does not have this effect upon these people. But postulating such items actually does bring about the condition.

R 2-47:
Body Differentiation

This process is done in the same manner as R2-46 (R2-46, R2-47 and R2-48 being a group of processes).

One has the preclear note the differences between himself and the bodies of the people he can see in his immediate environment. This process is done in a park, or a railroad station, or on the street seated in a car. The auditing command is:

"Point out a difference between that person's body and yours."

This command is used over and over.

R2-48:
Separateness

This is a key process attacking individuation. In his effort to control, a thetan spreads himself further and further from the universe. And in his failures to control, withdraws from things he has attempted to control, but leaves himself connected with them in terms of "dead energy." Thus we get the manifestation "buttered all over the universe."

This was the process which told me that we are not natively sprung from one "common body of theta." If you run Separateness, accentuating the difference in unity of a thetan from other thetans and things and spaces, he continues to gain in tone. If you run this process in reverse, how he is the same as or is connected to various items, he continues to dwindle in tone. By handling this latter process, one can press a thetan down into the rock-bottom state of aberration. We have long known that *differentiation* was the keynote of sanity and that *identification* was the basis of aberration. This fact is utilized in processing by running Separateness.

It can be concluded that the thetan is an individual, separate from every other thetan, and that he has never been part of any other thetan. There are many "phony" incidents implanted on the track, whereby an individual is made to feel that he is a result of an explosion having occurred to a larger body. He is also made to feel that he was at one time "whole" and is now only a splinter of himself. This is only an effort to reduce him. He has always been himself, he will always be himself, down to a time when he is entirely identified with this universe—at which time he would no longer be himself simply because he would no longer be conscious.

It seems that the "only" aberration can occur by *enforcing* Basic Truth (Axiom 35). Here we discover that the individual, being separate, is then *forced* to be separate and so develops a complex of the "only one" and tries to fend off the rest of the universe from himself and finally merges with it, with his impossibility of fending it off. All you have to do is accentuate the truth and force it home as an Other-determinism, in order to create an aberration. There is some Basic Truth, then, in whatever is wrong with a thetan. And, of course, the basic wrongness is that he is not a static.

Separateness is best run by having the preclear out in an open place inhabited by a great many people, as in R2–46 (Other People) and R2–47 (Body Differentiation).

The auditing commands are:

"Point out some things from which you are separate,"
"Point out some more things from which you are separate,"
"Point out some more things from which you are separate."

You might believe that there might be some value in having him point out some things from which he is *not* separate, in order to "As-is" his connections to things. However, if you started this process on having him find things from which he is not separate, you would very quickly discover that your preclear is deteriorating in tone and that he does not resurge. This is a one-direction process, having him point out things from which he *is* separate.

It should occur to you, as we learn in R2–43 (Fighting), that a thetan desires lots of opponents. Of course, the more separateness that he discovers, the more opponents he can have and the more fighting he can see before him. This makes him happy. By conceiving himself identified with an enormous number of things, he is of course rendered very scarce in opponents.

And this makes him unhappy and makes him choose out only things which he could then fight without being challenged, such as his engram bank or his body or his own machinery.

The basic reason a thetan conceives a great many remote viewpoints is to have a separateness from himself. A thetan can actually be separate from himself, as a remote viewpoint, and choose out himself, a thetan, as his opponent. Many a person who is thoroughly interiorized is being the body so he can fight himself, a thetan. This is also inverted. When I was making some of these basic discoveries, I was puzzled to encounter the fact that in many preclears, the preclear was entirely sold on the fact that he was "attacking a demon which was attacking his body." He would analytically conceive himself to be a thetan, but actually was being the body. And as the body and a remote viewpoint in it, was attacking a theta body which actually contained himself–a thetan. This complexity came about when he was not even permitted to fight the body.

As the totality of mis-emotion and weakness is exhibited solely when a thetan lacks opponents and feels he cannot have a fight, you will discover in running Separateness that many mis-emotions, weaknesses and so forth rise to the surface.

This is a relatively long process by itself, but it should be done in conjunction with R2-46 and R2-47.

Remember that the preclear should be absolutely certain that he is separate from the item. Do not take any "maybes."

R 2-49:
DEI Scale

The scale of Desire-Enforce-Inhibit is repeated over and over in that order as we go down the Tone Scale. And is therefore repeated in reverse order as we find a preclear rising. In running almost any process, it will be discovered that what the preclear is currently desiring will shortly be inhibited by the preclear, and what is being inhibited will shortly be enforced by the preclear, and what is being enforced by the preclear will shortly be desired by the preclear, and this in turn will again be inhibited by the preclear and so forth.

Step IV of SOP 8 (Expanded GITA) gives a great many items which are useful in raising tone. The number of items which produce the greatest effect, when used as prescribed in Step IV of SOP 8 (given in this book), follow:

Fighting

Self-determinism

Engrams

Health

Sanity

Peace

Evil

Present Time

Imagination

Control

Using any one of the above, fitted into the place of the blank in these auditing commands, one runs the DEI Scale in this fashion:

"Waste some fighting,"
"Have somebody else waste some fighting."

This is done until the communication lag is flat.

Then:

"Mock-up and pull in some fighting."

"Waste some _____,"
"Have somebody else waste some _____," and so forth, until the communication lag has been leveled.

"Mock-up and pull in some _____,"
"Mock-up and pull in some _____,"
"Mock-up and pull in some _____," again, until the preclear has no communication lag.

"Desire some _____,"
"Have somebody else desire some _____."

The DEI Scale, then, is approximated in processing by *waste* for inhibit, *accept* for enforce, and simply the idea for desire.

There are many other factors which could be utilized in this process and which have been utilized in this process, such as Problems, Healthy Bodies and so forth. But these are not as effective as the above-given list, which is the choice list of all the other factors which could be utilized.

Another list can be used, with considerable effectiveness, and this is the Know to Mystery Scale.

One would then have the preclear *waste, accept* and *desire,* in that order, the following items, in this order:

Mysteries

Problems

Sex

Eating

Symbols

Effort

Emotion

Vision

Hearing

Thought

It is interesting to note that a person who has sonic shut-off is hanging on to silence. One can have him *waste, accept* and *desire* sonic and vision pain and unconsciousness.

By running pain with the DEI Scale, one will discover that the thetan actually desires pain: Any sensation is better than no sensation.

R 2-50:
Changing Minds

The basic process of a thetan is simply getting him to change his mind. Most thetans fall below the level of mechanics. They have to be brought up to a point where they are not being handled by mechanics before they can simply change their considerations. If Changing Minds worked on any thetan, it would then be the only process in Scientology. But it does not work on thetans who are interiorized, since they are being other things than themselves. And when they start to change their minds, they are simply changing something else.

When you have a thetan exteriorized, all you have to do is ask him to change his mind. And unless he is still very badly burdened by mechanical considerations with which he is so thoroughly agreed that he cannot immediately change his mind, he will do so.

This process can be used on a non-exteriorized thetan, however, and on those who are uneasily exteriorized, by having them stand in one place with an idea that they have to *"appear there"* and then change their minds and *"disappear there."* Or simply have them stand in one place until they change their mind and then go to another place and change their mind. This is actually done by moving the body around, as most auditing these days is done.

The auditing commands for this would be:

"Walk over to this spot (indicating a spot to the preclear)*,"*
"Now decide you have to appear there,"
"Now change your mind and decide you have to disappear there,"
"Now change your mind and decide you have to appear there,"
and so on.

This can also be worked into Opening Procedure (R2-16) by having a preclear select a spot, then change his mind about the spot, select another spot, change his mind about that spot and select another spot–until he knows that he, himself, is changing his mind.

When exteriorized, the thetan can change his mind very easily on any subject simply when told to do so. Very often he does not realize that he can change the factors of his life around simply by changing his mind and so has to be asked to do so by the auditor.

A note of warning: This does not work on interiorized preclears with any great value.

R 2-51:
Rising Scale Processing

This is one of the older processes of Scientology. It consists of the individual being asked to get "whatever idea he can" about the buttons of the Chart of Attitudes and then "change his ideas upwards."

Using this process, the entire endocrine system of the preclear has been altered for the better.

The auditing commands would be dependent upon the Chart of Attitudes. The buttons of the Chart of Attitudes are:

Dead – Survives

Wrong – Right

No Responsibility – Fully Responsible

Owns Nothing – Owns All

Nobody – Everyone

Never – Always

Stopped – Motion Source

Hallucination – Truth

Distrust – Faith (Trust)

I Know Not – I Know

Full Effect – Cause

I Am Not – I Am

Lose – Win

Stop – Start

Identification – Differences

Had – Being

The auditing commands involved in this process follow:

"How close can you come to trusting everybody?"
"Now do you have that idea?"

And when the preclear has:

"All right. Shift that idea as high as you can toward trust."

Do this many times with the preclear on one item of the list before going on to the next.

R2-52:
Unknowns

One of the liabilities of Dianetics was that it took all the data off the bank and left on the bank *effort* and *unknown substances*. Efforts and unknowns were not As-ised.

One of the basic auditing commands of this is:

"Give me some unknown incidents."

The preclear, as he tries to do so, will immediately find known incidents turning up rapidly. He is As-ising unknownness.

One of the best ways of using Unknowns is with a group of Separatenesses (R2–48), where the preclear is outside looking at other people. Have him get how much is unknown to each one of these people, with the following auditing command:

"Now find a person and put some unknowingness into him,"
"Now find another person and put some unknowingness into him."

A variation of this is:

"Put unknownness of location into a person,"
"Now another person," and so on.

The reason why location is used is because it is part of the definition of "stupidity" (Axiom 38). One can also use time, with the following command:

"Put some unknown times into that person,"
"Now put some unknown times into that person," and so on.

Remember to always run the same auditing command, over and over and over, until a change has ceased to occur in the preclear.

R 2-53:
Repair

A four-star process.

It seems rather obvious that we should handle "repair" as a process, since that is what we have been doing in Dianetics and Scientology. If a preclear can't himself repair, he gets some help – a doctor, a minister. If the auditor can't repair, he won't run processes to make the preclear well. Granting of beingness has "repair" as a major part of its sphere.

The cycle-of-action of the MEST universe for this process could be:

Create-Repair (Change)-Deteriorate (Change)-Destroy.

The auditing commands for this process are:

"What wouldn't you mind repairing?"
"What wouldn't you mind letting others repair?"
"What would you mind repairing?"
"What would you mind others repairing?"
"What don't you know how to repair?"
"What don't others know how to repair?"

The above is the main process and should be heavily stressed. The communication lags are very long and the process must not be briefly run. Finish one command, reducing all lag by many times using it, get the question answered every time. Use for hours.

Other indicated questions are run by substituting the following for "repair" in the above question form:

> *Create, (Repair) Change, Deteriorate, Destroy,* or
> *Start, (Change)* and *Stop* – the factors of control.

CHAPTER FIVE
INTENSIVE PROCEDURE: ROUTE 2

A specific group of processes, which have been discovered to do a great deal for preclears, consists of R2-53 Repair, followed by R2-44 Must and Must Not Happen, followed by R2-43 Fighting, followed by R2-42 Pan-determinism. This series, run with the auditing commands as given, is enormously effective.

A complete audit of a preclear in very bad condition could follow this plan:

R2-16 Opening Procedure of 8-C, for several hours;

R2-17 Opening Procedure by Duplication, for several hours;

R2-20 Use of Problems and Solutions, using the commands given in the last paragraph of that section.

Then:

R2-53 Repair;

R2-44 Must and Must Not Happen;

R2-43 Fighting;

R2-42 Pan-determinism;

R2-39 Conceiving Something Interesting, as given in its last paragraphs;

R2-54 Flows;

R2-55 Importance.

Used in this exact order, continuous and very wonderful changes can be made to occur in a preclear even though he began the process as entirely psychotic. Many such routes could be designed, but this particular one happens to have been tested in this order on preclears and found workable.

R 2-54:
flows

The processing of flows has several times been tested in Scientology. And each time it has been discovered that there were many preclears who could not handle them with the processes which have already been advanced. Therefore, the static and the object were concentrated upon and flows were avoided. However, R2-54 overcomes this past difficulty. This is a very splendid way to make a preclear change his considerations. But it should be run long enough to take away the somatics which it turns on, for the somatics which R2-54 turns on can be severe.

The process is extremely simple to run, but must, like all other processes here, be run exactly as given to produce the desired result. It consists of having the preclear point out things which *inhibit, enforce* and *desire* flows.

The auditing commands would be as follows:

"Look around you and point out some things, one after the other, which inhibit flows,"
"Now point out some more,"
"Now point out some more."

Then:

"Look around you and point out some things which enforce flows,"
"Now point out some more,"
"Now point out some more."

"Now look around you and indicate some things which desire flows,"
"Now point out some more,"
"Now point out some more."

Chapter Five
Intensive Procedure: Route 2

"Now look around you and point out some things which inhibit flows,"
"Now point out some more,"
"Now point out some more," and so on.

If the preclear is indicating people, he will discover with some rapidity that people are enforcing and inhibiting flows. He will discover also that speech is a flow. He will discover also that the universe is built of these flows. The preclear should be permitted to discover these things for himself. He will find, for instance, that blackness forces a flow.

If a preclear wishes to know what a flow is, point out to him that a light bulb is flowing light waves out into the room and that an object is reflecting them.

This process is, of course, worked best as part of the group where the preclear is taken outside and made to point out people (R2-46, R2-47, R2-48) and actually belongs with that group.

This is definitely a four-star process.

R 2-55:
Importance

This is a five-star process.

It might be a very bad thing to run this process immediately and at once upon a preclear. And an auditor should never begin with such a process on a case. Auditors, today, begin only with Opening Procedure of 8-C and follow that with Opening Procedure by Duplication and ordinarily follow that with Problems and Solutions, and only then go off into processes as difficult as this process.

Although this is a difficult process, it is not difficult to do. It is difficult because it produces such rapid change upon the preclear that he is liable to be left in some state where he considers all things "unimportant" and is made, by the process, to be out of balance with the universe and his life and his environment. And if it were run on a preclear who was having a difficult time, without first running Opening Procedure of 8-C and Opening Procedure by Duplication, he would of course have a tendency to stop being audited. For he would be plunged into the unimportance of everything, including auditing.

The keynote of Importance is simply this: Anything which is important is solid or big. And the more important a person believes himself to be, the bigger he is liable to get. Or the more important a person believes something to be, the more solid he is liable to make it. Anybody who believes that minds are important is liable to make them solid. Hence, we immediately get the type of bank which some people have, with their solid facsimiles and, in consequence, masses and ridges.

We began to hit this a number of years ago when we discovered that whatever we validated became more prominent. I did not, at that time, know why this was and have now discovered that it is because things which are considered important become more solid.

This could also be called "Games Processing," for we are handling here the most important part of Importance–the fact that in order to have a game, there must be something important to defend, to have, to attack. There is no game unless one has some item which is important, for it would not be visible to anyone but himself if it were not solid.

"Important" and "solid" can be considered to be, for our purposes, synonyms.

The auditing commands which run this are very simple and are pursued for some time without change of command.

First:

"Tell me some things which are important,"

"Tell me some more things which are important,"

"Tell me some things which are important to other people,"

"Tell me some more things which are important to other people," back and forth on this.

Then:

"Point out some things which are important,"

"Point out some more things which are important,"

"Point out some things which other people consider important,"

"Point out some more things which other people consider important."

Then:

"Tell me some things which are unimportant,"

"Tell me some more things which are unimportant,"

"Tell me some things which are unimportant to other people,"

"Tell me some more things which are unimportant to other people,"
back and forth on this.

Then:

"Point out some things which are unimportant,"

"Point out some more things which are unimportant,"

"Point out some things which other people consider unimportant,"

"Point out some more things which other people consider unimportant."

In view of the fact that each consideration that something is important tends to add mass and each consideration that something is unimportant tends to detract mass, and in view of the fact that the consideration that something is important is the second postulate to the truth that it was unimportant, we discover the mechanism which causes minds to form large masses such as facsimiles and engrams.

At first one considered his mind unimportant, then he considered it important, and then again unimportant, and then again important. And this cyclic activity brings into existence the mind as mass—which is to say, creates the reactive mind.

We occasionally discover people who are having considerable difficulty—and the wide-open case and the occluded case—with considerable energy mass which they are calling their mind.

They do their thinking by facsimiles, they do their behaving at the orders of the facsimile. This can be traced immediately to the consideration that the mind is important, unimportant, important, unimportant, important, unimportant, in a repeating cycle.

An indicated process to remedy this condition would be:

"Spot some spots,"
"Spot some more," etc.

And:

"Spot some spots where others thought the mind was unimportant,"
"Spot some more such spots," and so forth.
"Spot some spots where you thought the mind was important,"
"Spot some more such spots," and so forth.
"Spot some spots where others thought the mind was important," etc.

This sequence of commands should be run, each one, until the communication lag is flat. And then, as in all such sequences in this book, should be gone through again several times.

A vital, if somewhat murderous process, very important to be run on Scientologists, is:

"Spot some spots where you thought thought was unimportant,"
"Some more,"
"Some more," etc.
"Spot some spots where others thought thought was unimportant," etc.

"Spot some spots where you thought thought was important," etc.
"Spot some spots where others thought thought was important," etc.

This crosses Importance with Conceiving a Static (R2–40).

Another indicated question is:

"What important things could you be?"
"Give me some more important things you can be."

And then:

"Give me some important things you could do as a thetan,"
"Give me some more important things you could do as a thetan."

A general formula on Importance would be to spot spots where the preclear considered everything on the Know to Mystery Scale important, emphasizing words, sounds, sights, blackness and energy. By running this process, you can expect a considerable regain of education on the part of the preclear.

Almost all education has been hammered into the preclear as a "terribly important activity." Actually, it will be as much use to him as it is considered casually. This accounts, in some measure, for the tremendous difference in the attitude toward education of one trained by casual and interested tutors and one trained between the millstones of the public school system, with all the horrors of the examination for passing. And accounts for the complete failure, on the part of universities, to educate into existence a leadership class. The secret lies entirely in the fact that education is as effective as it is pleasant, unhurried, casual, and is as ineffective as it is stressed to be important. For example, giving arithmetic the category of "something terribly important" is to bring the student at length into possession of a solid lump of energy which, utterly useless to him, will lie there as "arithmetic." This also accounts for the failure of the child genius. Generally, his parents consider his career so important that eventually his piano playing or painting will be an energy mass. He will be as good as, and as effective as, he can change his considerations. And one does not easily change his considerations in the face of such energy masses.

CHAPTER FIVE
INTENSIVE PROCEDURE: ROUTE 2

Auditors have often wondered at the resistance of the preclear toward turning on sonic and visio and at the persistence of blackness. Here, again, we have a problem of importance. The deafer a person becomes or the less sonic a person has, the more he tends to believe it is important for him to have this attribute. And, of course, the less he has it, for the more solid it gets. Solidity could be said to be "stupidity."

Here, also, we have the tremendous stress, as given in Book One, on words. The more important instructions are, the more important words are. The more important speech becomes, as in general semantics, the more buried and, therefore, the more effective words become in the reactive bank. If you were to choose a single process out of Importance, the one which would probably pay off best would be one which *wasted* words, *accepted* them and *desired* them, in brackets. And then, which caused the preclear to spot all the spots where words were considered *unimportant* and words were considered *important*, for himself and for others.

We are looking at the "master trick." A person is as well-off as he is free and lacking in uncontrolled energy deposits. But these gather to the degree that certain facets of existence are stressed as *important*.

R 2-56:
Games Processing

Games Processing 1954 is quite different than its predecessors, but the fundamentals are the same in Scientology as they have always been. The highest activity, action or ambition is "to have a game." A game requires that one create or have an opponent. The whole series centering around Fighting is actually the lower range of Games Processing (which accounts for its tremendous effectiveness).

Processing Games directly, the first indicated process would be one taken from Description Processing (R2–34) which would As-is certain undesirable characteristics. This would be done with the command:

"Give me some games which are no fun,"

"Give me some more games which are no fun,"

"Give me some more games which are no fun," until the Apathy and Antagonism toward games in general has been to a marked degree As-ised.

As an opponent is an essential part of games, the processing of opponents in general produces interesting results in a case. We could simply improve the *considerations* of the preclear, with regard to opponents, by asking him:

"What sort of opponents could you have?" and carrying this forward until all communication lag is gone.

Or one could have the preclear *waste, accept* and *desire* opponents, where the accepting is done by having him mock-up an opponent and remedying his havingness for it.

Another interesting process which produces excellent results is:

"Name some unromantic roles,"
"Name some more unromantic roles," and so forth.

"Name some romantic roles,"
"Name some more romantic roles," and so forth.

"Name some unromantic roles,"
"Name some more unromantic roles," and so forth, back and forth, until the preclear has regained the ability to imagine some roles.

Actually, he has been given roles by the motion pictures and television and his propaganda textbooks, until he will only accept a role which is generally approved by this society as represented in fiction. This could be said to be an intentionally fictionalized society. Marriages quite often go to pieces simply because Jim Jones and Mary Smith did not get married. Jim Jones, posing as Alan Ladd, marries Mary Smith, posing as Lana Turner. And a fictional Alan Ladd married to a fictional Lana Turner is going to be disappointed. Whereas, there is no reason under the sun why Jim Jones shouldn't be a good and interesting guy, doing an interesting role, and why Mary Smith should not be doing a role herself, as herself. For people are interesting to the degree that they can postulate and act into existence the roles required of them in life.

The Bard of Stratford-on-Avon said that "All the world's a stage," but didn't give us the process by which we could be "players." Your preclear has been "audience" and this process boots him out of being audience into being a player (which is more or less what the auditor is trying to do with a preclear). He can't have any games where everybody is being an audience and nobody is playing.

The scarcity of roles which a person can actually occupy in this society is such that we commonly discover a preclear continuing to act out any role, which he has been given in some school play, which he found romantic. I know several preclears whose total difficulty is that they have never ceased to be the gangster they did so well in the high school production of *Officer 666*, or the prostitute they did so excellently in the college drama club production of *Rain*.

A not-recommended and rather dead-end process would be involved in asking the preclear for things "worth fighting for." In that he can only *postulate* things worth fighting for and in that he is so far down the scale on this, the process is a difficult one but can be used.

A preclear quite commonly has "play" and "work" nicely and neatly separated.

The difference between play and work is that play is fun and work is no fun, in the common parlance, until today we have only work. In view of the fact that effort is stupidity, unless understood, working at trying to play is the general difficulty with people.

Quite often a medical doctor will advise somebody to "stop working so hard" and "start playing." The actual fact of it is, an executive quite commonly has his work as his only play (and really *plays* when he is working and he has to *work* to play) and so the medical doctor has consigned him to some hard work by telling him he has to play.

Thus we have an inversion.

"What kind of a game could you have?"
"Give me some more games you could have," is a useful process.

Chapter Five
Intensive Procedure: Route 2

"What would you have to be to have a game?"

"Some more things you would have to be to have a game," carried forward, interspersed with an actual description from the preclear of each game he lists, is very effective.

The following process ranks very high in effectiveness in all these procedures:

"What kind of a game could you have involving _____?"

In asking this question, the auditor points out some object in the immediate environment and the preclear is made to describe what kind of a game he could have with that object. The auditor then points out another object in the environment and asks:

"What kind of a game could you have involving _____?"

It will soon be borne home to the preclear that he has been trying to play games with the absence of opponents, that he has hung on to most of the disasters that have happened to him in his life because they meant the loss of opponents.

Here we find the child, who has been raised alone, dreaming up illusory opponents. And later on we discover him mocking-up demons. Any time we walk into an insane asylum and discover somebody involved with a battle with demons (or who has a demon, or who has a guardian angel, or who has any one of these mythical assistants or opponents), we are looking at somebody who found opponents so scarce that he had to mock them up. And having mocked them up, was unable to unmock them—for no new opponent came along.

The reason war mobilizes everyone into action and speeds up production in a country is because a tangible opponent has been introduced and people will accept tangible opponents above illusory opponents.

Man's activity in fighting himself, thetans' activities in fighting themselves, all stem from this effort to play games in the absence of opponents.

"What kind of a game could you have involving _____*?"* should be run until the preclear is cognizant of everything he is doing with regard to opponents, without ever mentioning opponents to him.

R2-57:
Processes

The processing of Processes actually belongs to Via (R2-41). It is an intensely important thing to do. Cells, trees, the whole of life is engaged in working processes. Normally they work them unconsciously.

One of the methods of straightening out this fixation on processes is to have the preclear plan to do something very simple, such as move an ashtray. Have him plan it out in its entirety and then have him execute it exactly as he planned it. One does this many times with many objects.

Another way of working this process is:

"Discover things in the environment which are using processes," and *"Discover things in the environment for which you could invent processes."*

R 2-58:
Loss

The subject of loss is an entire study in itself. It is the subject of havingness as well.

Loss results in *Degradation, Memory Failure, Blackness* and what we used to call "stuck on the track." So it is an important subject.

Loss, itself, can occur only when the consideration that one *wants, needs,* has to *have* has occurred first.

When one loses something "important," one supplants it by dragging in energy deposits, facsimiles on himself.

Here is the Scale of Substitutes Acquired by Reason of Loss:

    Cumulative Spiral
                Stopped Time
    Object
    Loss

sub Object owned
    Loss

sub Object others
    Loss

sub Mock-up
    Loss

sub Mock-up owned
    Loss

sub Mock-up others
    Loss

sub Problem
    Loss   ━━Lost by solution
                  ━━Lost by occlusion

sub Problem owned
Loss

sub Problems others
Loss

sub Blackness
(something in it?)
Loss

sub Blackness owned
Loss

sub Blackness others
Loss

sub Unconsciousness
Loss

sub Unconsciousness own
Loss

sub Unconsciousness others
Loss

sub Unconsciousness own
Loss

sub Unconsciousness
Loss

sub Blackness others
Loss

sub Blackness own

Hallucination

The Remedy of Havingness is a good process to overcome loss.

However, loss is a consideration.

The following processes remedy considerations involving havingness:

"What assistance do you need to survive?"
"What assistance do others need to survive?"

The most effective Straightwire on this is:

"Name some important possessions,"
"Some more," etc.
"Name some things it is important not to have."

As we have havingness going down to Ownership, then to Protection, then to Hiding, we have:

"Name some things it is important to protect."

"Name some things it is important to hide."

"Name some things it is important to display (exhibit)."

These are lower-level manifestations.

"Important possessions" will exteriorize.

R 2-59:
Survival

Whenever I have found a process unworkable in the past sixteen years, I have found that the unworkable process avoided the Dynamic Principle of Existence, Survive. In other words, it did not greatly matter how this principle was embroidered, if it was included in the process or rationale, some workability resulted.

The Dynamic Principle of Existence, Survive, and its application as the dynamics is easily the greatest discovery in Dianetics.

Even when we add to it the remainder of the curve of the cycle-of-action of the MEST universe, Create-Survive-Destroy, we find *Survive* is the potent truth in it.

So, Scientology or Dianetics, if we neglect *Survival* in our rationale, processes become unworkable.

Survive has as its dichotomy, Succumb. When one is below 2.0 on the Tone Scale, all Survival looks *evil* to him. LIVE = EVIL, in the succumbing case. To punish is to declare a thing evil. To be evil is to refuse Survival.

The dynamics are a breakdown of the dynamic Survival into eight parts. Each dynamic in turn breaks down into many parts. Thus we have life. And these interplays of Survival *are* life.

If your preclear is not Clear, he is avoiding Survival on one or many dynamics. His considerations about Survival are his personality.

I tell you this lest we forget. Dianetics is a *precision* science. It stems from this study and codification of Survival. Survival *is* the reason why.

Opening Procedure of 8-C (R2-16) works because the preclear, in spotting MEST, is recognizing "Look! After all I've been through, I've Survived."

Having a preclear spot, in a crowd, people's Survival potential is great processing.

The auditing command:

"Point out some things in your surroundings which aren't Surviving," will spring Grief or Apathy.

"Point out some things which are Surviving," is quite potent.

"Point out some unknown methods of Surviving," is one of these "fader" questions – he can almost answer it for hours.

As a thetan is immortal, he cannot do other than Survive. When he realizes this, his game may become, "How can I succumb?"

Survival has pay. That pay is the sensation of pleasure. This is acquired by Interest. One tries to Survive by being interesting. He demands of life that he be interested.

Thus, with the preclear in a crowd:

"What could that person (auditor indicating one) *(have, do, be) that would be uninteresting?"*
"What could that person (have, do, be) that would be uninteresting to your (ally)?"

The preclear has As-ised all the interest from life and has left intact uninteresting things. When he tries to get interested anew, uninteresting ridges soak up his interest.

"What dreams (goals) would you find uninteresting?" is interest + future = Survival.

A murderous auditing command, while the preclear is outside looking at people and the world, is:

"What dreams could that person have that would not interest you?"

"What dreams could that person have that would not interest your mother (and other allies)?"

Interest of allies make Survival possible. Anything which succeeds in interesting allies (orientation-points and symbols) then may be a successful mock-up for the preclear all his life. Syphilis, fatness, stupidity may be "interesting" enough to allies to leave the preclear with them all his life. For an interested ally means future and that is Survival.

Get a list of *all* people he has known since birth. Ask him, for each one, many times:

"What would be interesting to (ally)?" and you'll find his service facsimile and the source of his aberrations and psychosomatics.

"What dynamic could you abandon?" could be used on a Scientologist.

The most basic question about bodies, being cellular organisms, is:

"What wouldn't a cell Survive?"

"What else wouldn't a cell Survive?" and so on.

This is a very old but very potent Dianetic process for the repair of bodies. Organs, body parts and types of bodies can be substituted for cells in the above question.

Remember, your goal is to improve the preclear's Survival. If he thinks Survival is evil, if to succumb is the only way he can get interest, your road will be eased by remembering and processing the Dynamic Principle of Existence–Survive–on all or any dynamic by any type of process. And this is the rationale of Dianetics, which may be freely used by a Scientologist.

R 2-60:
The Hidden
Communication

"Spot some hidden knowingness," is an auditing command which, pursued properly, opens the gates to freedom.

In *Scientology 8-8008* you will find a scale which begins at its lowest rung with Hidden. Above that is Protection. Above that is Ownership. I have recently discovered that the DEI cycle and the above low scale join to make the scale read:

Curiosity

Desire

Enforcement

Inhibition

Ownership

Protection

Hidden

And I have discovered that the road upward through this scale is communication.

Knowingness condenses. Trying to know becomes the first level of communication. This "looking to know" condenses into "emoting to know," which condenses into "effort to know," which in turn becomes "thinking to know," which then condenses into "symbols to know," which (and this is the astonishing thing) becomes "eating to know," which becomes "sexual activity to know," which then turns into oblivion of knowing or "mystery."

An energy particle is a condensed knowingness. Trying to discover or move one is an action with the goal of knowingness.

Gravity, grim thought, becomes in the mind, and is, the effort to know, to pull in knowingness.

Other-determinism is only other knowingness.

The aspects of "know" are the common denominators of any scale in Scientology. When knowingness is done by communication, we get emotion and effort particles changing position.

This struggle to know is not just me and thee working on Scientology and gone mad in the process. It *is* life and all its manifestations, including space, energy, matter and time. Each is only a barrier to knowingness. A barrier is a barrier only in that it impedes knowingness. Barriers do not exist for complete knowingness.

And what is there to know? Only that knowingness can vary. One has to *invent* things to know. For there is only knowingness and knowingness has no data, since a datum is an invented, not a true knowingness. The motto of any particle below lookingness is "Only energy can tell you."

We handle R2-60, Hidden Communication, in this wise:

"Spot some hidden communications,"
"And now spot some more hidden communications," and so forth.

We may have to direct the preclear closely with:

"Point to the spot,"
"How far away does it seem?"
"Are you spotting a hidden communication there?" and such questions, meanwhile keeping good ARC.

He could be asked to spot specific kinds of hidden communications, as with this command:

"Spot some hidden disease communications,"

or

"Some hidden poisonous communications,"

or

"Spot some hidden but uninteresting communications."

But use the question to flatten all communication lags before you change it.

If he goes into the past, let him. He'll come back to the present. He'll find his chronic somatic and do many interesting things including, perhaps, the data in the text of R2-60 here.

It is curious that the above, *"Spot some hidden communications,"* does not seem to require a remedy of havingness. But it will turn on many heavy ridges and somatics.

Having thoroughly worked *"hidden communications,"* you can now use this command:

"Spot some protected communications."

And when that is null:

"Spot some owned communications."

And after that has no communication lag:

"Spot some inhibited (stopped) communications."

Then:

"Spot some enforced communications."

And then:

"Spot some desired communications."

Now, when all that is done, proceed as follows:

"Spot some hidden knowingness,"
"Are you spotting it in the physical universe?"

If so:

"All right, point at it,"
"How far away does it seem?"

"Spot some more hidden knowingness," and so on, until after an hour or two or six this command is communication lag flat.

Now start upscale as follows, making the preclear point and give the distance to the spot (even when trillions of miles away):

"Spot some protected knowingness."

And after many times of that, then:

"Spot some protected knowingness," many times.

Then:

"Spot some owned knowingness," many times.

Then:

"Spot some inhibited knowingness."

Then:

"Spot some enforced knowingness."

Then:

"Spot some desired knowingness."

Then:

"Spot some knowingness that people could be curious about."

In R2-60, Hidden Communication, we can use the Know to Mystery Scale:

"Spot some mysteries."

"Spot some hidden sex."

"Spot some hidden eating."

"Spot some hidden symbols."

"Spot some hidden thinking."

"Spot some hidden efforts."

"Spot some hidden emotions."

"Spot some hidden looking."

"Spot some hidden knowing."

Then:

"Spot some protected mysteries."

"Spot some protected sex," etc., etc.

You can, using the principles of hidden knowing and communication, combine any other part of Scientology with them, and discover an excellent process. However, the first commands given in R2-60 are the easiest to communicate and use.

R 2-61:
Good and Evil

The factors of good and evil are the factors of accepting Other-determinism (good) and accepting or giving blows (evil).

That which cooperates is "good."

That which is punished is "evil."

This is the totality of consideration involved.

"Good" and "evil" are Third Dynamic phenomena. But unlike most words one might process, these have definite emotional connotations which, to the preclear, speak louder than the words. These apply from Mystery up to Know.

Just as "good" and "evil" are the primary fixation of philosophy, so are they a primary fixation in a preclear. So confused are they, in philosophy or in preclears, that an enormous complexity results. Their resolution would resolve either philosophy or preclears.

The basic auditing commands to handle this extremely important process are:

"Spot a place where you decided to be good,"
"Now spot a spot in this room."

"Spot the place again,"
"Spot a spot in this room."

"Spot the spot again where you decided to be good,"
"Spot a spot in this room," etc., until all communication lag is gone for one distant spot where the decision was made to be good.

Then:

"Now find another spot where you decided to be good,"
"Spot a spot in this room," etc., and so on until many spots are "cleared."

Actually, the auditor wants the distant spot to come into present time before he leaves it. But at least reduce communication lag for each spot.

Now do exactly the same procedure using the following auditing command:

"Spot a place where another person decided to be good,"
"Now spot a spot in this room," alternating back and forth until communication lag is reduced.

The same is now done for "evil" with this slight variation:

"Spot a spot where you decided you were evil,"
"Spot a spot in this room."

"Spot the spot again where you decided you were evil,"
"Spot a spot in this room," etc., as for "good," picking out new single spots and clearing each one as far as possible.

Then follow the same procedure with the command:

"Spot a place where another person decided he was evil,"
"Spot a spot in this room," etc., reducing communication lag for each spot.

Then:

"Point out some unknown evils,"
"Point out what other people would find an unknown evil."

You may have to remedy havingness for the preclear, for this is very destructive of havingness.

The preclear will come up with many considerations and changing ideas. Let him voice them but continue with the process.

Don't let your preclear leave the session with a "good" or "evil" spot uncleared or in restimulation.

He will become neither saint nor devil from running this; he will become more capable of good action.

R 2-62:
Overt Acts and Motivators

One of the primary discoveries in Dianetics was the Overt Act-Motivator phenomena.

An *overt act* is a harmful act performed against another.

A *motivator* is an overt act performed against oneself by another.

If one receives a motivator, he then may consider himself licensed to perform an overt act against the person who harmed him.

When one commits an overt act *without* having received a motivator, he attempts then to "mock-up" or acquire a proper motivator or "justify" his own harmful action.

An *overt act* delivered in the absence of a motivator we call an *unmotivated act.*

A *justifier* is the technical term we apply to the "mock-up" or overt act demanded by a person guilty of an unmotivated act.

In that a thetan cannot possibly, actually, be harmed–having no mass, wavelength or actual location–*any* harmful act he performs is an unmotivated act. Thus a thetan basically cannot have a *motivator-overt act* sequence and always has an *unmotivated act-justifier* sequence.

The "catch" in this is the idea of "harmful" (good and evil). An act *must* be considered harmful or evil to be an overt act. To need a justifier, a person *must* have believed his act to have been harmful.

As the thetan cannot experience a *motivator-overt act* sequence, we have, then, the dwindling spiral. He is *always justifier hungry*. Thus he punishes and restimulates himself. Thus he is always complaining about what others do to him. Thus he is a problem to himself.

Only permit a thetan to get the idea that it is possible to harm others and you have, then, the dwindling spiral.

Use of these data in auditing is simple and intensely profitable.

For example, we have a preclear who continually complains about his father, how mean his father was to him. This means precisely that the actual facts of the past include many unmotivated acts against father by the preclear–*even though the preclear* seems to recall no such acts by himself and many overt acts against himself from father.

This is an excellent process to get a sudden result on a preclear. Ask him, Straightwire, for things he has done to his mother, father, any and all allies. Don't let him run things they have done to him.

"Can you recall doing something to your (father or other ally or person)*?"* is the only auditing question.

Having him remedy his havingness with motivators is also a fair process.

GUIDE TO THE MATERIALS

YOU'RE ON AN ADVENTURE!
HERE'S THE MAP.

Your journey to a full understanding of Dianetics and Scientology is the greatest adventure of all. But you need a map that shows you where you are and where you are going.

To obtain your **FREE Materials Guide Chart and Catalog**, fill out the following information and drop this card in the mail.

NAME _____ ADDRESS _____

CITY _____ STATE/PROVINCE _____

ZIP/POSTAL CODE _____ PHONE _____

E-MAIL _____

www.bridgepub.com

BUSINESS REPLY MAIL

FIRST CLASS MAIL PERMIT NO. 62688 LOS ANGELES, CA

POSTAGE WILL BE PAID BY ADDRESSEE

Bridge

PUBLICATIONS, INC.

4751 Fountain Avenue
Los Angeles CA 90029

R 2-63:
Accept-Reject

From Acceptance we get a ten-star process.

Whatever else you may do with a preclear, he must be brought to accept the physical universe *and* his own and other bodies, all in every kind of condition. *The way out is the way through.* In Eastern practices the goal was abandonment, desertion. Scientology's main difference from Eastern practices is this – it *accepts* to free. *And it frees.* That which one cannot accept chains one. For instance, revulsion to sex inclines at last to slavery to sex. A ruler's motto could be "make them resist" and his people would become slaves. In 1870 we find capitalists resisting Marx. In 1933 we find Marx the basic text of US government. Resistance and restraint are the barbed wire of this concentration camp. Accept the barbed wire and there is no camp.

On test, this process exteriorizes the worst case if run long enough.

This process is important because it is one of the few (like R2-16) which does not have Alter-isness as its operative factor. This is not, then, an altering process, confirming somatics and aberrations, it is a freeing process.

That which one cannot accept, he cannot As-is.

The commands of this process are as follows:

"Find something about yourself which you can accept,"
"Something else,"
"Find something else you can accept," etc., etc., until there is no communication lag.

Then:

"Find something about yourself you can reject,"
"Find something else about yourself you can reject," etc., etc.,
until there is no communication lag.

Then:

"Find something in this room you can accept,"
"Something else,"
"Find something else in this room you can accept," etc., etc.

"Find something in this room you can reject,"
"Find something else in this room you can reject," etc., etc.

Then:

"Find something about this universe you can accept," until
communication lag is flat.

Then:

"Find something in this universe you can reject."

Remember, this is not an altering process. It is a high-value
escape process. If your preclear keeps putting conditions of change
into everything before he can accept them, you must persuade
him to find things he can accept without changing them.

R 2-64:
Touching

Most thetans are inside because they are afraid to touch the outside. A baby is slapped out of touching things with its hands by mama *and* the MEST universe. Some thetans are afraid that if they touch MEST they'll stick to it and so remain "safely" inside.

There are two possible ways to run this. One is simply:

"What are you willing to touch?"

The other is:

"As a thetan, what are you willing to touch?"

If the preclear "no savvy" being a thetan, use the simpler form.

The command is:

"As a thetan, what are you willing to touch?"
"What else are you willing to touch?"
"What else are you willing to touch?" etc., etc.

Then:

"What are you willing to have touch you?"
"What else are you willing to have touch you?"

The mind can change without bringing Alter-isness into play. Changing the mind is the only possible way to improve without liability. This process alters only the mind.

This is a very valuable process. Eight stars.

R 2-65:
Alteration

As any energy or space condition survives only because it has been and is being altered, the primary unmotivated act would be changing the condition of energy, space and objects. The mind can change without liability. When a mind changes energy or space, we get a persistence of that energy or space. As persistence or Survival is good and bad only to those who desire to succumb, we do not see in alteration of energy or space any crime. But when we alter only "bad" conditions of space and energy, we make the "bad conditions" persist. Hence, it would be of value to a case to at least Straightwire out some of the times when he attempted to alter energy, spaces or the bodies of people. (To an auditor who works to exteriorize a preclear and change his mind, there is small liability and great personal advance. To an auditor who works only to change the body, the ridges, the somatics, there is failure, fixation of condition in the preclear and restimulation. *Successful* auditing of the thetan actually improves the auditor.) Failure is the biggest lock on Alter-isness, of course.

The preclear who is obsessively trying to change himself by self-auditing or whatever means, has *failed* many times to effect a change in the condition of this universe, or in the bodies of others, or has the space and energy of this universe as a stable constant.

The commands are:

"Can you recall a time when you failed to change some energy in this universe?" etc., etc.

And when this is flat:

"Can you recall a time when you failed to change some space?"

Then:

"Can you recall a time when you failed to change a body?"

This last is the one you stress. He may get nothing on the space question at all. *But* such incidents are in his recall or space would not exist at all for him.

Also:

"Can you recall a time when you failed to change a memory?" etc., etc.

Wherever or however the preclear is stuck in tone or condition, there he has failed to change something or somebody.

This can also be run on the "theta side of the ledger":

"Can you recall a time when you successfully changed something?" until the lag is flat.

Even more simply:

"Can you recall a time of change?"

R 2-66:
Electing Cause

Worry and anxiety have their root in the changing election of Cause.

People who elect Cause other than self are often shifting responsibility and refusing to fix actual Cause.

The "Black V" is a no-responsibility case.

This process is a brutal one, but it is a five-star process. It often sets off a "worry machine" and runs it out.

The auditing command is:

"Point out some things which are causing things,"
"Point out some more things which are causing things," etc., etc., until the lag is flat.

R 2-67:
Objects

To a person who cannot hold the two back corners of the room, the simple location of objects is valuable. When a person is self-auditing, this is a very valuable solo process.

The command is:

"Locate some objects," etc.

The person looks at them or puts his attention on them and notes what they are. This is all there is to the process. For variation, one locates some more objects.

By object is meant physical universe present time visible objects.

R 2-68:
Incomprehensibility

A thetan is understanding.

A space or mass is no understanding.

A thetan is no mass.

An object is mass.

Duplication is then difficult.

A thetan must be able to *be* a mass or a space and to experience, at will, incomprehensibility in order to see spaces and masses.

It is a new understanding to understand that something can be incomprehensible.

The Tone Scale is a study of varying degrees of ARC. ARC comprise understanding. With Knowingness at the top of the scale, we come down in "understanding" (Third Dynamic knowingness), then down through relative understandings and increasing incomprehensibility, until at bottom-scale (MEST) we have total incomprehensibility and total noncomprehension.

A "difficult" case is simply an *incomprehensible* case.

The processing on this is done by the command:

"Spot something incomprehensible," repeated many, many times.

This "ups" IQ and raises perception.

This is a good process.

R 2-69:
Please Pass the Object

(This process was developed by a long-time auditor. It is a very fine process and is recommended anywhere on the scale.)

Throughout the process the auditor doesn't say a word. He doesn't answer possible questions, he doesn't explain in words what he wants. Under all circumstances he makes like the Tar Baby and "don't say nuthin'." He uses any gestures necessary.

Step 1

a. Auditor stands in front of preclear, holding out a small object to him until the preclear takes it from his hand. As soon as the preclear takes the object, the auditor holds out his hand, palm up, until the preclear places the object in his palm. The auditor immediately offers it to the preclear again. This is continued until without communication lag. The object should be offered to the preclear from a variety of positions, once he has gotten the idea: from down near the floor, far off to either side, over the preclear's head. The palm should be held in a variety of positions for the return of the object. Both hands may be used. Get the preclear doing this really fast.

b. When Step I-a is going swiftly and easily, the auditor introduces a switch. After the preclear has just accepted the article, the auditor, instead of extending his palm for its return, places his hands behind his back briefly, then conveys by gestures that the preclear is to offer the object to him. When the preclear does so, the auditor takes the object from his hand but does not return it until the preclear holds out his own hand, palm up, to receive it.

This exchange is continued until the preclear is offering and accepting the object from as wide a variety of positions as the auditor used and all other communication lags are flat.

Step II

The auditor, just having accepted the object, makes a gesture that this part is over, then deliberately puts the object down where the preclear can see it, stands back, and indicates that the preclear is to pick it up. When the preclear picks it up, the auditor gestures that he is to put it down again anywhere he likes in the room. The instant the preclear does so, the auditor snatches it up and puts it somewhere else. This is continued until the auditor and preclear are racing around the room, seizing the object as soon as the other's fingers have let go of it. The object isn't necessarily placed in a different spot each time. It may be picked up and put down again in the same place, but it must be handled each time. All sorts of tacit rules and understandings will probably develop while this is being run.

This process rehabilitates the sense of play, validates nonverbal ARC, short-circuits verbal "machinery," lets the preclear position matter and energy in space and time, gets the preclear up to speed, murders "there must be a reason" for doingness, processes both auditor and preclear equally and, besides, it's fun.

R 2-70:
Expectance Level

This is a future type "acceptance level."

The command is:

"What do you expect from _____?" where the auditor fills the blank.

It is a cousin of Description Processing (R2–34).

Not for low cases.

R 2-71:
Answers

A relative of Problems and Solutions (R2-20) is:

"Give me some answers," as a constantly repeated question.

It is a valuable process.

R 2-72:
Security Processing

It is safe to do what your parents do–and that *is* evolution.

Death, failure, rejection are safe if your parents did them.

The auditing commands are:

"Tell me some things it is safe to be," etc.

"Tell me some things it is safe to do," etc.

"Tell me some things it is safe to have."

This works very well.

R 2-73:
Making Something for the future

The auditing command is:

"Point out some things which are making things for the future."

This is a brutal process.

R 2-74:
Processing (self-auditing)
(Reference: R2-57: Processes)

The auditing command is:

"Point out some things that are processing things."

This cures obsessive self-auditing.

R 2-75:
Knowingness

As everything is a condensation of knowingness, the following commands explain much and do much:

"Tell me something you wouldn't mind knowing."

"Something you wouldn't mind others knowing."

"Invent something to know."

A ten-star process.

R 2-76:
Communication Processing (Reference: Dianetics 55!)

The exact auditing commands to process Communications are:

Originated Communications

Auditor: *"Have somebody out there* (indicating a spot in the air) *start saying 'Hello' to you."*

The preclear does so, is himself silent.

When the process is long run:

Auditor: *"Start saying 'Hello' to a live spot out there."*

The preclear aloud, or as himself, does so.

Answers

Auditor: *"Have a spot out there start saying 'Okay' to you."*

The preclear does this many times.

Auditor: *"Start saying 'Okay' to a spot out there."*

Acknowledgments

Auditor: *"Have a spot out there start saying 'I did it.'"*

When the preclear has many, many times:

Auditor: *"Start saying 'I did it' to a spot out there."*

The command that turns on a somatic, repeated often enough, will turn it off.

When in doubt, remedy havingness.

The basic Communication command is:

"What wouldn't you mind communicating with?" in brackets.

R 2-77:

Games (Reference: Dianetics 55!)

The basis for this process is the observation that the MEST universe is a game.

One can have a game and know it. He can be in a game and not know it. The difference is his determinism.

Games require space and havingness. A game requires other players. Games also require skill and knowingness that they are games.

Havingness is the need to have terminals and things to play for and on.

When a game is done, the player keeps around tokens. These are hopes the game will start again. When that hope is dead, the token, the terminal, is hidden. And it becomes an automaticity–a game going on below the level of knowingness. Truthfully, one never stops playing a game once started. He plays old games in secret–even from himself–while playing or not playing new ones.

The only *real* game one can have is in present time. All others are in the past or the future. Anxiety for a game takes one into the past.

The command is:

"Invent a game."

And when the preclear has, again:

"Invent a game."

Then:

"Have somebody else invent a game."

Having established the fact that an auditing session is in progress and established some slight communication with the preclear, the auditor says:

"Invent a game."

When the communication lag on this is flat, the auditor then uses the command:

"Have somebody else invent a game."

This is the only phrase he utters. But he, of course, engages in two-way communication with the preclear when the preclear has something to say to him.

An auditor has to be a good auditor in order to use this process. Just because it is a simple "one-command" process is no reason why it will work for an auditor who is not cognizant with the Auditor's Code, cognizant of a two-way communication, and hasn't some experience in more basic levels of processing.

We use this process as a remedy for the scarcity of games and we use it in full awareness of the processes involved in two-way communication.

It is a murderous process and requires five or ten hours, in rough cases, to bring about an understanding of existence.

This is not necessarily a recommended process. It is a workable process, it does function, it is fast.

But remember that it has the frailty of the ability of the auditor himself. It has the frailty of failing when a two-way communication is not maintained with the preclear. It will fail if the preclear, in volunteering information, finds no attention from the auditor. It will fail if the auditor does not acknowledge the fact that the preclear has done this. But, if these things are considered, it will work.

This process can be abused by the preclear. He can wander from it. He can sit there in the auditing chair doing other things. But we depend upon the skill of the auditor to see that the preclear is not doing other things and that he is actually doing the process.

The preclear will "pick his bank clean" rather than invent, he will have doubts that he *is* inventing. But we persevere–and we win.

INTENSIVE PROCEDURE: L'Envoi

"...these same persons being run on R2-16 have, day after day, with an hour or two of such running per day, commenced steady and stable gains which they have retained."

Intensive Procedure:
L'Envoi

As a summary comment on these processes, it cannot be indicated too strongly that a preclear who is psychotic, neurotic or who is having any psychosomatic difficulty, must be run on Opening Procedure of 8-C (R2-16) for many, many, many, many hours. It will be discovered that on such preclears the use of subjective processes, which is to say, those processes which intimately address the internal world of the preclear, is fruitless. The processes which produce large results and effects will not make the preclear well.

As an example of this, many persons have been run by the "best processes" for fifty hours or more only to have their cases remain stagnant. And then these same persons being run on R2-16 have, day after day, with an hour or two of such running per day, commenced steady and stable gains which they have retained. When in doubt, then, on any process, run R2-16. And when the case claims that nothing is happening, run R2-16. And when the case is going very jumpily forward, with many losses and few gains, run R2-16. And when R2-16 has been thoroughly run, then turn to R2-17.

The reason why R2-16 is so effective is that it immediately addresses the problem of barriers. The preclear who is having difficulty will be found to be confounded by mechanics, which is to say, the barriers of space, energy and mass, and that these barriers have entered into his own universe so that he himself, in his own thinking, is encountering barriers. By making the preclear put his attention on objects, walls, floors, ceilings, the preclear will eventually come into the state where he himself is stopping his sight on the barrier, rather than the barrier stopping the sight of the preclear, for all perception is done by stopping the perception on what is looked at. This is only one of the reasons why Opening Procedure 8-C works. Use it.

GROUP

"Keep them in contact with present time and out
of their facsimile bank and you'll get
Group Processing Clears."

PROCESSING

Chapter Six

GROUP PROCESSING

FOR SUCCESSFUL GROUP PROCESSING the following are near absolutes.

1 The Group Auditor *must* be able to grant beingness to the group.

Stage fright and timid commands have no place in Group Auditing.

An auditor who is afraid of a group will "Q and A" with the group (as soon as it gets an effect, he changes the process – he changes commands when the group changes aspect).

2 Commands must be simple, clear, concise, evenly spaced, without sudden breaks of pace or jarring interjections of loudness.

3 The processes should be objective–addressing the environment, not the thinkingness of the group. Opening Procedure, adapted to a group, run long enough, would exteriorize everyone present.

4 Every command given should be run long enough to flatten every communication lag present.

5 Every process used should be run long enough consecutively to "flatten" the process itself.

6 The Auditor's Code in full should be obeyed.

If these rules are vigorously followed, good results can be attained in Group Processing.

Here are some standard processes for groups. Each is a one-hour session.

Session 1

"Spot some spots on the front wall,"
"Spot some more spots,"
"Spot some more spots," etc., for some time.

Then:

"Spot some spots on the floor,"
"Spot some more spots on the floor," etc., for some time.

Then:

"Without turning around, spot some spots on the back wall,"
"Some more spots," etc.

Then spot spots on the front wall again, then the floor, then the back wall. If the ceiling is used in this, their necks get tired very quickly.

Session 2

"Spot some spots in your body."

Pause.

"Spot some spots in the room."

Pause.

"Spot some spots in your body."

Pause.

"Spot some spots in the room."

Alternate these two commands for at least one hour.

Session 3

"Examine your chair."

Pause.

"Examine the floor."

Pause.

"Examine your chair."

Pause.

"Examine the floor."

And alternate these for at least one hour.

Session 4

"Where's your face?"

Pause.

"Where's your face?"

Pause.

"Where's your face?"

Pause.

"Where's your face?"

Pause.

And so on for at least one hour.

Session 5

"Start laughing."

Pause.

"Keep on laughing."

Pause.

"Laugh."

Pause.

"Keep on laughing."

Just these for at least an hour.

Session 6

"Where are you?"

Pause.

"Where are you?"

Pause.

"Where are you?"

Pause.

For at least one hour.

Session 7
Opening Procedure by Duplication

A very arduous one.

Have group, each one, hold two objects, one in each hand. Be very sure, as an auditor, not to vary your commands:

"Call the object in your left hand Object One,"
"Call the object in your right hand Object Two."

"Look at Object One,"
"What is its color?"
"Temperature?"
"Weight?"

"Look at Object Two,"
"What is its color?"
"Temperature?"
"Weight?"

"Look at Object One,"
"What is its color?"
"Temperature?"
"Weight?"

"Look at Object Two,"
"What is its color?"
"Temperature?"
"Weight?"

Use these over and over for at least an hour. Never give less than an hour of Opening Procedure by Duplication–never do it for only half an hour, much less fifteen minutes.

This is the first step of what Scientologists call "Dirty 30."

For convenience of the auditor this list is given:

Object One:
　　Color.
　　Temperature.
　　Weight.

Object Two:
　　Color.
　　Temperature.
　　Weight.

Session 8
Duplication by Attention

This is very arduous.

Put up two black pieces of material somewhat above eye level, at least 90 degrees apart for the preclear. Hang them up on the walls, ahead of the group so all can see them. (One on forward right wall, one on forward left wall is best.) Describe them to the group as Object One and Object Two.

"Put your attention on Object One,"
"Now put your attention on Object Two."

"Now put your attention on Object One,"
"Now put your attention on Object Two."

Do this without variation for at least an hour. On duplication processes, somebody in the audience usually claims this is "hypnotism," for it *runs out* hypnotism. It induces no trances. People who think so simply don't know much about hypnotism.

Session 9

This is in four parts. Do each part exactly fifteen minutes. It is run with the group's eyes closed.

"Find the two back corners of the room, hold on to them and don't think."

The auditor repeats this quietly and reassuringly every few minutes until fifteen minutes is reached. Then, at fifteen minutes past the hour, he says:

"Now find a third back corner of the room,"
"Hold on to three of the back corners of the room,"
"Sit still and don't think."

He repeats:

"Hold on to three of the back corners of the room and sit still and don't think."

At the half hour, he says:

"Now find all four back corners of the room, hold on and don't think."

He repeats every few minutes:

"The four back corners of the room and don't think."

When the forty-five minute mark of the process has been reached, the auditor says:

"Now locate the eight corners of this room, hold on and don't think," and repeats *"Eight corners, don't think"* every few minutes.

At the hour mark, the process *could* be repeated. If so, do it again exactly as above.

Session 10
Description Processing

Description Processing should not be done on groups, some of whose members have questionable stability. Use only Sessions 1 to 6 on such groups. When a group has been much run, almost any form of Description Processing can be used. Session 10, however, consists entirely of one command which is not changed for at least half an hour. This is:

"How close does your body seem to you now?"

Pause.

"How close does your body seem to you now?"

Pause.

"How close does your body seem to you now?" etc.

Summary

In processing groups, duplication of command is part of the process.

Keep it simple. Grant them beingness. Keep them in contact with present time and out of their facsimile bank and you'll get Group Processing Clears.

Make it complicated, make them "figure," be shy, and the group won't come back.

Never worry about boring them.

The reason they're spun in is because "the body and the confusion were so interesting."

"Scientology has opened the gates to a better world."

REFERENCES

References

THIS IS
THE SCIENCE

"Knowledge itself is certainty."

SCIENTOLOGY

OF CERTAINTY

The Journal of Scientology 16-G
1 June 1953

FOREWORD

FOR NEARLY A QUARTER of a century, I have been engaged in the investigation of the fundamentals of life, the material universe and human behavior. Such an adventure leads one down many highways, through many byroads, into many back alleys of uncertainty, through many strata of life, through many personal vicissitudes, into the teeth of vested interests, across the rim of Hell and into the very arms of Heaven. Many before me have made their way across these tumultuous oceans of data, where every drop of water appears to be any other drop of water and yet where one must find *the* drop. Almost everything I have studied and observed has been evaluated otherwise somewhere, at some time, in relation to this or that.

What equipment must one have to venture upon these wastes? Where are the rules-books, the maps, the signposts? All one perceives when he peers into the darkness of the unknown are the lonely bones of those who, reaching before, have found their hands empty and their lives destroyed. Such a thing is a lonely drama; one must cheer one's own triumphs and weep to himself his despair. The cold brutality of the scientific method fails far back, almost at the starting point. The airy spiralings and dread mysteries of India, where I drank deep, lead only into traps.

The euphoria of religion, the ecstasies of worship and debauchery become as meaningless as sand when one seeks in them the answer to the riddle of all existence. Many have roved upon this unmapped track. Some have survived to say a fraction of what they knew, some have observed one thing and said quite another, some looked knowing and said naught. One engaged upon such a quest does not even know the answer to that most important question of all: Will it be good for Man to loose upon him, all in a rush as an avalanche, the knowingness of eternity?

There are those who would tell you that only a fiend would set you free and that freedom leads at best into the darkest hells. And there are those to inform you that freedom is for you and not for them. But there are also men of kind heart who know how precious is the cup and drink of wide, unbounded ways. Who is to say whether Man will benefit at all from this knowledge hardly won? You are the only one who can say.

Observation, application, experience and test will tell you if the trek has been made and the answer found. For this is the science of knowing how to know. It is a science which does not include within it cold and musty data, data to be thrust down the throat without examination and acceptance. This is the track of knowing how to know. Travel it and see.

Che Factors

ummation of the considerations and examinations
of the human spirit and the material universe
completed between 1923 and 1953 A.D.)

1 Before the beginning was a Cause and the entire purpose
of the Cause was the creation of effect.

2 In the beginning and forever is the decision and the
decision is TO BE.

3 The first action of beingness is to assume a viewpoint.

4 The second action of beingness is to extend from the
viewpoint, points to view, which are dimension points.

5 Thus there is space created, for the definition of space is:
viewpoint of dimension. And the purpose of a dimension
point is space and a point to view.

6 The action of a dimension point is reaching and
withdrawing.

7 And from the viewpoint to the dimension points there are connection and interchange: thus new dimension points are made: thus there is communication.

8 And thus there is LIGHT.

9 And thus there is energy.

10 And thus there is life.

11 But there are other viewpoints and these viewpoints outthrust points to view. And there comes about an interchange amongst viewpoints; but the interchange is never otherwise than in terms of exchanging dimension points.

12 The dimension point can be moved by the viewpoint, for the viewpoint, in addition to creative ability and consideration, possesses volition and potential independence of action: and the viewpoint, viewing dimension points, can change in relation to its own or other dimension points or viewpoints and thus comes about all the fundamentals there are to motion.

13 The dimension points are each and every one, whether large or small, *solid*. And they are solid solely because the viewpoints say they are solid.

14 Many dimension points combine into larger gases, fluids or solids: thus there is matter. But the most valued point is admiration, and admiration is so strong its absence alone permits persistence.

15 The dimension point can be different from other dimension points and thus can possess an individual quality. And many dimension points can possess a similar quality and others can possess a similar quality unto themselves. Thus comes about the quality of classes of matter.

16 The viewpoint can combine dimension points into forms and the forms can be simple or complex and can be at different distances from the viewpoint and so there can be combinations of form. And the forms are capable of motion and the viewpoints are capable of motion and so there can be motion of forms.

17 And the opinion of the viewpoint regulates the consideration of the forms, their stillness or their motion, and these considerations consist of assignment of beauty or ugliness to the forms and these considerations alone are art.

18 It is the opinions of the viewpoints that some of these forms should endure. Thus there is survival.

19 And the viewpoint can never perish; but the form can perish.

20 And the many viewpoints, interacting, become dependent upon one another's forms and do not choose to distinguish completely the ownership of dimension points and so comes about a dependency upon the dimension points and upon the other viewpoints.

21 From this comes a consistency of viewpoint of the interaction of dimension points and this, regulated, is TIME.

22 And there are universes.

23 The universes, then, are three in number: the universe created by one viewpoint, the universe created by every other viewpoint, the universe created by the mutual action of viewpoints which is agreed to be upheld–the physical universe.

24 And the viewpoints are never seen. And the viewpoints consider more and more that the dimension points are valuable. And the viewpoints try to become the anchor points and forget that they can create more points and space and forms. Thus comes about scarcity. And the dimension points can perish and so the viewpoints assume that they, too, can perish.

25 Thus comes about death.

26 The manifestations of pleasure and pain, of thought, emotion and effort, of thinking, of sensation, of affinity, reality, communication, of behavior and being are thus derived and the riddles of our universe are apparently contained and answered herein.

27 There *is* beingness, but Man believes there is only becomingness.

28 The resolution of any problem posed hereby is the establishment of viewpoints and dimension points, the betterment of condition and concourse amongst dimension points and, thereby, viewpoints, and the remedy of abundance or scarcity in all things, pleasant or ugly, by the rehabilitation of the ability of the viewpoint to assume points of view and create and uncreate, neglect, start, change and stop dimension points of any kind at the determinism of the viewpoint. Certainty in all three universes must be regained, for certainty, not data, is knowledge.

29 In the opinion of the viewpoint, any beingness, any thing, is better than no thing, any effect is better than no effect, any universe better than no universe, any particle better than no particle, but the particle of admiration is best of all.

30 And above these things there might be speculation only. And below these things there is the playing of the game. But these things which are written here Man can experience and know. And some may care to teach these things and some may care to use them to assist those in distress and some may desire to employ them to make individuals and organizations more able and so could give to Earth a culture of which Earth could be proud.

Humbly tendered as a gift to Man
by L. Ron Hubbard
April 23, 1953

THIS IS SCIENTOLOGY

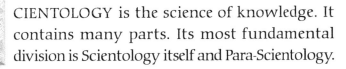

S CIENTOLOGY is the science of knowledge. It contains many parts. Its most fundamental division is Scientology itself and Para-Scientology.

Scientology

Under Scientology, we group those things of which we can be *certain* and only those things of which we can be certain. Knowledge itself is certainty. Knowledge is not data. Knowingness itself is certainty. Sanity is certainty, providing only that that certainty does not fall beyond the conviction of another when he views it. To obtain a certainty, one must be able to *observe*.

But what is the level of certainty we require? And what is the level of observation we require for a certainty or a knowledge to exist? If a man can stand before a tree and by sight, touch or other perception, know that he is confronting a tree and be able to perceive its form and be quite sure he is confronting a tree, we have the level of certainty we require. If the man will not look at the tree or, although it is observably a tree to others, if he discovers it to be a blade of grass or a sun, then he is below the level of certainty required and would not be able to grasp Scientology. Some other person, helpfully inclined, would have to direct his perception to the tree until the man perceived without duress that it was indeed a tree he confronted. That is the only level of certainty we require in order to qualify knowledge. For knowledge is observation and is given to those who would *look*.

Things about which there is observational difficulty, such as mirror mazes, items hidden in smoke, objects guessed at in the dark, are outside the boundaries of Scientology.

Three Universes

In order to obtain knowledge and certainty, it is necessary to be able to observe, in fact, *three universes* in which there could be trees.

The first of these is *one's own universe*. One should be able to create, for his own observation, in its total form, for total perception, a tree.

The second universe would be the *material universe*, which is the universe of matter, energy, space and time, which is the common meeting ground of all of us.

The third universe is actually a class of universes which could be called the *other fellow's universe*, for he and all the class of "other fellows" have universes of their own.

A complete clarity on all three universes would be well above any goal attempted, even in Scientology, and it is not necessary that one be as certain as this of three universes before one can be certain of Scientology. For certainty of Scientology requires only the same order of certainty one would have to have to know he was confronting a physical universe tree.

Para-Scientology

Para-Scientology is that large bin which includes all greater or lesser uncertainties. Here are the questionable things, the things of which the common normal observer cannot be sure with a little study. Here are theories, here are groups of data, even groups commonly accepted as "known."

Some of the classified bodies of data which fall in Para-Scientology are: Dianetics, incidents on the whole track, the immortality of Man, the existence of God, engrams containing pain and unconsciousness and yet all perception, prenatals, Clears, character and many other things which, even when closely and minutely observed, still are not certain things to those who observe them. Such things have relative truth. They have, to some, a high degree of reality. They have, to others, non-existence. They require a highly specialized system in order to observe them at all. Working with such uncertainties, one can produce broad and sweeping results. One can make the ill well again, one can right even the day which went most wrong. But those things which require highly specialized communication systems remain uncertain to many.

Because Dianetics is placed in this category does not mean it is disowned. It means simply that it is a specialized thing based on theory which, no matter how workable, requires specialized observation. It does not mean that Dianetics will cease to work, but it means that Dianetics is not easily or quickly forwarded into a complete certainty. Yet Dianetics is more of an exact science than many which have before borne that name. And Dianetics is an intimate part of Scientology, for it is through its special communication processes that the data was won which has become Scientology.

Also under the heading of Para-Scientology, one would place such things as past lives, mysterious influences, astrology, mysticism, religion, psychology, psychiatry, nuclear physics and any other science based on theory.

A doctor, for instance, may seem entirely certain of the cause of some disease. Yet it depends upon the doctor's certainty for the layman to accept that cause of the disease.

Here we have a specialized communications system. We may have an arduously trained observer, a highly mechanistic observation resting upon a theory which is not (even at this late date) entirely accepted even in the best circles. That penicillin cures certain things is a certainty to the doctor, even when penicillin suddenly and inexplicably fails to cure something. Any inexplicable failure introduces an uncertainty, which thereafter removes the subject from the realm of an "easily obtained certainty."

Hypnotism, no matter how certain the hypnotist may be that he is effective on some people, is a wild variable and even in expert practice is a definite uncertainty.

The use of drugs or shock produce such variable results that they class far down a gradient scale, which would begin with a fair degree of certainty and which would end with almost no certainty of any kind.

Certainty and Sanity

We have here, then, a parallel between certainty and sanity.

The less certain the individual on any subject, the less sane he could be said to be upon that subject. The less certain he is of what he views in the material universe, what he views in his own or the other fellow's universe, the less sane he could be said to be.

The road to sanity is demonstrably the road to increasing certainty. Starting at any level, it is only necessary to obtain a fair degree of certainty on the MEST universe to improve considerably one's beingness. Above that, one obtains some certainty of his own universe and some certainty of the other fellow's universe.

Certainty, then, is clarity of observation. Of course, above this, vitally so, is certainty in creation. Here is the artist, here is the master, here is the very great spirit.

As one advances, he discovers that what he first perceived as a certainty can be considerably improved. Thus we have certainty as a gradient scale. It is not an absolute, but it is defined as "the certainty that one perceives," or "the certainty that one creates what one perceives," or "the certainty that there is perception." Sanity and perception, certainty and perception, knowledge and observation, are then all of a kind. And amongst them we have sanity.

What will Scientology do? It has already been observed by many who are not that doubtful thing, the "qualified observer," that people who have traveled a road toward certainty improve in the many ways people consider it desirable to improve.

The road into uncertainty is the road toward psychosomatic illness, doubts, anxieties, fears, worries and vanishing awareness. As awareness is decreased, so does certainty decrease. And the end of this road is a "nothingness" quite opposite from the nothingness which can create. It is a nothingness which is a total effect.

Simplicity, it would be suspected, would be the keynote of any process, any communications system which would deliver into a person's hands the command of his own beingness. The simplicity consists of the observation of three universes.

The first step is the observation of one's own universe and what has taken place in that universe in the past.

The second step would be observation of the material universe and direct consultation with it to discover its forms, depths, emptinesses and solidities.

The third step would be the observation of other people's universes or their observation of the MEST universe, for there are a multitude of viewpoints of these three universes.

Where observation of one of these three is suppressed, hidden, denied, the individual is unable to mount, beyond a certain point, into certainty.

The Triangle of Certainty of Awareness

Here we have a triangle, not unlike the Affinity, Reality, Communication Triangle of Dianetics. These three universes are interactive to the degree that one raises all three by raising one. But one can raise two only so far before it is restrained by the uncertainty on the third. Thus any point on this triangle is capable of suppressing the other two points and any point of this triangle is capable of raising the other two points.

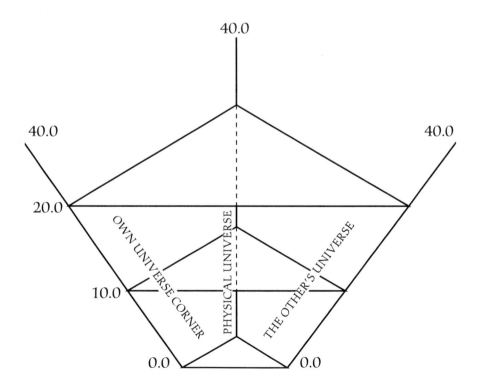

This drawing could be called the Scale of Awareness. It is also the Scale of Action and the Cycle-of-Action. The numbers represent entirely arbitrary levels which yet can be found to mean "levels of predictable attitudes." It would be found on the Tone Scale that humanity at this time hovers, in terms of awareness, at the level of 2.0 (slightly above or slightly below). Here is scarcely any awareness at all compared to the awareness which is available. It is very puzzling to people at higher levels of awareness, why people behave toward them as they do. Such higher level people have not realized that they are not seen, much less understood. People at low levels of awareness do not *observe*, but substitute for observation *preconceptions, evaluation, suppositions* and even *physical pain* by which to attain their certainties.

In the field of Zen Buddhism, there is a practice of administering a sudden blow, by which is obtained a feeling of certainty. Here is a relatively false certainty—the certainty of impact—although all certainty actually *is* derived, below the level of 10.0, from prior impact for its conviction. After a brutal accident or operation under anesthetic, it can be observed that individuals will sometimes react with an enormous conviction which yet does not seem to be based upon any fact. A certainty has been carried home to them in terms of a physical impact. This, then, is not a self-determined certainty—and the self-determined certainty carries one into high echelons. The mistaken use of shock by the ancient Greek upon the insane, the use of whips in old Bedlam, all sought to deliver sufficient certainty to the insane to cause them to be less insane. Certainty delivered by blow and punishment is a non-self-determined certainty. It is productive of stimulus-response behavior.

At a given stimulus, a dog who has been beaten, for instance, will react invariably providing he has been sufficiently beaten.

But if he has been beaten too much, the stimulus will result only in confused bewilderment. Thus, certainty delivered by blows, by applied force, eventually brings about a certainty as absolute as one could desire–total unawareness.

Unconsciousness itself is a certainty which is sought by many individuals who have failed repeatedly to reach any high level of "awareness certainty." These people then desire an "unawareness certainty." So it seems that the thirst for certainty can lead one into oblivion if one seeks it as an effect.

Uncertainty: "Maybe"

An uncertainty is the product of two certainties. One of these is a conviction, whether arrived at by observation (causative) or by a blow (effected). The other is a negative certainty. One can be sure that something *is* and one can be sure that something is *not*. He can be sure there is something (no matter what it is) present and that there is nothing present. These two certainties, commingling, create a condition of uncertainty known as "maybe." A "maybe" continues to be held in suspense in an individual's mind simply because he cannot decide whether it is nothing or something. He grasps and holds the certainties each time he has been given evidence or has made the decision that it is a somethingness and each time he has come to suppose that it is a nothingness. Where these two certainties of something and nothing are concerned with and can vitally influence one's continuance in a state of beingness, or where one merely supposes they can influence such a state of beingness, a condition of anxiety arises.

Thus anxiety, indecision, uncertainty, a state of "maybe" can exist only in the presence of poor observation or the inability to observe. Such a state can be remedied simply by eradicating from the past of the individual:

First, the conviction that the matter is *important*;

Next, the conviction that it is totally *unimportant*;

Next, all the times when he was certain of the *somethingness*;

And then, all the times he was certain of the *nothingness*.

One merely causes the individual to observe in terms of the three universes.

Analytical and Reactive Minds

We face, then, two general types of mind.

One is an analytical thing, which depends for its conclusions upon perception, or even creation of things *to* perceive, and bases its judgment on observation in terms of three universes. This we call the "analytical mind." We could also call it the "spirit." We could also call it the "awareness of awareness unit." We could call it "the conscious individual himself in the best of his beingness." We could call it the mathematical term "thetan." Whatever its name, we would have precisely the same thing–a viewpoint capable of creation and observation of things created, which concludes and directs action in terms of the existing state of three universes as they are observed directly.

The other type of mind resembles nothing if not an electronic brain. It receives its data in terms of conviction, delivered by force. It is directed by and reacts to hidden influences, rather than observed influences, and is to a large extent the reverse image and has reverse intentions to the analytical mind. This we call the "reactive mind." It is an actual entity and it operates in terms of experience and theory. It sets up thinking machinery around uncertainties and the course of its thinking is downward. It seeks to direct and dictate out of pain and the effort to avoid pain.

The primary difference between these two "minds" is that one (the analytical mind) is without finite duration and the other (the reactive mind) is susceptible to death.

These two minds are a certainty since they can be observed by anyone, even in himself. He knows he is aware of things around him and he knows that he has definite desires which are perfectly reasonable. And he knows, if he is a Homo sapiens or animal, that internal commands and compulsions, even those which tell him to eat and tell his heart to beat, are not directly within his control.

All thinking can then be divided, for our purposes, into:

Thinking based upon *direct observation* and *conclusions from observation*; and,

Thinking which has to *know* before it can *be* or *observe*.

Analytical thought can be called "analytical thought" because it directly observes and analyzes what it observes in terms of observations which are immediately present. The reactive mind concludes and acts entirely on experience and with only a fragmentary regard to things present which could be observed. The reactive mind begins and continues with uncertainties. And where the course of the analytical mind is progressively upward, the course of the reactive mind is progressively downward.

The reactive mind comes into being as a servant of the analytical mind and is set up by the analytical mind to work upon and store data about the basic uncertainty that there *might be something* and there *might be nothing*. The reactive mind, then, continues in growth and from the servant, if the analytical mind does not observe it, tends to become the master.

Survival

The goals of the two minds are not separate goals. The reactive mind is a makeshift effort, on the part of the viewpoint, to perceive things which it believes to be unperceivable except by comparison of uncertainties. Both minds are seeking to persist and endure through time–which is to say, *survive.* The analytical mind can (unless it becomes too uncertain and, by that uncertainty, has set up too many reactive mechanisms) persist *indefinitely.* The reactive mind pursues the cycle of *life span.*

The analytical mind seeks by *creation* to cause an effect. The reactive mind seeks by *duplication, borrowing* and *experience* to cause an effect. Both minds, then, are seeking to cause an effect and this is their entire motivation for action.

Each of the three universes seeks to persist indefinitely. Each is continuously caused and each is continually receiving an effect. Each has its own adjudication of what it should receive as an effect and what it should cause.

Time itself consists of a continuous interaction of the universes. Each may have its own space. Each has its own particular energy.

The urge of any of these three universes toward survival is subdivisible, for each of the three universes, into eight dynamics.

There are, then, four groups of eight dynamics each:

The eight dynamics of one's *own universe;*

The eight dynamics of the *physical universe;*

The eight dynamics of the *other's universe;* as well as

The eight dynamics of the *triangle* itself.

These dynamics could be subdivided as follows:

The First Dynamic would be that one most intimate to the universe which could be said to be the dynamic urging the survival of self.

The Second Dynamic would be that one of the persistence of admiration, in many forms, in one's own and the other's universe. This admiration could take the form of sex, eating or purely the sensation of creation (such as sex and children). In the physical universe, it would be that light emanation similar to sunlight.

The Third Dynamic could be said to be that dynamic embracing persistence of groups of objects or entities.

The Fourth Dynamic would concern itself with an entire species.

The Fifth Dynamic would concern itself with other living species and would embrace all other living species.

The Sixth Dynamic would embrace, in terms of survival, the space, energy, matter and forms of the universe, as themselves.

The Seventh Dynamic would be the urge to survive of the spirits or spiritual aspects of each universe.

The Eighth Dynamic would be the overall creativeness or destructiveness as a continuing impulse.

Each impulse is concerned wholly with systems of communication. Communication requires a *viewpoint* and a *destination*, in its most elementary form. And as this grows more complex and as it grows more "important," communication grows more rigid and fixed as to its codes and lines.

The reason for communication is to *effect* effects and *observe* effects.

Triangle of Affinity, Reality and Communication

Each of the three universes has its own Triangle of Affinity, Reality and Communication. These three things are interdependent one upon another and one cannot exist independent of the other two.

Affinity is the characteristic of the energy as to its vibration, condensation, rarefaction and, in the physical universe, its degree of cohesion or dispersion.

Reality depends upon coincidence or noncoincidence of flow and is marked mainly by the direction of flow. It is essentially agreement.

Communication is the volume of flow or lack of flow.

Of these three, Communication is by far the most important. Affinity and Reality exist to further Communication.

Tone Scale

Under Affinity, we have, for instance, all the varied emotions which go from Apathy at 0.1, through Grief, Fear, Anger, Antagonism, Boredom, Enthusiasm, Exhilaration and Serenity, in that order. It is Affinity and this rising scale of the characteristics of emotion which give us the Tone Scale. The Tone Scale can be a certainty to anyone who has seen other beings react emotionally, who has himself felt emotion and who has seen the varied moods of the physical universe itself. The periodic chart of chemistry is itself a sort of Tone Scale.

There is a downward spiral on the Tone Scale and an upward spiral. These spirals are marked by decreasing or increasing awareness. To go upscale, one must increase his power to observe with certainty. To go downscale one must decrease his power to observe.

There are two certainties here. One is a complete certainty of total *awareness*, which would be at 40.0 on the Tone Scale. And the other is a certainty of total *unawareness*, which would be 0.0 on the Tone Scale (or nearly so). Neither end, however, is itself an absolute for the analytical mind and the analytical mind can go below 0.0 of the reactive mind. However, these two classes of certainty are very wide in their satisfaction of the qualifications of a certainty. Because the two extremes of the scale are both zeros in terms of space, it is possible to confuse one for the other and so make it appear that total awareness would be total unawareness. Experience and observation can disabuse one of this idea. The scale is not circular.

The characteristics and potentiality of the top of the scale, or near the top of the scale, are:

Unbounded creation
Outflow
Certainty
Going-awayness
Explosion
Holding apart
Spreading apart
Letting go
Reaching
Goals of a causative nature
Widening space
Freedom from time
Separateness
Differentiation

Givingness of sensation
Vaporizingness
Glowingness
Lightness
Whiteness
De-solidifyingness
Total awareness
Total understanding
Total ARC

The bottom of the scale and the vicinity around it includes:

Death
Inflow
Certainty
Coming-backness
Implosion
Letting-come-together
Pulling together
Holding together
Withdrawing
Effect goals (ambition to be an effect rather than a cause)
Contracting space
No time or infinite time in a moment
Connectingness
Identification
Identity
Receivingness of sensation
Condensation
Blackness
Solidification
No-awareness
No understanding
No ARC

These various characteristics or intentions are observable for any dynamic and any universe.

Between these two extremes is the mean of action where complete freedom to do any of these things – of the top or bottom of the scale – is exercised. Therefore, somewhere between 3.5 on the Tone Scale and 36.5, there is action.

The above conditions of top and bottom of the scale, of course, reach away from the extreme and toward each other.

As awareness becomes more fixed, intentions become less flexible in action, communications systems become more rigid, more complex and less susceptible of alteration. One alters these communications systems, however, by raising or lowering certainty on the three universes.

Viewpoint

The principal difference between the analytical mind (in a state of awareness itself) and the reactive mind is that the analytical mind, highly aware, knows that it is not "the thing" but is the "viewpoint" of things. Of this it can be very certain as it increases in awareness. The reactive mind conceives itself to be "the thing."

The analytical mind is in a state of *becoming* without reaching the point of *being*. The reactive mind conceives itself to be in a state of *being* and so resists *becoming*.

Perception is accomplished by the analytical mind, in a high state of awareness, by its own outflow and inflow or by its receipt of inflows which it can outflow. The reactive mind perceives by inflow only and makes complete recordings of the inflow.

The analytical mind is capable of developing its own energy. It is the energy of the analytical mind which empowers the reactive mind. But the reactive mind can be empowered, as well, by the energy of other minds and by the life energy contained in any living thing. Thus the reactive mind can become the servant of all things. It can believe it is anything. It can believe it is owned or has the identity of anyone, regardless of whom it was created to serve. The analytical mind serves itself in a continuing knowledge of serving itself. But it serves, as well, and knows it serves the other two universes.

The analytical mind extends from it points, or observes points extended from it, and thus conceives space. Space is only "the viewpoint of dimension." The dimension depends upon those points which give it boundary. Within these dimensions, called space, the analytical mind can create energy and form and thus, by change of form, beget time.

Energy: Two-Terminal Universe

Whether created by or within any one of the three universes, flow of energy is accomplished by setting up a terminal and flowing toward it, from a viewpoint, a stream of energy. Or, by setting up two terminals and causing a flow between them.

Each universe could be said to be a *two-terminal universe*, but flows can be set up on a basis of more than two terminals. The basic unit of any universe, in terms of energy, is two. This, however, does not restrict nor qualify the number of viewpoints which any universe can have. A physical universe, however, is observably a two-terminal universe and a two-point universe. And it is also observable that the other two universes set up, almost invariably, two terminals or more and utilize two viewpoints each.

Very low on the scale, in terms of awareness, the analytical mind conceives itself to be the reactive mind and so does not act or perform to put out dimension points, so as to get space, and does not generate, for its own accountability, energy. It does, however, always generate energy—whether it admits it is doing so or not.

Attention

The concern of two viewpoints is *attention*. Each viewpoint is apt to be curious about or desire the attention of another viewpoint.

Admiration

The most valuable part of an attention interchange is *admiration*. Admiration is a special particle. It is a universal solvent. It is the very substance of a communication line. And it is that thing which is considered desirable in the game of the three universes. Admiration goes into the interplay of the universes in the form of made-up objects or even in the form of bodies. These made-up objects could be called "creative pictures." These, as they become more complex in form, take on the aspect of a life of their own and become animated beings.

Two viewpoints, setting up terminals to be viewed by the other viewpoint, demand attention one from the other and will invent all manner of "reasons" to command the continuing attention of the other viewpoint. One of the primary methods of operation is to make one's object, or action of object, so strange that the other viewpoint cannot look away. Another is to make the object, or action of object, so artistic or colorful or interesting that the other viewpoint cannot look away. Another method is the command by force for attention. Another method is to inhibit the attention so as to invite it solely to one's objects.

One can plot this as a cycle of Demand for Attention, with Curiosity below 40.0, Desire below that, Enforcement down to as low as 1.5 on the scale and Inhibition at 1.1 on down. The lowest methods of this scale are quite observable among men. And the primary operation, very low on the scale, is Inhibition of attention *elsewhere*. By cutting the communication lines of another viewpoint, an effect is created on the other viewpoint by which that viewpoint fixes with whatever emotion (since any attention is better than no attention) upon the products or objects of that one who cut the communication line. There are many methods of cutting communication lines. A common one could be summarized as "It's too horrible over that way for you to look." Viewpoints are thus given the understanding that they are surrounded by horrible things which they have never perceived and which, indeed, have never existed, but which are said to be there so that they will be forced to give attention.

Hidden influences are the commonest methods of enforcing attention. Of course, any analytical mind is itself a hidden influence since it cannot, as itself, be perceived. Only its energy and objects can be perceived. Thus comes about the worship of the hidden influence, the fear of the hidden influence, the neurosis about hidden influences.

Eating and Sex

The goal of "seeking attention" is to receive the particle admiration. One creates effects simply in order to create effects. But he is given the bonus of admiration when he creates sufficient effect or, what is most important, when he demands, commands and is able to effect admiration by duress.

It might be said that there was no eating until one was so furious about not being admired that one slew as a punishment. The tiger walking through the woods with his beautiful stripes, it could be humorously offered, would never have eaten a thing and would not be eating today if some monkey had not chattered insults at him instead of admiring him. The tiger compelled the admiration of the monkey by pinning him down and eating him up. It can be observed that the eating of living flesh or live cells delivers a kind of admiration to the taste.

301

And it can be observed that under torture, duress of all kinds, the tortured one will suddenly, if degradedly, admire his torturer.

Energy pictures which we call "mock-ups" are created things which themselves contain admiration. It could be said that these are prior to bodies.

The acquisition of admiration by pain, by eating, or by devouring something that belongs to somebody else, was later succeeded by a better communications system which would prevent eating on such a rigorous scale. This thing was sex, which is an interchange of condensed admiration particles which forwards new bodies into being. So far as the body of Homo sapiens is concerned, its desire not to be eaten has been answered, evidently, by sex. And sex performs the function of continued survival of form. Thus, so long as one has the symbol of sex to offer, one feels relatively secure. And when he does not have that symbol to offer, one feels insecure.

But of this evolution of admiration and of evolution itself, we have no high degree of certainty as we first begin to observe. And it is offered here as an explanation of why it is a thing we do not particularly need and a thing of which we will or will not gain a future certainty as we go up the Scale of Awareness. Many things are non-existent low on the scale. Many things are uncertain on the scale at low levels, which become high-level certainties up on the scale. But this certainty only depends on the positiveness of observation or the positiveness of observation which says the thing does not exist.

Processing—Gradient Scale to Certainty

It is not the purpose of Scientology to present an uncertainty and then demand that it be accepted. For here is the gradient scale of a process by which one can become more certain. If there be immortality, or even the lack of necessity on the part of the analytical mind to be a specific object, then one will find it out in due course as he is processed. If they do not exist, again, one will find it out. This would be a matter of progressive observation. Where a thing exists in the form of an uncertainty, it has a tendency to plague the reactive mind. For the reactive mind itself deals only with uncertainties and its convictions are based entirely on blows and pain.

Applause–Cause and Effect

A very basic uncertainty comes about on the subject of *applause*. High on the scale, one performs for an effect and knows that it is an effect, whether or not there is any attention or admiration–which is to say, applause. A little lower on the scale, one desires a nod or the actual substance of admiration. If it does not come, he is not concerned. But even lower on the scale, the individual actively invites and requests applause. Lower than that, he becomes Angry in the absence of applause. Lower than that, he exhibits Fear, Grief and Apathy in the lack of applause. Apathy is the realization that there will never be any applause for any effect.

That which is not admired tends to persist, for the reactive mind does not destroy. One can become fixed upon producing a certain effect simply by insisting that it be admired. The longer it is not admired, the longer one is likely to persist in demanding that it be admired (which is to say, exhibiting it), until at length it breaks downscale to a lower level and he realizes it will not be admired, at which time he becomes the effect of it. Here one has become the effect of one's own cause. Here is the psychosomatic illness which began as a pretended infirmity in order to create an effect. Perhaps it was once applauded, but not sufficiently.

And after a while, was not applauded at all and one was forced to applaud it himself and believe it himself. And so it came into existence and was, for him, a certainty.

This, too, is the course of responsibility which degenerates into irresponsibility. At the top of the scale, one knows that he is causing the effect. Lower on the scale, he says he is not causing the effect (even though he is causing the effect, only *he* knows he causes it). Even lower on the scale, he does not take the middle step. He causes an effect and instantly believes that something else caused the effect, rather than himself, and that he is the effect of the effect.

One can see cause and effect working in terms of viewpoints. If one has not been applauded for many things, one will begin to take the position of the audience. One does the trick, creates the thing and then goes out front, sits down over the whole theater and applauds it. For one can be a knowing viewpoint from many places. This is often the case with a writer, who is seldom confronted by his readers. Indeed, most editors are so low-toned that they cut off all the admiring letters of a writer and leave him to wonder. As other things influence the writer, he goes downscale to a point where he believes the things he writes are not admired and so he has to "go out and sit in the audience." This is the first step to becoming the effect of his own cause. After a while he thinks he is the audience. When he does this, he is no longer the writer. Thus with the painter, thus with anyone.

Evaluation and Perception

The little child is quite bent on causing effects and getting things admired. He is continually being evaluated in terms of what is to be admired.

Evaluation is the reactive mind's conception of viewpoint. The reactive mind does not *perceive*, it *evaluates*. To the analytical mind, it may sometimes appear that the reactive mind has a viewpoint. The reactive mind does not have a viewpoint, it has an *evaluation* of viewpoint. Thus, the viewpoint of the analytical mind is an actual point from which one perceives. Perception is done by sight, sound, smell, tactile, etc. The reactive mind's "viewpoint" is an opinion based on another opinion and upon a very small amount of observation. And that observation would be formed out of uncertainties. Thus the confusion of the word "viewpoint" itself. It can be a point from which one can be aware (which is its analytical definition) and it can be somebody's ideas on a certain subject (which is the reactive definition).

Because the analytical mind and reactive mind in men can become confused one with the other, one is most prone to assume the actual perception point of that person who has most evaluated for him. Father and mother, for instance, have evaluated about art, habits, goodness, behavior, badness, how one should dress, what manners are, to such a degree that the child has no choice, it seems to him, but to assume their "points to look from." And so we will find the child observing things as his father or mother would observe them and even wearing his father's glasses or his mother's glasses as he grows older. He has confused evaluation with actual perception.

Where he has been told that he is bad looking, ugly, ridiculous, unmannerly, crude and so forth by somebody else continually, his reactive mind (which, like a prostitute, cares nothing for its master and serves anyone) eventually causes him to lose his viewpoint of himself and he sees himself, not by observation, but by evaluation, as something undesirable.

Of course, he would rather be something than nothing. He has, indeed, a horror of being nothing. So it is better to be something ugly about which he is guessing than to be nothing at all. And so he persists and continues as he is. Furthermore, because he has been talked to so much about talking, about looking, about perceiving in general, he has gotten the idea that his communications system is unalterable. His whole business of living actually is a communications system with the motivation of causing effects. Thus, the lower he is on the Tone Scale, the more he persists without change–except downward.

Reaching and Withdrawing

The characteristic actions of the energy produced by the analytical mind are summarized above, in terms of the top and bottom of the scale. However, the most important of these seem to be *reaching* and *withdrawing*. In the MEST universe, we have *start*, *stop* and *change* as the characteristics of motion. The analytical mind, however, with its dimension points is more concerned with reaching and withdrawing. This is the way it perceives. It can control by creating or using energy, such as that in the physical universe, and it uses this energy to start, stop and change other energy. But in itself, its handling of dimension points direction consists of reaching and withdrawing. Compulsive reaching, compulsive withdrawing bring about many odd and interesting manifestations.

The sensation of pain is actually a sensation of loss. It is a loss of beingness, a loss of position and awareness. Therefore, when one loses anything, he has a tendency to perceive less, for there is less to perceive. Something has withdrawn from him without his consent. This would be the definition of loss. This brings about, eventually, a condition of darkness. This could also be called an ARC break. If he has lost something, the guilty party is probably in the other two universes. It is either the physical universe or another's universe which has caused the loss. Thus he has less communication, since he is unwilling to communicate–which is to say, put out things in the direction of something which is going to take them and carry them away without his further consent. This brings about a reduction of the desire to be aware, which is the reduction of affinity, reduction of agreement (reality) and the reduction of communication in general. In a moment of severe disappointment in one's fellow man, the universe around him actually grows dark. Simply as an experiment, one can say to himself that he has the only viewpoint there is, that all other viewpoints are simply mocked-up by him. He will get an almost immediate diminution of lightness around him. This is the same mechanism as the mechanism of loss. The result of too much loss is darkness.

Another mechanism of the darkness and unawareness settling over a person is brought about by the loss of a viewpoint which has greatly evaluated for one. One has had a mother or a father who overevaluated about everything and then this parent (or guardian or ally in life, such as a teacher) died or inexplicably disappeared. One was depending for actual looking, seeing, hearing, upon the continued existence of this individual. Suddenly that individual goes and all becomes dark. After that, one is not able to perceive one's own universe. For one was most of the time actually perceiving the lost person's universe and now that universe is no longer there, which gives one the idea that he has no universe to perceive. This even dims his perception of the physical universe, of course, because of the interdependence of the triangle of the three universes.

When one has had an insufficient amount of admiration from sexual partners, the physical body, which depends mainly upon sex for its sensation and continuance to almost as great a degree as upon eating, will actually begin to change viewpoint to the other sex. Thus we find some older men becoming as women, some older women becoming as men. Thus we get the failure of the androgen and estrogen balances and the resultant decay of the body. Here, in the matter of sex, one finds reaching and withdrawing rising to considerable magnitude. The reactive mind, operating the body, conceives itself to be withdrawing and does not know from what it is withdrawing. For it perceives itself to be under the compulsion of reaching and does not know for what it is reaching. In terms of processing, it is withdrawing from or reaching toward sexual partners. When it withdraws a great deal or when it has been withdrawn from a great deal, the reactive mind conceives the body to be covered with blackness.

This resolves in terms of *sex* and *eating*. It should be fully understood, however, that this is the resolution of the problem of the body. And this resolution is employed only when the analytical mind cannot be brought, itself, into an immediate height of awareness using SOP 8. When one addresses the body, itself, and only the body, one addresses the subject of *sex* and the subject of *eating* in terms of *reaching* and *withdrawing*.

Matched Terminaling and Double Terminaling

The particular processes used on this are called "Matched Terminaling" or "Double Terminaling." This is done in the following fashion:

Even when the individual cannot create forms of his own, he can at least create two ideas in front of him. He can put a form with an idea, or an idea itself, facing another idea out in front of him—both of them exactly alike:

"Withdrawing from sex,"
"Reaching toward sex."

He will very often find other terminals he did not create suddenly appearing. When he has run withdrawing, those things he puts up will be black and the object from which it is withdrawing will be white. He should get the idea that the whitish object is reaching and the blackish object is withdrawing. He should then run this identical terminal as though it is being put up by somebody else (not himself), again with withdrawing for blackness, reaching for grayness. And then he should run it as though somebody is putting it up for somebody else (other than himself). These three causations ("brackets") of putting up this identical idea facing itself are *himself, another for him* and *others for others*. This is called Matched Terminaling.

Double Terminaling simply puts up two pairs of matched terminals. The pairs may each be of two different things, but each pair contains one thing the same as the other pair. In other words, husband and wife is one pair and husband and wife is the other pair. These, parallel, give one the two-terminal effect necessary for a discharge. One will find that these terminals discharge one against the other. However, this is a physical body technique and it is limited in use. If one becomes very ill in doing it, he should turn to what is called (later on) an "unlimited technique." Or he should do the next-to-last list, in the book *Self Analysis in Scientology*, and do it over and over. Or he should simply go straight through Short 8. It has many remedies.

This Matched Terminaling (for oneself, others for oneself and others for others) on the subject of reaching and withdrawing on sex can, of course, be considerably expanded as a technique.

It can have in it compulsion to reach, compulsion to withdraw, compulsion to reach while somebody else is withdrawing, compulsion not to reach. And it can be addressed in terms of all those "complexes" and things which Sigmund Freud observed empirically while investigating in his practice.* Sigmund Freud observed, even as you may have observed, that a person's concern and trouble with his body commonly began at the age of puberty. And that a curve of his ups and downs did sudden changes at those points where he was defeated sexually, where his sexual impotence ceased and where it increased. Dr. Freud unfortunately developed no fast or deeply workable techniques to resolve problems posed by these observations, mainly because the selection of sex as the prime motivator was not the selection of the basic mechanics of beingness. However, the brilliance of Freud's theories and his extrapolations from a limited amount of data, and his courage in standing before a whole world and declaring that an unpopular subject was the root of all evil, has no parallel in history. The complexes he mentioned, each and every one, are discoverable in the mind by direct observation or electropsychometry and are resolvable in the body by the technique of "Matched Terminals in Brackets" (which is the proper name for the above).

Where the level of the case is Step IV or Step V or below (in SOP 8), it is necessary to free the analytical mind of the grip of the body. The analytical mind cannot withdraw. The body is most swiftly reduced to compliance by running the Second Dynamic. This is very far from the end of all of processing, but it is the fastest method I have developed for remedying occlusion or accomplishing exteriorization in low-step cases.

---

*L. Ron Hubbard studied Freudian psychoanalysis under the tutelage of Commander Thompson, (MC) USN, who was one of Freud's star pupils. Commander Thompson studied under Freud himself in Vienna to introduce to the United States Navy the theory and practice of psychoanalysis and was sent to Vienna for that purpose.

In sex and eating, the body desires to be an effect most strongly. And in these things one does find the strongest desire, on the part of the body, in terms of immediate accessibility. The analytical mind, on the other hand, can create its own sensation, but it has become dependent upon the body. Even so, it is that part of the beingness which desires to give sensation rather than receive it. Thus one has the conflict of desire to give sensation crossed with the desire to receive sensation on the part of the reactive mind. The body's desire to receive sensation is so strong that an extremely powerful and persistent uncertainty ("maybe") develops and the primary conflict of the analytical mind and the body's reactive mind comes about.

I cannot help but give forth my own admiration to a man who, working without prior art, without electropsychometry, without nuclear physics, without any broad observation of primitive tribes or ethnology in general, separated from his conclusion by every convention of his age, yet hit upon and set forth, with the weight of logic alone, the center of disturbance in the human body. He did not live to see his theory completely validated. He was deserted by his students who began to write fantastic theories, completely unworkable and far from the point, which yet were better accepted. In discouragement at the end of his career, he wrote a paper called *Psychoanalysis, Terminable and Interminable*. Freud, with no method of direct observation, spoke of prenatals, birth trauma and, verbally, if not in writing, of past existences and of the continuing immortality of the individual. No praise can be great enough to give such a man and the credit I give him for my own inspiration and work is entirely without reservation or bounds. My only regret is that I do not know where he is today to show him his 1894 libido theory completely vindicated and a Freudian psychoanalysis delivered beyond his expectations in five hours of auditing.

Processing the Analytical Mind

The analytical mind can be processed directly and it improves simply by *changing its mind* about things. But so long as it believes itself to be closely dependent upon the reactive mind and the body, it cannot change its opinions. These opinions, however, are not simple shifts of mind. They are changes of experience. The analytical mind must discover that it can perceive, that it can perceive accurately in three universes, that it does not need to be dependent upon the body and that it can handle any reactive mind. This is done by increasing its powers of *perception*, increasing the number of viewpoints it can *assume* and increasing its ability to *locate* spaces, actions and objects in time and space and by increasing its ability, above that, to *create* space, energy and objects. This is done by drills and by the procedures of the first three steps of SOP 8.

It should not for one moment be thought that one is trying to perform, by the gradient scale of increasing certainties in Scientology, all the tricks and exhibitions of which the ancients speak. We are not even vaguely interested in moving physical universe objects, throwing lightning about, or in creating solids which can be seen by others. We are only interested in the rehabilitation of the analytical mind to a point where it can handle any reactive mind, whatever its proximity to that reactive mind. We are not interested, in other words, in the objective reality (from another viewpoint) of the capabilities of the analytical mind in performing various types of tricks. Whether it can do these things or not do these things falls into the realm of Para-Scientology, for it is completely beyond the "ability to be certain" where the analytical mind is not processed well up and where the observer is very low on the Tone Scale. We are not trying to achieve the certainty of mysticism, necromancy or, to be blunt, the Indian rope trick. We are trying to make sane, well beings.

The analytical mind, when it is in close proximity to the body, is unwittingly continually restimulating a reactive mind which, some say, evolved through very difficult and savage stages. Just as Freud said, the suppression in the mind is the suppression of things so bestial, so savage, that the preclear undergoing professional processing is extremely shocked. Almost anything and almost any impulse, including a thirst for pain and a desire to create any kind of effect, no matter how bad, will manifest itself while processing the reactive mind. Cannibalism, purely for sensation, so as to get the last remnants of admiration of the tortured and dying being, becomes a subjective certainty to the preclear who undergoes processing and has to have his reactive mind addressed before he can be *himself* (which is, of course, his *analytical mind*). The more suppression this reactive mind gets, the more it restimulates its beastliness.

The analytical mind is basically good. It has suffered from this proximity to the reactive mind. It is no wonder that Plato wrote as he did in an essay about the conduct and behavior of Man. It is no wonder that states are completely convinced that Man is a beast and must be held in check at pistol point. The wonder is that, in a civilized world, so few crimes are committed. Our desire is to reach the basic goodness of the individual and bring him into a level of activity where he does not have to do terrible and gruesome things in order to produce an effect. There are various levels, as one goes upscale, where these manifestations seem to be the all and everything of existence. One becomes completely downhearted at the thought that one goes upscale simply to get to a point where he can kill and maim and hurt with impunity. One's feelings of honor, ethics, all his finer beingness, is revolted at the idea that this is, in actuality, life. He should say, instead, that this is life in a stupid conflict of uncertainties. The goal is not to get above such things and ignore them. The goal is to achieve the basic decency which is inherent in all of us.

Processing Techniques

Although I have given you here Matched Terminal Brackets on the subject of reach and withdraw, with particular attention to sex, you must understand that this is a professional auditor's technique. The first three steps of SOP 8, when they can be done, can be done by alert, interested people. From Step IV down, a professional auditor is not simply desirable, he is completely necessary. This technique which I have given you here turns on, when one runs its compulsive aspects (particularly when one runs *must* reach and *can't* reach), the emotion which we see in sanitariums which is called insanity. And although the turn-on is brief and temporary and would wear away in about three days, an inexperienced auditor could become quite frightened. Simply by carrying on with the technique, or by getting back to "unlimited techniques," or by taking *Self Analysis* with its next-to-last list, these things could be remedied. But these techniques walk on the rim of Hell where they are addressed to cases below the level of IV. If the test subject or the preclear cannot make space (which is to say, Step III of SOP 8), let a professional auditor have him. The professional auditor, by using Matched Terminal Brackets of reach and withdraw with attention to sex, will be able to exteriorize this analytical mind and turn on its perceptions. This is skilled work, however, and is a little too shockingly intimate to the seamier side of life for tender hands and tender minds.

Even the operation of "wasting," which is contained in Expanded GITA, is capable of turning on a vast amount of illness and somatic on the part of the preclear. Expanded GITA is a "limited technique"–which is to say, it can be audited perhaps only for ten minutes and at the most for fifty or sixty hours, without finding the preclear on the downgrade. One has to turn to an "unlimited technique," such as contained in Short 8, if the preclear becomes too ill trying to *waste* things.

Just because an unlimited technique is labeled "unlimited" is no reason why it is a faint technique. These unlimited techniques are extremely powerful. They're very simple, but, again, when one of them becomes too strong for the preclear, it is necessary to turn to something simpler and easier.

Simply getting the idea in two places (the idea, so to speak, facing the idea), "*There is nothing*," will turn on a sick sensation in many preclears. This fear of being nothing is very great. He will be anything rather than nothing.

A safe technique is that technique which always – I repeat, always – deals in things of which the preclear is certain. When one deals with uncertainties, one is dealing with circuits. One can use Double Terminaling (which is to say, two pairs of matched terminals) of the preclear being certain of things. One never runs things or puts the preclear up against things of which one is uncertain, or of which the preclear is uncertain, if one wishes the preclear to come on up the Tone Scale. As an example of this, on any object, thing or idea, on any psychosomatic ill or any numb portion of the body, one has only to run:

"*There is something there*,"
"*There is nothing there*."

Have it saying:

"*There is something here*,"
"*There is nothing here*."

One can do a complete bracket on this having the numb or painful or injured area saying:

"*There is something here*,"
"*There is nothing here*."

Having it then say:

"There is something there,"
"There is nothing there."

Having the preclear say about the area:

"There is something there,"
"There is nothing there."

And then the preclear about himself:

"There is something here,"
"There is nothing here."

This makes a complete bracket. This turns on and off interesting somatics. A professional auditor could get the somatic or numb area to get the feeling *it* is reaching while the *preclear* is withdrawing, the *preclear* reaching while *it* is withdrawing, and bring about a change in any somatic.

As one is dealing with communications systems, one must realize that communication depends upon certainty of *despatch* and *receipt* and certainty of *what it is* that is being despatched and received. Thus one does not deal in uncertainties. *"There is something," "There is nothing"* are, of course, observable certainties, because one is top-scale, the other is bottom-scale. One does not say what the something is and, of course, nothingness needs no qualifications.

In the case of the person who has *been* and is trying to *become* again, one should run out by "concepts" the former successes, the triumphs of that person and the times when he was absolutely certain he had failed. One does this with Double Terminals or Matched Terminal Brackets. This is a professional technique.

The Road to Certainty

It was mentioned to me by Meredith Starr, one of the great mystics from Cyprus, that Jung had once had a great experience and had sought ever since to recover it. He gave this as another man's opinion of Jung. This gives you some clue as to what happens to someone who has a great triumph. He ever afterwards is not seeking to duplicate the triumph, he is seeking the triumph itself. This puts him back on the time track. This is particularly applicable to old people. One hangs, then, on to certainties. The certainties are important. The uncertainties are important only in their production of psychosis.

It is possible to take a sick animal and rehabilitate his idea that he is dangerous by dodging every time he strikes out, no matter how faintly, at one. It is possible to rehabilitate an individual who is very low on the Tone Scale merely by coaxing him to reach out and touch the material universe and, touching it, to be certain that it is there and, having touched it, to withdraw the touch and to be certain that he could withdraw.

Certainty is a wonderful thing. The road toward realizing what certainty is, has led these investigations through many uncertainties. One had to find out what *was* before one could find out what *could be*. That work is done. It is possible to take large groups and, using Short 8, to bring them, each and every one, into higher levels of certainty. And bringing them into higher levels of certainty brings them into higher levels of communication–communication not only with their own bodies, but with others and with the material universe. And as one raises that level of awareness, one raises also the ability to *be*, to *do*, to *live*.

Today, this world suffers from an increasing incidence of neurosis brought about by a dependency upon mechanical things which do not think, which do not feel, but which can give pain to those that live. It suffers with an overdose of agreement that there is only one universe. So long as it believes that there is only one universe, that there is only one universe to study, to be studied, only one universe to agree with, it will continue to seek the lowest end of the scale–which is to say, that point where all universes become one universe. Where the triangle vanishes to a single point, it vanishes completely. And where one studies but one corner of the triangle and ignores the other two corners of the triangle and agrees only with one corner of the triangle (such as the *physical universe*), one will tend toward that point where that corner of the triangle is coincident with the other two corners. And this is *death*.

The curse of this world is not actually its atom bomb, though that is bad enough. The curse of this world is the irresponsibility of those who seeking to study but one universe–the physical universe–try to depress all beings down to the low order of mechanically motivated, undreaming, unaesthetic things. Science, as a word, has been disgraced. For the word "science" means truth and truth means light. A continual fixation and dependence upon only one universe, while ignoring the other two universes, leads to darkness, to despair, to nothingness. There is nothing wrong with the physical universe. One should not cease to observe the physical universe, but one certainly should not concentrate upon it so that he can "agree" with it and its laws only. He has laws of his own. It is better, far better for the individual to concentrate upon his own universe, than to concentrate upon the MEST universe. But this, in itself, is not the final answer. A balance is achieved in the three universes and certainty upon those universes.

318

All control is effected by introducing uncertainties and hidden influences: "Look how bad it is over there, so you'll have to look back at me." Thus slavery is effected solely by getting people to fix on one thing. That one thing, in this case, is the physical universe. Science, so called, today produces machines to blow your nose, produces machines to think for you, produces every possible argument as to why you should consider your body frail and unexpendable. Science, under the domination of capital, creates scarcity. It creates a scarcity of universes in fixing one upon one universe only.

Those things which are scarce are those things which the individual has lost his faith in creating, in having. An individual who cannot create has to hold on to what he has. This leads him into holding on to what he has had. Where he has had a certainty in the past that something existed, he begins to grip it closer and closer to him. His space lessens, his beingness lessens, he becomes less active. The reactive mind that cannot create children has lost its hope of creation. It then can influence the analytical mind into believing that it can no longer create. The analytical mind creating artistically in the MEST *universe*, and not in its *own universe* at all and not in *other people's universes* that it can recognize, goes downscale until it meets, on its own level, the reactive mind. And here, at this level, we find the enslaver, the person who makes things scarce, the fellow who uses his ethics, so called, to enforce his crude judgments and to make "things" out of beings that could be *men*.

Here, where the reactive mind and the analytical mind have come into a parity, we have the only effect that can be produced—the effect of pain. Where we have an active desire for pain masking in a thousand guises, where every good impulse high on the scale is turned into a mockery, here we have crime, here we have war.

These things are not awareness. These things merely act on a stimulus-response mechanism.

Upscale is the high, bright breadth of being, breadth of understanding, breadth of awareness. To get there, all one must do is to become aware of the existence of the three universes by direct observation.

STANDARD
OPERATING PROCEDURE 8

HE BASIC TECHNOLOGY of this operating procedure is to be found in *The Factors*, *Scientology 8-8008* and the Professional School.

In using this operating procedure, the auditor should give every heed to the Auditor's Code. Further, he should audit the preclear in the presence of a third person or another auditor.

This operating procedure is best done by an auditor who has been thoroughly trained in all processes involving the reduction of the past and its incidents. The untrained auditor may encounter manifestations with which only a professional auditor would be familiar.

This operating procedure retains the most workable methods of preceding procedures and, in itself, emphasizes *positive gain* and the present and future, rather than *negative gain* of eradication of the past.

The thetan, exteriorized and rehabilitated, can handle and remedy, by direct address of his own energy to the body and the removal of old energy deposits, all body malfunctions or mental aberrations attacked by older processes. The goal of this procedure is not the rehabilitation of the body, but of the thetan. Rehabilitation of a body incidentally ensues.

The goal of this procedure is *Operating Thetan*, a higher goal than earlier procedures.

The auditor tests the preclear for each step, from Step I on, until he finds a step the preclear can do. The auditor then completes this step and then the next higher step until the thetan is exteriorized. With the thetan exteriorized, the auditor now completes all seven steps regardless of the steps performed before exteriorization. He may complete all these steps and all parts of these steps rapidly. But they must be done to obtain a Theta Clear and they must be done thoroughly to obtain an Operating Thetan.

The techniques involved herein were tested on a wide variety of cases. It is doubtful if any earlier process of any kind in any age has been as thoroughly validated as this operating procedure. However, it works only when used as stated. Disorganized fragments of this material, given other names and emphases, may be found to be harmful. Irresponsible and untrained use of this procedure is not authorized. Capricious or quasi-religious exteriorization of the thetan, for other purposes than the restoration of his ability and self-determinism, should be resisted by any being. *The goal of this process is freedom for the individual to the betterment of the many.*

Step I

Ask preclear to be three feet behind his head. If stable there, have him be in various pleasant places until any feeling of scarcity of viewpoints is resolved. Then have him be in several undesirable places, then several pleasant places. Then have him be in a slightly dangerous place, then in more and more dangerous places until he can sit in the center of the Sun. Be sure to observe a gradient scale of ugliness and dangerousness of places. Do not let the preclear fail. Then do remaining steps with preclear exteriorized.

Step II

Have preclear mock-up own body. If he does this easily and clearly, have him mock-up own body until he slips out of it. When he is exteriorized and knows it thoroughly (the condition of all exteriorization) do Step I. If his mock-up was not clear, go to Step III immediately.

Step III: Spacation

Have preclear close his eyes and find upper corners of the room. Have him sit there, not thinking, refusing to think of anything, interested only in the corners until he is completely exteriorized without strain. Then do a Spacation (constructing own space with eight anchor points and holding it stable without effort) and go to Step I. If preclear was unable to locate corners of the room easily with his eyes closed, go to Step IV.

Step IV: Expanded GITA

(This is an extension of Give and Take Processing.) Test preclear to see if he can get a mock-up he can see, no matter how vague. Then have him *waste, accept under duress, desire* and finally be able to *take or leave alone* each of the items listed below. He does this with mock-ups or ideas. He must do the sequence of waste, etc., in the order given here for each item. He wastes it by having it at remote distances in places where it will do no good, being used or done or observed by something which cannot appreciate it. When he is able to waste it in vast quantities, the auditor then has him accept it in mock-up form until he no longer is antagonistic to having to accept it even when it is unpleasant and great force is applied to make him take it.

Then again, with mock-ups, he must be able to bring himself to desire it even in its worst form. Then, by mock-ups of it in its most desirable form, he must come to be able to leave it entirely alone or take it in its worst form without caring. Expanded GITA remedies contra-survival abundance and scarcity. It will be found that before one can accept a very scarce (to him) thing, he has to give it away. A person with a milk allergy must be able to give away, in mock-up, enormous quantities of milk, wasting it, before he can accept any himself. The items in this list are compounded of several years of isolating what factors were more important to minds than others. The list lacks very few of the very important items, if any. Additions to or subtractions from this list should not be attempted. *Viewpoint, work* and *pain* should be heavily and often stressed and given priority. Next in importance are *incidents, looking, sensation, talking* and *knowing.*

Waste, Have Forced Upon, Desire, Be Able to Give or Take, in that order, each of the following (order of items here is random):

Viewpoint, Work, Pain, Incidents, Looking, Sensation, Talking, Knowing, Beauty, Motion, Engrams, Ugliness, Logic, Pictures, Confinement, Money, Parents, Blackness, Police, Light, Explosions, Bodies, Degradation, Male Bodies, Female Bodies, Babies, Children Male, Children Female, Strange and Peculiar Bodies, Dead Bodies, Affinity (Love), Agreement, Beautiful Bodies, People, Attention, Admiration, Force, Energy, Lightning, Unconsciousness, Problems, Antagonism, Reverence, Fear, Objects, Time, Eating Human Bodies, Sound, Grief, Beautiful Sadness, Hidden Influences, Hidden Communications, Doubts, Faces, Dimension Points, Anchor Points, Anger, Apathy, Ideas, Enthusiasm, Disagreement, Hate, Sex, Eating Parents, Eaten by Parents, Eating Men, Eaten by Men, Eating Women,

Eaten by Women, Starts, Spoken Communications, Written Communications, Stillness, Exhaustion, Stopping Motion Women, Stopping Motion Men, Changing Motion Women, Changing Motion Men, Changing Motion Babies, Changing Motion Children, Starting Motion Men, Starting Motion Women, Starting Motion Children, Starting Motion Objects, Starting Motion Self, Omens, Wickedness, Forgiveness, Play, Games, Machinery, Touch, Traffic, Stolen Goods, Stolen Pictures, Homes, Blasphemy, Caves, Medicine, Glass, Mirrors, Pride, Musical Instruments, Dirty Words (written on paper, in air), Space, Wild Animals, Pets, Birds, Air, Water, Food, Milk, Garbage, Gases, Excreta, Rooms, Beds, Punishment, Boredom, Confusion, Soldiers, Executioners, Doctors, Judges, Psychiatrists, Liquor (Alcohol), Drugs, Masturbation, Rewards, Heat, Cold, Forbidden Things, God, the Devil, Spirits, Bacteria, Glory, Dependence, Responsibility, Wrongness, Rightness, Insanity, Sanity, Faith, Christ, Death, Rank (Position), Poverty, Maps, Irresponsibility, Greetings, Farewells, Credit, Loneliness, Jewels, Teeth, Genitalia, Complications, Help, Pretense, Truth, Lies, Assurance, Contempt, Predictability, Unpredictability, Vacuums, White Clouds, Black Clouds, Unattainables, Hidden Things, Worry, Revenge, Textbooks, Kisses, The Past, The Future, The Present, Arms, Stomachs, Bowels, Mouths, Cigarettes, Smoke, Urine, Vomit, Convulsions, Saliva, Flowers, Semen, Blackboards, Fireworks, Toys, Vehicles, Dolls, Audiences, Doors, Walls, Weapons, Blood, Ambitions, Illusions, Betrayal, Ridicule, Hope, Happiness, Mothers, Fathers, Grandparents, Suns, Planets, Moons, Waiting, Silence, Not Knowing, Fac One, Remembering, Forgetting, Auditing, Minds, Fame, Power, Accidents, Illnesses, Approval, Tiredness, Acting, Drama, Costumes, Sleep, Holding Things Apart, Holding Things Together, Destroying Things, Sending Things Away,

Making Things Go Fast, Making Things Appear, Making Things Vanish, Convictions, Stability, Changing People, Silent Men, Silent Women, Silent Children, Symbols of Weakness, Symbols of Force, Disabilities, Education, Languages, Bestiality, Homosexuality, Invisible Bodies, Invisible Acts, Invisible Scenes, Accepting Things Back, Rules, Players, Restimulation, Sexual Restimulation, Space Reduction, Size Reduction, Entertainment, Cheerfulness, Freedom for Others to Talk, Act, Feel Pain, Be Sad, Thetans, Personalities, Cruelty, Organizations, Nothing. Try first: Healthy Bodies, Strong Bodies, Good Perception, Good Recall.

WARNING: Should your preclear become unstable or upset doing this process, take him to Step VI. Then return to this list.

COMMENT: The mind is sufficiently complicated that it can be expected to have computations on almost all the above. Thus there is no single clearing "button" and search for it is at the dictate of a circuit, the mechanism of circuits being to search for something hidden. Thus your preclear may begin to compute and philosophize and seek to find the "button" that will release all this. All this releases all the buttons, so tell him to relax and go on with the process every time he starts to compute.

NOTE: Running the above will bring to the surface, without further attention, the "computation on the case" and the service facsimile. Do not audit these. Run Expanded GITA.

Step V: Present Time Differentiation. Exteriorization by Scenery

Have preclear, with his body's eyes, study and see the difference between similar real objects such as the two legs of a chair, the spaces between the back, two cigarettes, two trees, two girls.

He must see and study the objects – it is not enough to remember the objects. The definition of a Case V is "no mock-ups, only blackness." Have him continue this process until he is alert. Use liberally and often.

Then exteriorize by having the preclear close his eyes and move actual places on Earth under him, preferably places he has not been. Have him bring these up to him, find two similar things in the scene and observe the difference between them. Move him over oceans and cities until he is certain that he is exteriorized.

Then, preferably while exteriorized, have him do Step I.

This case has to *know* before he can *be*. His viewpoint is in the past. Give him present time viewpoints until he is a Step I by the methods given for Step V.

COMMENT: Present Time Differentiation is a very good general technique and resolves chronic somatics and improves tone.

Assume other people's viewpoints as a drill – not what they think about things, but as they look at things in the material universe. Attempt to be in the location of a leaf, blade of grass, car headlamp, etc., and view the universe.

Step VI: ARC Straightwire

ARC Straightwire using next-to-last list of *Self Analysis in Scientology* (which asks the preclear to recall something really real to him, etc.). Then use the lists in *Self Analysis*. This level is the neurotic. It is identified by the preclear having mock-ups which will not persist or which won't go away. Use also Present Time Differentiation. Then go to Step IV. At any drop in tone, return case to Step VI.

Step VII: Psychotic Cases

(Whether in or out of body.) The psychotic appears to be in such desperate straits that the auditor often errs in thinking desperate measures are necessary. Use the lightest possible methods. Give case space and freedom where possible. Have psychotic *imitate* (not mock-up) various things. Have him do Present Time Differentiation. Get him to tell the difference between things by actual touch. Have him locate, differentiate and touch things that are really real to him (real objects or items). If inaccessible, mimic him with own body, whatever he does, until he comes into communication. Have him locate corners of the room and hold them without thinking. As soon as his communication is up, go to Step VI. But be very sure he changes any mock-up around until he knows it is a mock-up, that it exists and that he himself made it. Do not run engrams. He is psychotic because viewpoints in present time are so scarce that he has gone into the past for viewpoints which at least he knew existed. By Present Time Differentiation, by tactile on objects, restore his idea of an abundance of viewpoint in present time. If he has been given electric shock, do not process it or any other brutality. Work him for very brief periods, for his attention span is short. *Always* work psychotics with another auditor or a companion present.

NOTE: All steps for all cases. If in doubt as to condition of case, test with Step VI.

NOTE: An Operating Thetan must also be able to manufacture particles of admiration and force in abundance.

Appendix to SOP 8 No. 1

(Any alterations in SOP 8 will appear in appendices as they are expected to be minor and to make no radical change in the design of the steps in general.)

Step I

The Operating Thetan must be able to manufacture and experience, to his complete satisfaction, all sensations including pain in mock-up form and all energies such as admiration and force. It will be found that some Step I cases will not be able to manufacture admiration particles.

Step II

Be very careful not to make a lower-step preclear, while still in a body, mock-up his own body too long. Any mock-up will appear if it is simply put there often enough and long enough–providing the preclear doesn't spin in the process. The long-term manufacture of mock-ups of one's own body and of admiration may not produce quite the results expected–communication lines which should remain shut may open with bad results. These lines that are shut appear like hard, black cords to the preclear.

There are two types of techniques in general: *positive gain* and *negative gain* (as defined in the above text). Positive can be administered in unlimited amounts without harm. Negative gain techniques, such as the reduction of engrams and locks, Double Terminaling, Black and White, are often limited in the length of time they can be given. After a few hundred hours of early-type auditing, the case could be found to slump.

Thus we have in positive gain the *unlimited* technique which improves the analytical mind. In negative gain we have a *limited* (in terms of the time it can be audited) technique. In SOP 8 the following steps and processes may be audited without limit: Step I, Step III, Step V, Step VI, Step VII. The following steps are limited and should not be audited many hours without changing to another type (unlimited) for a while, after which the following steps could be resumed: Step II, Step IV. The following steps can be used on groups: Step III, Step V Part 1 and Part 2, Step VI, Step VII.

Appendix to SOP 8 No. 2
Certainty Processing

The anatomy of "maybe" consists of uncertainties and is resolved by the processing of certainties. It is not resolved by the processing of uncertainties.

An uncertainty is held in suspense solely because the preclear is holding on so hard to certainties. The basic thing he is holding on to is, "I have a solution," "I have no solution." One of these is positive, the other is negative. A complete positive and a complete negative are, alike, a certainty. The basic certainty is, "There is something," "There is nothing." A person can be certain there is something, he can be certain there is nothing.

"There is something," "There is nothing" resolves chronic somatics in this order.

One gets the preclear to have the center of the somatics say:

"There is something here,"
"There is nothing here."

Then he gets the center of the somatic to say:

"There is nothing there,"
"There is something there."

Then the auditor has the preclear say toward the somatic:

"There is something there,"
"There is nothing there."

And then he gets the preclear to say, about himself:

"There is something here,"
"There is nothing here."

This is a very fast resolution of chronic somatics. Quite ordinarily three or four minutes of this will resolve an acute state and fifteen or twenty minutes of it will resolve a chronic state.

This matter of certainties goes further. It has been determined by my recent investigations that the reason behind what is happening is the desire of a *cause* to bring about an *effect*. Something is better than nothing, anything is better than nothing. Any circuit, any effect, any anything is better than nothing. If you will Match Terminals in brackets "There is nothing," you will find that a lot of your preclears become very ill. This should be turned around into "There is something."

The way one does Matched Terminals is to have the preclear facing the preclear or his father facing his father—in other words, two of each of anything, one facing the other. These two things will discharge, one into the other, thus running off the difficulty. By "bracket" we mean, of course, running this with:

The preclear putting them up as *himself to himself;*

As though they were put up by *somebody else* (the *somebody else facing the somebody else*);

And the matched terminal again put up by *others facing others.*

The clue to all this is positive and negative, in terms of certainties. The positive plus the negative in conflict make an uncertainty. A great number of combinations of things can be run. Here's a list of the combinations.

The button behind sex is:

"I can begin life anew,"
"I cannot begin life anew."

"I can make life persist,"
"I cannot make life persist."

"I can stop life,"
"I cannot stop life."

"I can change life,"
"I cannot change life."

"I can start life,"
"I cannot start life."

A very effective process is:

"Something wrong _____,"
"Nothing wrong _____," with *you, me, them, my mind, communication,* various allies.

A very basic resolution of the lack of space of an individual is to locate these people and these objects which you've been using as anchor points (such as father, mother and so forth) and putting them into Matched Terminal brackets with this:

"There is father,"
"There is no father."

"There is grandfather,"
"There is no grandfather."

In the compulsive line this can be changed to:

"There must be no father,"
"There must be a father."

One takes all the allies of an individual and runs them in this fashion.

The basic law underneath this is that a person becomes the effect of anything upon which he has had to depend.

This would tell you immediately that the Sixth Dynamic, the MEST universe, is the largest dependency of the individual.

This can be run out, but then any dynamic can be run out in this fashion:

"There is myself,"
"There is no self."

And so on, up the dynamics.

"(Any dynamic) is preventing me from communicating,"
"(Any dynamic) is not preventing me from communicating," is intensely effective.

Any such technique can be varied by applying the Sub-zero Scale.

One runs any certainty out because he knows that for this certainty there is an opposite negative certainty and that between these lies a "maybe" and that the maybe stays in suspense in time. The basic operation of the reactive mind is to solve problems. It is based on uncertainties about observation. Thus one runs out certainties of observation. The most general shotgun technique would have to do with:

"There is sex,"
"There is no sex."

"There is force,"
"There is no force."

This could be run, of course, in terms of Matched Terminal brackets or even as concepts. But one must not neglect to run the overt act phenomenon (which is to say, getting somebody else getting the concept).

The processing out of certainties would then embrace:

"I have a solution,"
"There is no solution."

These two opposite ends would take care of any individual who was hung on the track with some solution, for that solution had its opposite. People who have studied medicine begin by being certain that medicine works and end by being certain that medicine doesn't work. They begin by studying psychology on a supposition that it is the solution and finish up believing that it is not the solution. This also happens to superficial students of Dianetics and Scientology. Thus, one should also run:

"Dianetics is a solution,"
"Dianetics is not the solution."

This would get one off the maybe on the subject.

We are essentially processing communications systems. The entire process of auditing is concentrated upon withdrawing communications from the preclear, as predicated on the basis of the body and the preclear cannot handle communications.

Thus:

"The preclear can handle communications,"
"The preclear cannot handle communications," is a shotgun technique which resolves maybes about his communications.

An intensely interesting aspect of Certainty Processing is that it shows up intimately where the preclear is aberrated. Here is the overall basic technique. One runs:

"There is _____,"
"There is not _____," the following: *communication, talk, letters, love, agreement, sex, pain, work, bodies, minds, curiosity, control, enforcement, compulsion, inhibition, food, money, people, ability, beauty, ugliness, presents,* and both the top and bottom of the Chart of Attitudes, positive and negative in each one.

Basic in all this is the urge of the preclear to produce an effect, so one can run:

"I can produce an effect upon Mama,"

"I cannot produce an effect upon Mama," and so forth for all allies and one will resolve the fixations of attention on the part of the preclear.

Thus fixations of attention are resolved by Certainty Processing, processing out the production of effect.

One can occasionally, if he so desires, process the direct center of the maybe (which is to say, doubt itself) in terms of Matched Terminals. This, however, is risky–for it throws the preclear into a general state of doubt.

The key to any such processing is the recovery of viewpoints.

"I can have grandfather's viewpoint,"

"I cannot have grandfather's viewpoint," and so on, particularly with sexual partners, will prove intensely interesting on a case.

"There are viewpoints,"
"There are no viewpoints."

"I have a viewpoint,"
"I don't have a viewpoint."

"_____ has a viewpoint,"
"_____ has no viewpoint," resolves problems.

One should also realize that when one is processing facsimiles, he is processing at one time energy, sensation and aesthetics. The facsimile is a picture. The preclear is being affected by pictures, mainly, and so:

"There are no pictures,"

"There are pictures," forward the case toward handling pictures (which is to say, facsimiles).

A person tends to ally himself with somebody whom he considers capable of producing greater effects than himself, so:

"(I, she, he, it) can create greater effects,"
"(I, she, he, it) can create no effect," should be run.

When one is processing, he is trying to withdraw communications. Reach and Withdraw are the two fundamentals in the action of theta. Must Reach and Can't Reach, Must Withdraw and Can't Withdraw are compulsions which, when run in combination, produce the manifestation of insanity in a preclear.

"I can reach,"
"I can't reach."

"I can withdraw,"

"I can't withdraw," open up into the fact that remembering and forgetting are dependent upon the ability to reach and withdraw.

You will find that a preclear will respond to:

"You must _____"
or
"You can _____,"

"You must not _____"
or
"You cannot _____."

"There is _____,"
"There is not _____," forgetting and remembering.

The only reason a person is hanging on to a body or facsimile is that he has lost his belief in his ability to create. The rehabilitation of this ability to create is resolved, for instance, in a person who has had an ambition to write, with:

"*I can write,*"
"*I cannot write,*" and so forth.

The loss of this creative ability made the person hang on to what he had. The fact that a preclear has forgotten how to or no longer can himself generate force, makes him hold on to stores of force. These are very often mistaken by the auditor for facsimiles. The preclear doesn't care for the facsimile. He simply cares for the force contained in the facsimile because he knows he doesn't have any force anymore.

It should be kept in mind that Reaching and Withdrawing are intensely productive of reaction in a preclear. But that preclear who does not respond to Reaching and Withdrawing and Certainty thereon, is hung up in a very special condition: *he is trying to prevent something from happening.* He also prevents auditing from happening. He has lost allies, he has had accidents and he's hung up at all those points on the track where he feels he should have prevented something from happening. This is resolved by running:

"*I must prevent it from happening,*"
"*I cannot prevent it from happening.*"

"*I must regain control,*"
"*I must lose all control.*"

Blackness is the desire to be an effect and the inability to be cause.

"*I can create grandfather* (or ally),"
"*I cannot create grandfather* (or ally)," solves scarcity of allies.

"I want to be aware,"
"I want no awareness," is a technique which is basic in attitudes.

Run this as others, in Matched Terminal brackets or in Expanded GITA:

"Certainty there is a past,"
"Certainty there is no past."

"Certainty there is a future,"
"Certainty there is no future."

"Certainty it means something else,"
"Certainty it does not mean anything else."

"Certainty there is space,"
"Certainty there is no space."

"Certainty there is energy,"
"Certainty there is no energy."

"Certainty there are objects,"
"Certainty there are no objects."

SHORT 8

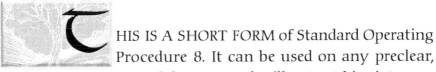

HIS IS A SHORT FORM of Standard Operating Procedure 8. It can be used on any preclear, without any survey of the case, and will not get him into any difficulties and should resolve his various computations. This can also be used on groups. Just do the lettered steps in order.

A. Next-to-last list in *Self Analysis* (recalling something *real*, etc.) until auditor is certain preclear has and can do so easily. In a group, ask for a show of hands the moment something real is recalled. Take those hands that went up in a couple of seconds and use them for the rest of this. Take the no-hands or slow hands as a special group under somebody else and simply drill them on this step until their speed is well up. Then put them back into the main group, or keep all in one group and go on.

B. Examine and compare two similar MEST objects or spaces and tell the difference. Keep this up for at least twenty minutes. It can be kept up for hours with astonishing case improvement.

C. Run *wasting* Healthy Bodies, then *accepting them under duress,*
then *wasting them,* then *accepting them under duress.* Do this
for twenty minutes or an hour, until preclear or group shows
signs of relief or amusement.

D. Run next-to-last list of *Self Analysis* for five minutes.

E. Run Duplication. This process is the basis of making facsimiles.
Have preclear or group look at a MEST object. Then have him
or them mock-up a "mock-up" similar to it, but beside it.
Have the MEST object and the "mock-up" compared to tell the
difference. Some people get none of the duplicates for quite a
while, but will eventually. Some start making much fancier
objects of the same sort. In any result, keep this up for twenty
minutes.

F. Have preclear or group close eyes and locate the corners of
the room behind them and keep interested in those corners
and not thinking for several minutes.

G. Have preclear or group move MEST scenery under them
individually but at the command of the auditor. The scenery is,
preferably, that not before viewed by the preclear or preclears.
Don't let them invalidate what they see. This is Exteriorization
by Scenery. Keep up for twenty minutes.

H. Do next-to-last list of *Self Analysis.* Five minutes.

I. Examine and compare two present time objects.

J. Have one of the members go to the window and look out of
the window. Have the remainder of the group assuming his
viewpoint to see what he sees out of the window. Do this for
ten minutes.

K. Start at beginning again and use list over and over. What they *waste* each time through, can be changed to "Work" and "Anchor Points." Avoid pain with this Short 8. Run "Healthy Bodies" for it instead.

"The highest theory of SOP 8-C is that
the being is engaged upon a game
called 'Physical Universe.'"

SOP 8-C

The Journal of Scientology 24-G

31 January 1954

SOP 8-C:
THE REHABILITATION OF THE HUMAN SPIRIT

SCIENTOLOGY, the science of knowing how to know, has been developed for various applications in the field of human experience.

Where it is utilized by skilled persons to enhance the personal ability and knowledge of others, the recommended process is Standard Operating Procedure 8-C (SOP 8-C).

SOP 8-C was developed after almost a year of observing SOP 8 in action, in other hands than mine, and after observing the frailties and talents of human auditors. SOP 8-C might be called "SOP 8 modified for clinical, laboratory and individual human application."

The goal of this system of operation is to return to the individual his knowledge, skill and knowingness, and to enhance his perception, his reaction time and serenity.

It is entirely incidental that SOP 8-C is effective on "psychosomatic" illness, on human aberration and social difficulties. It is not the intent or purpose of Scientology to "repair." The science is a creative science. If the fact is that human illness, disability and aberration uniformly cease to be because of Scientology, the effect is not intended to be primary and the goal of SOP 8-C is not their remedy. Indeed, if SOP 8-C is used to remedy these only, it fails as a system. SOP 8-C succeeds only when it is addressed toward higher knowingness and beingness.

Ironically, in using it, human ills vanish only when the auditor concentrates on the goals of the system and neglects the obvious physical disabilities of the preclear.

In that one creates that which one concentrates upon, a treatment of illness which validates it in treatment will always tend to be unsuccessful.

SOP 8-C was the subject of the Camden Indoctrination Course B,* from November 16 to December 23, as well as the subject of the Phoenix International Congress of December 28, 1953.

Specifically, the use of these processes obtains, when correctly used, without further evaluation for or indoctrination of the preclear, the knowledge that he is not a body, that he is a creative energy-production unit and demonstrates to him his purposes and abilities.

This energy-space production unit we call a "thetan," that being a coined word taken from a mathematical symbol–the Greek letter "theta." This *is* the preclear. One does not send "one's thetan" anywhere. One goes *as* a thetan. When a preclear is detected being in one place and finding "his thetan" in another ("I'm over *there*"), he is not exteriorized. To be exteriorized, the preclear must be *certain* that he is outside his body. An uncertain "exteriorization" requires more work before it becomes an exteriorization.

SOP 8-C brings about a condition designated as "Theta Clear." This is a relative, not an absolute term. It means that the person, this thought unit, is clear of his body, his engrams, his facsimiles, but can handle and safely control a body.

The state of "Operating Thetan" is higher than Theta Clear and means that the person does not need a body to communicate or work. It is accomplished with SOP 8-O.

2nd American Advanced Clinical Course.

SOP 8-C
The Rehabilitation of the Human Spirit

The highest theory of SOP 8-C is that the being is engaged upon a game called "Physical Universe." This is a game requiring barriers—which is to say, walls, planets, time and vast distances (which last two are also barriers). In engaging upon this game, he has at last become so conscious of barriers that he is limited in his actions and thoughts. He thinks, in the case of Homo sapiens, that he is a body (a barrier) hemmed in by vast distances (barriers) and pinned in a time stream (a system of moving barriers) so as to reach only the present. These combined barriers have become so formidable that they are not even well-perceived but, from being strong, have become unreal to him. The matter is further complicated by "invisible barriers," such as the eyes or glasses.

In actuality, the thetan is a knowingness total, in a cleared state, who yet can create space and time and objects to locate in them. He reduces his knowingness only to have action. Knowingness is reduced by assuming that one cannot know or knows wrongly. Knowingness is reduced by assuming one must be in certain places to perceive, and so know, and that one cannot be in certain places.

Space is, but does not have to be, the first barrier of knowingness. With Scientology, we have the first definition of space: "Space is a viewpoint of dimension." Given a viewpoint and four, eight or more points to view, one has space. Space is a problem of observation, not of physics.

There is no question here of whether space, energy or objects are *real*. Things are as real as one is certain of their reality. Reality is, here on Earth, "agreement as to what *is*." This does not prevent barriers or time from being formidably *real*. It does not mean, either, that space, energy or time are not illusions. It is as one knows it is. For one makes, by a process of continuous automatic duplication, all that one perceives.

So much for theory. In application, this theory obtains results of considerable magnitude in changing beingness.

The thetan is continuously engaged upon cycles-of-action. The basic cycle-of-action is: "*create,* resist effects *(survive)* and *destroy.*" This can be stated in various ways: "create an object, have it resist effects (survive) and then destroy it." Or: "create a situation, continue it and change it, and destroy or end it." When a thetan leaves a cycle which is important to him unfinished, he tends to strive to finish it elsewhere or later in disrelated circumstances. Further, he can become overly concentrated upon *creating* or persistence *(surviving)* or upon *destroying*—and so form an unbalanced state of beingness.

Time exists in those things a thetan creates. It is a shift of particles, always making new space, always at an agreed-upon rate. A thetan does not change in time but, as he can view particles (objects, spaces, barriers) from many viewpoints, he can consider himself to be in a "time stream" which he is not. A thetan's ideas (postulates, commands, beliefs) change. Particles change. The thetan does not change, either in space or in time.

Just as he is making an effort to do something he cannot help but do, *Survive,* he is also fighting against doing the only thing he does—sit fixed in one "position."

The thetan, to produce interest and action, operates as a paradox. He cannot die, so he firmly insists and proves continually that he can die. He never changes location, but only views new locations, and constantly lives in horror of being fixed in time and space. Above that, he knows the past and the future and all of the present, and so fights to obscure the past and guess the future.

Less theoretically, the individual who is processed is, at first, usually "in" the body and perceiving with the body's eyes.

SOP 8-C
The Rehabilitation of the Human Spirit

When exteriorized (placed three feet back of his head), he is actually out of the body and still "in" physical universe space. He can, exteriorized, move about and be in places just as though he had a body, seeing without eyes, hearing without ears and feeling without fingers – ordinarily better than with these "aids." This is not like "astral walking," which is done by the individual who "sends a body" or a viewpoint to some other place and perceives with it. A thetan is as much present where he is, as if he were there in body. He isn't "somebody else" than the preclear moving dimly about. He *is* the preclear, he *is* there. At first, he may be uncertain as to what he is seeing. This faculty becomes better as his ability to look, hear and feel, while exteriorized, improves. SOP 8-C improves this perception. Because the body only perceives what the thetan is perceiving anyway, looking, feeling, hearing of the body are also better with SOP 8-C. But this is only incidental.

When a thetan believes too thoroughly he is a body, he is generally unhappy, afraid, doubts his own (and validates the body's) existence and worries about his inabilities. When he is out of the sphere of influence of the body (a very small one), he becomes serene, confident and knowing. He can handle a body better, can act faster, can recall more and do more while exteriorized than he can while in a body.

Society, thirsting for more control of more people, substitutes religion for the spirit, the body for the soul, an identity for the individual and science and data for truth. In this direction lies insanity, increasing slavery, less knowingness, greater scarcity and less society.

Scientology has opened the gates to a better world. It is not a psychotherapy. It is a body of knowledge which, when properly used, gives freedom and truth to the individual.

It could be said that Man exists in a partially hypnotized state. He believes, on other-determinism, in many things to his detriment. He will be as well as he is self-determined. The processes of Scientology could be described as methods of "unhypnotizing" men to their own freer choice and better life.

THE USE OF
SOP 8-C

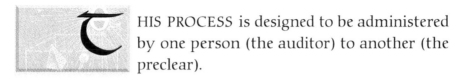

HIS PROCESS is designed to be administered by one person (the auditor) to another (the preclear).

SOP 8-C is first used step by step, from Step I on, until the person to whom it is addressed *knows* he is back of his head and no longer in the body. If the preclear is very difficult to exteriorize, the person should be referred to an auditor trained at the HAS Clinical Center (for there are special methods of exteriorization for difficult cases, which are contained in, but are not at once visible, in SOP 8-C). The first three steps are exteriorization steps. They should be repeated over and over until certain exteriorization takes place.

The auditor can go through the first steps many times (one after the other) with the preclear until exteriorization occurs. Doing Steps IV to VII on a person not exteriorized should be minimized. (Earlier SOPs used all seven steps for exteriorization, a practice not followed in SOP 8-C where only the first three steps are used.)

When the preclear has exteriorized, one then begins again with Step I and continues to Step VII (in order) with the preclear exteriorized. Here, in SOP 8-C, the emphasis is upon an exteriorized thetan. When the auditor has taken the exteriorized preclear thoroughly and *correctly* through Steps I to VII at least twice, one has then what may be considered a Theta Clear.

To repeat, one uses SOP 8-C Steps I to III, in that order. On one of these, the first time through, the majority of people exteriorize with certainty. As soon as exteriorization takes place, the auditor starts with Step I again, does it thoroughly on the exteriorized preclear, then the auditor applies Step II thoroughly, and so on, until all seven are done.

The auditor knows when the preclear exteriorizes by asking him or by the preclear volunteering the information.

CAUTION: Do not ask the preclear to look at his body.

If the preclear fails to exteriorize sometime during the first three steps, the auditor should simply do them again. If the preclear fails the second time, the auditor patiently goes through them a third time, and so on. If the matter then seems too difficult, contact an auditor trained during late 1953 (at Camden) by the HAS itself.

The least possible result in going over these first three steps many times will be a considerably bettered condition of the preclear, superior to all past results. Only a very few preclears fail to exteriorize after Steps I to III have been several times repeated.

CAUTION: Although this process is as foolproof as it can be made, it can be maliciously used in this wise: By giving the preclear constant losses; by giving him no chance to win; by bullying him; by evaluating for him; by insisting he is "outside" when he is not; by invalidating him; by pretending to see him or his mock-ups; or, saying that one does if he does.

SOP 8-C
FORMULAS AND STEPS

Opening Procedure:
(Ten Minutes to Two Hours – with MEST Body)

a. Send preclear to exact places in the room, one place at a time.

b. Have preclear select places in room and move to them one at a time, still under auditor's direction.

c. Have preclear drill in physically holding on to and letting go of objects and spaces on his own decision to hold on, decision to let go.

Step 1: Location

PRELOGIC: *Theta orients objects in space and time.*

AXIOM: *In life experience, space becomes beingness.*

FORMULA I:

Permitting the preclear to discover with certainty where people and things are not in the present, past and future recovers sufficient orientation to establish his knowledge and certainty of where he is and they are. The application of this is accomplished by negative orientation of *beingness, havingness* and *doingness,* on each of eight dynamics, in the *present, past* and *future.*

Step I

a. Ask preclear to be three feet back of chair. Ask him for things, people which are not giving him directions (orders). For things, persons he is not giving orders to. For things, persons which are not giving directions to other things. Ask preclear for goals he does not have. For goals another does not have. For goals others do not have for others. For goals another does not have for him. For goals he does not have for another. For persons he is not. For animals he is not. For objects he is not. For places where he is not. For places others are not. For places animals are not. Where bacteria is not. Where objects are not. For places where he is not thinking.

NOTE: All of the above are done in "brackets" for present, past and future.

b. (If exteriorized) Have him drill, while exteriorized, into holding on to and letting go of objects on his specific decision. Ask him to be in places which are safe, dangerous, pleasant, unpleasant, beautiful, ugly.

Step II: Bodies

AXIOM: *In life experience, energy becomes doingness.*

AXIOM: *Compulsive position precedes compulsive thinking.*

AXIOM: *That which changes the preclear in space can evaluate for him.*

FORMULA II:

Permit the preclear to discover that he handles bodies and allow him to handle bodies, in mock-ups and actuality, and remedy his thirst for attention which he has received by contagion from bodies.

SOP 8-C
FORMULAS AND STEPS

Step II

a. Have preclear mock-up bodies and unmock them. Have him get somethingnesses and nothingnesses of bodies until he feels better about them. Ask him to be three feet back of chair.

b. (If exteriorized) Have him complete IIa many times and then move body while he is outside.

Step III: Space

PRELOGIC: *Theta creates space and time and objects to locate in them.*

DEFINITION: *Space is a viewpoint of dimension.*

AXIOM: *Energy derives from imposition of space between terminals and a reduction and expansion of that space.*

FORMULA III:

Permit the preclear to regain his ability to create space and impose it upon terminals, to remove it from between terminals and to regain his security concerning the stability of MEST space.

Step III

a. Have preclear hold two back corners of room and not think.

b. (If exteriorized) Have preclear complete Spacation.

NOTE: If not exteriorized, return to Step I.

Step IV: Havingness

AXIOM: *In life experience, time becomes havingness.*

OBSERVATION: *To a thetan, anything is better than nothing.*

357

OBSERVATION: *Any preclear is suffering from problems of too little havingness and any reduction of his existing energy, if not replaced, will cause him to drop in tone.*

FORMULA IV:

a. The remedy of problems of havingness is accomplished by creating an abundance of all things.

b. As the preclear has rendered automatic his desires and ability to create and destroy, and has thus placed havingness beyond his control, the auditor should place in the control of the preclear his automaticities of havingness and unhavingness and permit him, on his own self-determinism, to balance his havingness.

c. How to make havingness: Have preclear put out eight anchor points of size, thus creating a space. Have him pull in these eight to the center and have him retain the resulting mass. Do this using large and various objects for anchor points. Do this until he is willing to release such *old* energy deposits as engrams and ridges, but still continue to make havingness.

Step IV

Have preclear remedy problems of havingness by mocking-up and pulling together sets of eight anchor points. Do this many times. Do not have him make anchor points explode in this fashion. Have him save masses thus created. Have preclear adjust anchor points in body.

Step V: Terminals

AXIOM: *Space exists by reason of anchor points.*

DEFINITION: *An anchor point is any particle or mass or terminal.*

DESTINATION: TOTAL FREEDOM

The *Classification, Gradation and Awareness Chart of Levels and Certificates* is your Bridge to Total Freedom. It tells you which step to take, one after the other, to achieve that destination. Reach for your eternity. Fill out the information below, mail this card and receive a *free* copy of the chart.

NAME

ADDRESS

CITY

STATE/PROVINCE   ZIP/POSTAL CODE

PHONE   E-MAIL

www.scientology.org

BUSINESS REPLY MAIL
FIRST CLASS MAIL PERMIT NO. 62688 LOS ANGELES, CA

POSTAGE WILL BE PAID BY ADDRESSEE

PUBLICATIONS, INC.

4751 Fountain Avenue
Los Angeles CA 90029

AXIOM: *Energy is derived from mass by fixing two terminals in proximity in space.*

AXIOM: *Self-determinism is related to the ability to impose space between terminals.*

AXIOM: *Cause is a potential source of flow.*

AXIOM: *Effect is a potential receipt of flow.*

AXIOM: *Communication is the duplication at a receipt-point of that which emanated at a cause-point.*

AXIOM: *Wrongness in terms of flow is inflow.*

FORMULA V:

The thetan is rehabilitated as to energy and terminals by remedying his postulates about outflow and inflow and drills relating to the outflow and inflow of energy according to the above axioms.

Step V

a. Ask preclear for times he could do something. Times when he couldn't do anything. For things he can do. For things he can't do. For things other people can, can't do. For things other people can do for others. For things another specific person can't do for him. For things he cannot do for another or others.

b. Ask preclear for objects, actions, persons, ideas he is not destroying. For objects, actions, persons, ideas he is not making survive (persist). For objects, actions, persons, ideas he is not creating. Present, past and future. In brackets. (NOTE: Ideas are the most important here.)

c. Ask preclear for objects, persons, energies, times which are not touching him. Which he is not touching. Which are not reaching for him. For which he is not reaching.

For objects, persons, times from which he is not withdrawing. Which are not withdrawing from him. In brackets.

d. Ask preclear for sights which will not blind him. For people he will not blind if they see him. For noises that will not deafen him. For people he will not deafen. For spoken words that will not hurt him. For spoken words which will not hurt others. In brackets.

e. Ask preclear for ideas that will not destroy, cause to survive (persist), create or upset others. In brackets.

f. Ask preclear for ideas, sounds, sights that will not fix people or unfix them from specific places.

g. Ask preclear for ideas he is not trying to fix in things. For ideas he is not trying to unfix from things. In brackets.

h. Have him unmock and mock-up terminals and move them together and apart until he can make them generate currents.

Step VI: Symbolization

DEFINITION: *A symbol is an idea fixed in energy and mobile in space.*

FORMULA VI:

The thetan who has been moved about by symbols is strengthened by mocking-up and moving about and fixing in space ideas which have formerly moved him.

Step VI

Have preclear create symbols which mean nothing.

Ask preclear for ideas he is not trying to destroy. For ideas he is not trying to make survive (persist). For ideas he is not trying to create.

NOTE: The above are done in brackets. Have him mock-up ideas and move them about.

Step VII: Barriers

AXIOM: *The MEST universe is a game consisting of barriers.*

DEFINITION: *A barrier is space, energy, object, obstacles or time.*

FORMULA VII:

Problems of barriers or their lack are resolved by contacting and penetrating, creating and destroying, validating and neglecting barriers by changing them or substituting others for them, by fixing and unfixing attention upon their somethingness and nothingness.

Step VII

a. Have preclear reach and withdraw (physically, then as himself) from spaces, walls, objects, times.

b. Have preclear do Six Ways to Nothing.

c. Have him create and destroy barriers.

Step VIII: Duplication

FUNDAMENTAL: *The basic action of existence is duplication.*

LOGIC: *All operating principles of life may be derived from duplication.*

AXIOM: *Communication is as exact as it approaches duplication.*

AXIOM: *Unwillingness to be cause is monitored by unwillingness to be duplicated.*

AXIOM: *Unwillingness to be an effect is monitored by unwillingness to duplicate.*

AXIOM: *An inability to remain in a geographical position brings about an unwillingness to duplicate.*

AXIOM: *An enforced fixation in a geographical position brings about an unwillingness to duplicate.*

AXIOM: *Inability to duplicate on any dynamic is the primary degeneration of the thetan.*

AXIOM: *Perception depends upon duplication.*

AXIOM: *Communication depends upon duplication.*

AXIOM: *In the MEST universe, the single crime is duplication.*

FORMULA VIII:

The primary ability and willingness of the thetan to duplicate must be rehabilitated by handling desires, enforcements and inhibitions relating to it on all dynamics.

Step VIII

a. Ask preclear for actions, forms and ideas which do, do not duplicate specific other people. For actions, forms, ideas by which specific other people do, do not duplicate specific others. For actions, forms, ideas of others which do, do not duplicate him.

b. Have preclear duplicate physical objects and people and possess himself of the duplicates.

c. Have him make "no-duplicates" of objects and people.

d. Have him duplicate somethings and "nothings."

Group C

"Group C" is a process used on large numbers of people. It is composed of the following steps of SOP 8-C: Step Ia, Step IIa, Step IIIa, Step Va to h, Step VI, Step VII, Step VIII.

Glossary

PRECLEAR: A person being processed.

MOCK-UP: A self-created image the preclear can see.

BRACKET is done as follows: For preclear, for another, others for others, others for self, another for preclear, preclear for another. See Step Ia.

SPECIAL NOTE: The first three steps of SOP 8-C could be classified as *beingness* steps. The remaining five steps of SOP 8-C could be classified as *havingness* steps. SOP itself, in all eight steps, constitutes *doingness*, thus approximating (as described in *Scientology 8-8008*) the Space-Be, Energy-Do, Time-Have Triangle.

SPECIAL NOTE: In its entirety, SOP 8-C could be considered as various exercises in Formula H, which involves the most basic action of the thetan (which is reaching and withdrawing).

SPECIAL NOTE: It will be noted that the negative orientation techniques are done in such a way as to make the preclear, without his being told to do so, create space. The auditor should pay specific attention, when the preclear is discovering where things are *not*, that the preclear be caused to note specifically each time the exact location and position where the thing does not exist. This calls the preclear's attention to various positions which, in themselves, thus located, create space. Thus, throughout SOP 8-C the rehabilitation of space is also to be found, the definition of space being: "Space is a viewpoint of dimension."

SPECIAL NOTE: In his auditing, if the auditor does not get a communication change on the part of the preclear, whether better or worse, every five or ten minutes, either the auditor is using the wrong step at the time (in which case he should progress on into the steps) or the preclear, even if he says he is, is not complying with the auditor's orders. The auditor, thus, should remain in continuous communication with the preclear, so far as possible, and should ascertain with great care what the preclear is doing after he indicates that he has complied with the direction, and to discover every five or ten minutes if there has been a change in certainties or communication.

Source of failures

The commonest source of failure, in any step in SOP 8-C, is a failure on the part of the preclear to execute the orders given as they were intended to be executed, or on the part of the auditor in failing to ascertain whether or not the preclear is executing properly or if there has been a communication change. A careful check of auditors and preclears utilizing SOP 8-C has demonstrated, in each case where its use was becoming lengthy, that the auditor was failing to ascertain from the preclear whether or not there had been communication changes. And it was also uniformly discovered that the preclear, who was failing to get results while being audited with SOP 8-C, was not doing the steps as directed, but was either avoiding by not doing them at all (although he said he was doing them) or was failing to understand the direction and so was executing the step in some other way.

Preclear Willingness

The first goal which an auditor must achieve is "willingness in the preclear to receive directions."

The condition of the preclear is such, in nearly all cases, that he has chosen as a main point of resistance in life "direction of himself other than his own." Because the physical universe is designed to resist and overcome that which resists it, a continuous resistance to "other direction than one's own" results, finally, in a loss of ability, to greater or lesser degree, to direct oneself.

In that it is the ability to direct himself which the auditor is seeking to return to the preclear, it must be demonstrated to the preclear, solely by the process of good auditing, that "other direction" is not necessarily harmful or in the worst interest of the preclear. Thus, to some degree he ceases to resist incoming direction and, by ceasing to resist it, no longer validates it as a barrier and so is not concentrating attention on resisting direction, but is able to use it freely in his own self-direction.

The self-determinism of a preclear is proportional to the amount of self-direction he is capable of executing and deteriorates markedly when a great deal of his attention is devoted to preventing other direction. Directing himself, the preclear becomes capable of execution. Preventing direction of himself (resisting the direction of others) brings about a condition where he is mainly devoted to resisting his environment. The latter results in a diminishing of space of the preclear.

The first step in the rehabilitation of the preclear in self-direction is therefore a limiting of the amount of resistance he is concentrating on "other direction" and demonstrating to him that his following of the steps of SOP 8-C, under the direction of an auditor, is not harmful but, on the contrary, increases his command and control of himself and brings him at last to the point where he can neglect and ignore the continuous stimulus-response operation of the physical universe.

It can be seen clearly, then, that the auditor who sets himself up to be resisted will fail, for the preclear is mainly concentrating upon resisting the auditor. This is the primary factor in all auditing.

The preclear is brought to a point of cooperation, in terms of direction, without the use of hypnosis or drugs and without argument or "convincingness" on the part of the auditor–by which is meant, overbearing demeanor. At the same time, it should be the sole intention and operation of the auditor that his own directions be carried out explicitly by the preclear and that these be performed with a minimum of communication break and with a maximum of affinity, communication and reality.

Opening Procedure

Using the axiom that "that which changes the preclear in space can evaluate for him," the auditor in using SOP 8-C should use at the beginning of the first session, and in any session where the preclear becomes unreasonably uncooperative in following simple directions, the following procedure:

> The auditor has the preclear walk to specific points in the room, touch, hold and let go of various specific objects. The auditor should be very exact in his directions. The auditor should do this, even on an apparently cooperative case, at least twenty minutes before going on to the next step in Opening Procedure.

When the preclear, drilled in this fashion, has at length realized (without being told) that the auditor's directions are quiet, reliable, exact and to be performed, and not until then, the auditor uses this process:

> Preclear is asked to send himself to various parts of the room and do specific things. The auditor is very specific

and exact about this, in that he has the preclear decide on his own determinism (and before moving from the spot where he is standing) what part of the room he is going to send himself to. When the preclear has decided this, and only then (but not necessarily telling the auditor), the preclear then takes himself to that part of the room. The auditor must be very exact that the *decision* to go to a certain part of the room, and to reach or withdraw from a certain thing, is made before the preclear takes an actual action. And then, the auditor should make sure that the preclear has done exactly what he decided he would do before he moved. In such a wise, coached by the auditor, the preclear is led to direct himself to various parts of the room until he is entirely sure that he is directing himself to certain parts of the room and that the orders are coming from nobody but himself. (Of course, before each new place is chosen, the auditor tells the preclear to choose a new place and tells him when to go there.)

The third stage of this Opening Procedure is, then, as follows:

The auditor has the preclear be in one spot in the room and then has the preclear decide, there, to go to another spot in the room. The preclear leaves. The auditor has the preclear change his own mind and go to yet another spot. This last is done to lessen the preclear's fear of changing his mind, to strengthen his decision and to lessen his reaction to his own mistakes.

The last two steps of Opening Procedure are done at some length. It is profitable (by the experience of many auditors) to spend as much as an hour on Opening Procedure, even in a case which is not in poor condition. When Opening Procedure is omitted or is not carried on far enough, the auditor may discover that it will take him from five to ten hours to "get the case working."

This time is saved by the expenditure of much less time in using Opening Procedure. Even when the preclear is complacent, even when the preclear is an obvious "Step I," even when the preclear shows no outward sign of resistance to other direction than his own, the first communication lag lessening which the auditor will perceive on the case will probably occur during the use of Opening Procedure. Further, the certainty of the case is heightened. Further, Opening Procedure is, for any level of case, an excellent process.

The preclear who is familiar with SOP 8 may conceive that he is doing a step which is "reserved for psychotics." The preclear should be disabused of such a concept, since the step is used today on all cases.

In the case of a preclear who is very resistive, Opening Procedure can be used with considerable profit for many hours. For such activity, however, an auditing room of the usual dimensions is usually too constrictive and the drill may be carried on as well out of doors, even if only on a street.

Auditor Patter

The "patter" for the first part of Opening Procedure would be, for the auditor:

"Go to that corner of the room and touch the wall."

Preclear complies.

"Go to the lamp and take hold of the lamp,"
"Now let go of it."

"Now take hold of it,"
"Now let go of it."

"Go to the door and touch the doorknob,"
"Now withdraw from the doorknob."

"Go to the chair and sit down,"

"Get up and sit down in the other chair."

"Go to the closet door and touch the top of it," etc.

The auditor's patter for the second part of Opening Procedure is:

"Stand there in the corner and decide on some other part of the room to send yourself to,"

"Now have you decided on a place?"

"Go there," etc.

Auditor patter for the third stage of Opening Procedure would be:

"Stand there and decide some part of the room to go to,"

"Decide on an exact spot,"

"Now do you have that?"

"Now change your mind and go to another spot," etc.

It is noteworthy that the more exact the spot to which the preclear is sent and the more exact the action he is to take, the better the results of the process. A preclear is probably interiorized during the entirety of Opening Procedure. The auditor does not bother to find out, nor does he begin to exteriorize the preclear until he has entered Step Ia of SOP 8-C.

Opening Procedure can be run using much wider space, with great profit on a case, after he has been exteriorized.

When Opening Procedure has been accomplished, and not until then, the auditor begins on Step Ia.

His patter would be as follows:

"Be three feet back of your chair." (The preclear's attention is never called to the body and he is never asked to look at the body until his perceptions are excellent, or at least until he has done the mock-up portion of Step II.) Auditor makes no further inquiry for whether exteriorized with certainty, or uncertainty, or not at all. The procedure would be the same, although it is much better if a certain or even an uncertain exteriorization has been effected. Continuous auditing of a preclear *in* a body is destructive. In the case of a certain exteriorization, again, the auditor makes no further reference to the matter.

The auditor now says to the seated (not reclining) preclear:

"Give me three goals you did not complete." (The preclear is *not* to name them. Nods when he has them.)
"Now three goals another did not complete,"
"Three goals another did not complete for somebody else,"
"Three goals another did not complete for you,"
"Three goals you did not complete for another."

Auditor goes over this list many, many, many times.

"Give me three people you are not." (The preclear does not vocalize who these three people are, but simply nods when he has all three of them.)
"Give me three people who are not you,"
"Give me three people who are not specifically other people." (The correct reply is that "so-and-so is not so-and-so, so-and-so is not so-and-so, so-and-so is not so-and-so." The incorrect reply would be that "so-and-so isn't anybody else but himself.")

This can be done again, around two or three times, or even carried on for a very long time, but the auditor should ask when he has done it *once:*

"Have you noted any change of perception?"

If the preclear has not, when the auditor has done this around three times, the auditor should immediately go on to the next step:

"Give me three animals you are not,"
"Give me three animals who are not you,"
"Give me three animals who are not specifically other animals."
(Make the preclear be specific, that a certain dog is not a cat, and so on.)

This carried on, for some little time, will resolve problems of eating. And as eatingness is the lowest stage of attention, the process can be quite effective.

"Give me three objects you are not,"
"Give me three objects who are not you,"
"Give me three objects which are not specifically other objects."

The auditor may achieve several communication changes on the preclear while doing this stage of Step Ia. But if he does not, he should go on quickly to the next part of Step Ia and should not endlessly continue the first portion.

"When a person has just been exteriorized,
get his attention onto the environment."

SOP 8-O

SOP 8-O:
GOALS OF
OPERATING THETAN

GOALS OF OPERATING THETAN:

1 To be able to tolerate nothingness.

2 To be able to have or not-have without consequences to memory.

3 To be in universes at will with full perception in them.

4 To communicate or receive communications in all those ways used by the body.

5 To take apart and put together in working form all automaticities.

6 To be able to handle any kind of body.

7 How do you endow and disendow any kind of body or new kinds of bodies so as to be able to create new life forms? This is a study and an art.

These are not roughly done in this order. The individual becomes more and more capable all along this line as Operating Thetan level is reached.

Operating Thetan should be able to fix and unfix ideas in energy, i.e., to be able to fix into a car an idea that "it can't be stolen," and it won't be.

Demonstration of prowess *in order to prove* is very low-toned, the work of a fakir.

Operating Thetan is merely a state of mind. It is a contest between being an Operating Thetan and an inmate of the MEST universe. This universe is an interiorizing universe and if any sole aberration comes in upon the thetan, it is resisting interiorization. And that which one resists one becomes. This universe puts upon the Operating Thetan the stress of resisting interiorization unless he customarily keeps himself entirely away from any phobia about havingness.

The phobia to *have* (obsession to have something) follows as a direct result of the DEI cycle. The thetan *inhibits* inflow and *desires* it and then *inhibits* it and then he has it *enforced* upon him.

Interiorization is 360 degree flow inward. This is why exteriorization is the top goal in processing him. He gets the idea that his ideas are fixed in energy. And the more ideas fixed in energy, the less *effective* they are as postulates; the more an idea is fixed in energy, the less *pervasive* it is as a postulate. Energy doesn't have to accompany an idea in any way, shape or form for it to be effective. The idea is as effective as it is not cloaked in energy. When it gets fixed in energy, it pulls in a symbol. We find this to be a direct index of the sanity of an individual. He is as sane as he doesn't have energy kicking around in his bank.

SOP 8-O:
EXAMPLE
OF AUDITING

WHEN A PERSON has just been exteriorized, get his attention onto the environment. The reason why the preclear is in the body is because he hasn't been able to endow the environment with life.

Don't run "concepts" when exteriorized. Running a concept is endowing something with life.

A person would like to feel alive, so he makes the body feel alive. Those Straightwire techniques which give him a different environment are the best:

"Pretend you have just exteriorized from a lion."

We never ask an individual to look at his body. The dwindling spiral is a smaller perimeter of aliveness until the person is alive only in the body. Ask the preclear to expand his awareness:

"Be alive now through this room."

When you ask him to be the space of his body, you are to some extent energizing the body. Have him be the space behind his chair, around his body and in the environment.

Ask the preclear to put emotion in something and then feel a different one himself:

"Pick out the realest object in the room."

"Put some apathy in it," while you tell the preclear, *"Now you feel some boredom."*

"Have the pillow feel apathy while you feel resentment," etc.

When the preclear looks at the body, he is to some extent energizing it. Co-experience and sympathy with the body makes a person feel he is a body.

The thetan can be deteriorated by "not-knowingness." So you ask him for:

"Three areas of blackness you don't have to know about."

This will desensitize his "not-knowingness." If one has a compulsion to know, it is an admission that he doesn't know. The black case is being effect and the only reason he is being effect is because he doesn't know.

Avalanches have served their purpose:

"You should turn around now and turn on the outward avalanche."

Have him pitch things away in "mock-up" until you find something he can "reject." This will break down the "never must happen again" computation.

Start this reverse avalanche on one object at a time. You won't get dust and bones to fly away from him, or upper echelon life forms. You build him up to where he can start rejection avalanche.

You will never go wrong if you keep his attention on the environment. Keep attention off his body.

EXAMPLE OF AUDITING THAT WILL BRING A THETA CLEAR UP THE LINE:

"Give me three places where you are not,"
"Give me three places where you are not thinking,"
"Give me three places you don't have to go,"
"Give me two particles you are not trying to hold apart,"
"Give me two particles you are not trying to hold together."

"Give me three places you are not,"
"Give me three places you don't have to go,"
"Give me three places you don't have to be."

"Be ten feet back of your chair,"
"Get the idea you have just exteriorized from a cat's body,"
"Duplicate him,"
"Duplicate him,"
"Duplicate him,"
"Duplicate him,"
"Duplicate him,"
"Throw it away."

"Duplicate a cat's eyes,"
"Duplicate the eyes for use,"
"Throw them away."

"Get three barriers not in front of you,"
"Get three things you don't have to run away from,"
"Get three things you don't object to having at this moment."

"Get something you can throw away,"
"Get some more things you can throw away."

"Give me three places in the environment you wouldn't mind having alive."

"Get a nothingness around you,"

"Duplicate it,"
"Duplicate it,"
"Duplicate it."

"What is the realest object in the area?"
Person says *"microphone."*
"Okay. Put the emotion of fear in the microphone, you feel boredom,"
"Keep fear in the microphone and you feel resentment,"
"You feel apathy,"
"Now feel grief,"
"Feel exhilaration,"
"Feel you are a very personable person."

"Now change the emotion on the microphone. Have the microphone being happy,"
"While it is being happy, you be angry,"
"You feel excited,"
"You feel serene,"
"You feel apathetic,"
"You feel grief,"
"You feel enthusiasm,"
"You feel much happier."

"Name yourself,"
"Give yourself a different name."

"Name the ceiling something,"
"The floor something,"
"Let's give the microphone a name,"
"Let's get it a personality,"
"While the microphone has a personality, you take on a different personality."

"Feel like yourself."

"Be up on the roof."

"Give me three places you don't have to jump into."

"Let's check off three goals you don't have."

"While you are on the roof, throw a remote viewpoint down in traffic,"
"Now blow up the viewpoint."

"Put another viewpoint down in traffic,"
"Blow it up."

"Be a hearing point in traffic,"
"Remain on the roof,"
"Blow it up."

"Put a hearing point into something that is very noisy around town,"
"Now hear it."

"Be a thousand feet up,"
"A thousand feet above the Moon,"
"A thousand feet above the Sun."

"A hundred feet above the Earth,"
"Above the Sun,"
"The Moon."

"The Earth,"
"The Sun,"
"The Moon."

"The Earth,"
"The Sun,"
"The Moon."

"Here."

"Did you feel any gravity pull?"

"Be near the Moon,"
"The Earth."

"The Moon,"
"The Earth."

"Switch back and forth rapidly from Moon to Earth."

"Be at a real hot place,"
"Make it feel hotter,"
"Make it feel cooler."

"Cold,"
"Hot."

"Cold,"
"Hot."

"Be outside the Moon,"
"In center of the Moon."

"Outside,"
"Center."

"Outside,"
"Center."

"Flip back and forth as rapidly as you can."

"Be at the place you entered the MEST universe,"
"Be here."

"Entrance,"
"Here."

"Entrance,"
"Here."

SOP 8-O
EXAMPLE OF AUDITING

"Entrance,"
"Here."

"Entrance,"
"Here," etc., etc.

"Outside,"
"Entrance,"
"Outside."

"Flip back and forth."

"Let's be outside the biggest star you can find in the MEST universe—a dark one."

"Be in the center of it,"
"Be outside of it."

"Center,"
"Outside."

"Center,"
"Own it."

"Outside of it,"
"Own it."

"Outside of it,"
"Inside of it."

"Outside,"
"Be in the center of it and savor it."

"Feel a little courage,"
"Be inside feeling courage and outside feeling courage."

"Flip in and out a number of times feeling courage."

"Be inside and feel some enjoyment,"
"Be outside and feel some enjoyment."

"Inside and outside feeling enjoyment."

"Flip back and forth feeling enjoyment."

"Be inside and feel density of it,"
"Be outside and feel density."

"Be inside and feel its density,"
"Be outside and feel its density."

"Be on the roof,"
"See the whole area blue,"
"See the whole area gold,"
"See the whole area green,"
"See the whole area gold,"
"See the whole area blue,"
"See the whole area black,"
"See the whole area blue,"
"See the whole area red,"
"See the whole area infrared."

"See the whole area all colors, at once,"
"See the whole area and separate its colors."

"See the whole area all colors,"
"See the whole area and separate its colors."

"See in any way you please."

"Start an avalanche of sound,"
"Build it up,"
"More different kinds of sound avalanching in on you."

"Put some more out there to avalanche in on you,"
"Let's start them in selectively,"
"You make them and start them in."

"Throw all those away."

SOP 8-O
EXAMPLE OF AUDITING

"Let's outflow some sound,"
"Some more sound,"

"Throw it away."

"Be 1,000 feet up and let's divebomb the roof."

"Be 1,000 feet up and soar around Phoenix* like a sea gull."

"Now be here."

"End of session."

---

*This process was originally delivered to students in Phoenix, Arizona.

ADVANCED

"A problem with universes is primarily
a problem in spaces."

COURSE
DATA & PROCEDURE

10 April 1954

ADVANCED COURSE: DATA SHEET

Goals:

Life has solutions for many things. It has never had a solution for aberration until now. The target of the auditor is not simply the eradication of aberration. It is the relegation of aberration to the status of a solved problem.

Primary in auditing procedures is getting the preclear to change his mind. When he can shift postulates easily and at will, he will continue to be in good condition. When he cannot, his is a problem of other universes in which he is "trapped." In any universe, one is subject to the postulates of the god of that universe. Therefore, when a preclear cannot be brought to change his postulates, he must be having trouble with other universes.

A problem with universes is primarily a problem in spaces. Secondarily it is a problem in energy and matter. Any preclear having difficulty with other universes is having difficulty with space.

The definition of space is "a viewpoint of dimension." Thus other universes are created by other viewpoints. When a preclear has been changed in space a great deal by another viewpoint, and when he has many impacts in common with it, he may believe that he is in another universe. And, mechanically, this is so.

In such a way, a preclear may be found in mother's universe, in father's, in a pet's, in his body's and is, of course, in the MEST universe where the postulates (he conceives) are those of God. The nuclear physicist studies God's postulates.

Whenever a preclear cannot change his own postulates easily, we conceive that he is operating upon other postulates than his own and, thus, that he is in another universe. We resolve space only insofar as we need to resolve other universes.

Where the preclear is in a universe which operates upon psychotic postulates, he is immediately pressed to face aberration.

This is an E-Meter problem (that of other universes) and is resolved by asking the preclear, while on the meter, whose commands he would obey–whether father's, mother's, etc. The meter will experience its biggest drop on those universes where he is having the greatest conflict. However, the meter will not necessarily respond on universes in which he is entirely enclosed. Removing the "reacting" (biggest drop) universes one at a time will exteriorize the preclear from all universes. The key command in all Universe Processing is:

"*Where* (father, mother, wife, pet) *would be safe.*"

The preclear must then spot points in space where he is certain the person in question would be safe. Various regular phenomena then occur. The replies are not, of course, very rational. Getting the preclear to spot spots in space is of the essence. He must be brought to spot spots in MEST space.

It will be found that spotting a spot in space is almost impossible for some preclears. They give conditions, not locations. Or, even in using Opening Procedure, they cannot easily spot a location in space without their attention flicking quickly to objects.

Know–Sex Scale:

There is a scale of behavior, patterned on the Tone Scale, which starts at the top with Know and goes (as follows) downscale. This is also a Scale of Tolerance of Viewpoints, or Tolerance of Space, or Interiorization in Universes, and furnishes a fast diagnosis.

Know–can create space.

Look–is creating space.

Emote–is combining space and energy.

Effort–is condensing space.

Think–is wandering in condensed spaces.

Symbols–has codified spaces into words and other significances.

Eating–is content with spaces already condensed, but belonging to others.

Sex–finds no space tolerable for present beingness, but looks to other and future beingnesses as the only chance for universes.

Communication:

The graph of communication is:

Cause to Effect
or
Cause, Distance, Effect
or
C Distance E

A perfect communication occurs when whatever is at Cause-point is duplicated exactly at Effect-point. Thus a perfect communication contains *duplication*. A thetan, seeking to communicate, seeks to send impulses or particles from himself at C to the receipt-point at E *without form*. Thus a thetan has *no-form* as a condition of a perfect communication.

A body, on the other hand, when it communicates, places the condition of *form* into any communication it sends. Thus a thetan, working obsessively, would seek to make *no-form* at all Effect-points, while a body would attempt to create *form* at Effect-points. A body seeks to make something out of every communication, hence significance and "deeper meanings" and "prior causes." A thetan seeks to make *no-form* out of all communication, hence a nothingness. These are the mechanics of communication. They are also the mechanics of human behavior. The perfect duplication of a communication is seldom possible, hence the dwindling spiral. *But* harm in communication only occurs when there is no *knowing* about communication. Impulsive or obsessive communication alone takes exception: on the part of a thetan, to *something*; on the part of the body, to *nothingness*.

Non-Exteriorized Cases:

When cases are difficult to exteriorize, the auditor is involved, basically, with a tangle of universes. The thetan cannot *look* because he is in another universe where looking (the making of space) is forbidden. Occlusion of various kinds, facsimile looking, are present only when the thetan is in another universe than his own. In his own, he can easily look–even into other universes. Occlusion and non-exteriorization are, then, stemming from the same cause:

THE MORE DIFFICULT THE CASE, THE LESS TOLERANCE OF SPACE.

This is resolved by having the preclear spot space, using the body perception or not. He can do this via Opening Procedure as well as by spotting distant MEST spaces. The *spot* in space is more important than the object in space. Thus one has him spot spots until he can with ease. One then begins the task of separating him from universes, using Universe Processing.

Change of Space:

This process has been standard for some time. It is not used on preclears until they are exteriorized. It can be approximated by non-exteriorized cases by having them spot spots in space. The goal of Change of Space is bringing the preclear up to present time in all MEST spaces. Rapid spotting or changing into various locations where the preclear has been in difficulty keynotes this process.

Interiorization-Exteriorization:

The preclear must be able to interiorize into and out of objects and spaces at will. Drills which interiorize and exteriorize him rapidly, time after time, from the interior to the exterior of rocks, planets, animals and people, remedy his ability. It must be noted, however, that this decreases havingness and this decrease must be remedied.

Havingness:

The preclear has so long *had* that he believes he must *have*. This lack of havingness is run by discovering what is acceptable to the preclear in the way of mass and having him pull many such objects in upon him. Pulling in enough mass will run out the engram bank. Engrams are in restimulation only because they represent energy which the preclear or the body pulls in. Universe Processing, run correctly, *does not upset havingness* and is the one process which escapes it. Avalanches of planets and stars can be started inward and outward by remedying havingness.

This is beneficial rather than otherwise. Such avalanches should be put into the control of the preclear with starting, stopping and changing their inflow and outflow.

Grand Tour:

This is the process of taking the newly exteriorized preclear to various locations in this solar system and is Change of Space and Interiorization–Exteriorization combined. The preclear is sent to places near the Earth, the Moon, the Sun, Mars, etc. This is done rapidly and many times. He is then exteriorized-interiorized out of and into these heavenly bodies. He is made to move down to planet surfaces and to centers, as opposed to being *in* positions, but he is also made to be in positions. In other words, he is rapidly changed in space and is also, during other intervals, made to move through space. A Grand Tour is completed, actually, by Change of Space through all the important spots (where he has had experience on the whole track) of the MEST universe.

SOP 8-C:

This process, as developed, continues to be successful in general hands and is recommended for instruction of auditors in other than the Advanced Clinical Course and for use by Book Auditors. It is a powerful weapon and is chalking up many successes.

Other Processes:

There are many patch-up and emergency processes. They are of varying value. None of them have been abandoned. Where an auditor has these as part of his know-how, he should use them in relationship to their effectiveness in his experience. He should not, however, compulsively continue with a process which he is not finding very useful in his hands simply because it "makes nothing" or "makes something" of the preclear. A case in point is the obsessive use, by many auditors, of the early processes of Dianetics. These auditors have fixated on "making nothing of pictures." In Scientology, we have better processes and have had better processes for some time. In fact, Scientology processes are so much better than this that we terminated the temporary use of the word "Dianetics." Older processes and emergency processes, in particular, have not been invalidated. Auditors would, for instance, discover that engrams can be made to vanish by having the preclear remedy his havingness or by *"Finding places where pictures would be safe"* for a few hours. Any phenomena can be remedied by 8-C or Universe Processing. The results of these have the great advantage of being stable when attained.

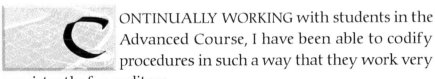

ADVANCED COURSE:
PROCEDURE

CONTINUALLY WORKING with students in the Advanced Course, I have been able to codify procedures in such a way that they work very consistently for auditors.

First:

Establish a two-way communication with the preclear, either by discussion or questioning in generalities. Get him to talk a little. Then run next-to-last list of *Self Analysis* to measure his communication lag for future reference and to avoid falling into "one of *those* cases" unawares.

Second:

Run from ten minutes to two hours of Opening Procedure (a) until the preclear is happy to take orders from an auditor and (b) until the preclear can locate spots in space without his attention snapping onto MEST objects.

Third:

Run SOP 8-C Step I. If at this point preclear exteriorizes with certainty, run the remainder of this procedure (Advanced Course Procedure). If preclear does not exteriorize easily, he is having a major problem with universes. This problem with universes must be resolved somewhat before he can be made to exteriorize. Resolve some of the universe problems, then go to the second step (Advanced Course Procedure) above, then run this step (8-C Step I) again. If he still doesn't exteriorize, resolve more universe problems. To run Universe Processing, have preclear first spot spots in space. Then have him find places where E-Meter reacting personnel (mother, father, etc.) *"are safe."* This is actually all there is to the process. One stays with the person selected until the charge is greatly lessened or until the phenomenon of "separating universes" takes place.

The key command is:

"Where are viewpoints safe?"

Have the preclear actually spot spots in space and make sure that he *is* certain that the viewpoint (or the person) is safe there. The clue to this "safe" is, of course, "senior survival." The preclear gets into the winning valence because that had senior survival. Thus he takes the viewpoints of MEST objects or people which have senior survival. Beingness Processing is another process similar to, but less powerful than (but complementing), Universe Processing.

Fourth:

Beingness Processing, by which the auditor has the preclear *be* various things until he finds things the preclear can be with certainty. The goal here is to get the preclear able to be anything in any universe or to be any universe–which is to say, to assume the viewpoint of anything. This clears up spots which the preclear cannot tolerate, also forms of which he is afraid. When the preclear is discovered being something compulsively, one finds where that *"would be safe"* (for it is a winning valence). This includes getting the preclear to be his first piece of space, his first piece of energy. The reason one does this last is to "undercut" his first period of "unknowingness." The preclear is asked to be the space, then himself, back and forth many times. Then to be the energy, then himself, back and forth many times. A variation, when the preclear is compulsively discovered being something, is to have him be that thing, then to find places where a thetan would be safe from the viewpoint of that thing he is being. Again, the goal is to get the preclear to a point where he can be any object or space in any universe.

Fifth:

Universe Processing and Step I of 8-C on the *exteriorized* preclear, alternating.

NOTE: When the preclear goes into Apathy on Universe or Beingness Processing, the auditor should take care that he himself, by communication breaks, has not brought on the condition. Running Opening Procedure on a case which has heavily bogged into Apathy is a good repair measure. But Apathy results in Beingness Processing when the thetan has been something compulsively and is just beginning to be himself in that situation. Asking him to be the object and then be himself will run out this Apathy. The Apathy is the halfway mark of coming out of a winning valence and is rather inevitable. Apathy is more alive than the object the preclear was being.

Sixth:

The Grand Tour (see earlier). The Grand Tour now includes Change of Space to the entrance point of the MEST universe, etc., etc., etc. It also includes Exteriorization-Interiorization drills.

NOTE: If preclear boils-off or gets dull, *remedy havingness.* If this does not alter the condition, it is a problem in universes and Universe Processing should be used.

Seventh:

Run SOP 8-C in its entirety on preclear, including brief Opening Procedure.

Eighth:

SOP 8-O.

GRAND TOUR

 HIS IS A LIST TO BE RUN BY CHANGE OF SPACE
PROCESSING:

1. The first geographic location of the thetan in the MEST universe as soon as he came from the Home Universe

2. The geographic location where he created his first facsimile

3. Where the thetan committed his first overt act in the MEST universe

4. Where the thetan received his first motivator in the MEST universe

5. Where he started the first spiral. Also the end of the spiral. Do this with all spirals up to present time.

6. The geographic location where the thetan first was in contact with a body in any way

7. The Jack-in-the-Box

8. The Obsession

9. The first Blanketing

10. The Halver

11. Facsimile One

12. Before Earth

13. Before MEST universe

14. The Joiner

15. The Assumption

16. His first Borrowing

17. His first Nipping

18. The Ice Cube

19. The first Between-Lives area

20. The Emanator

21. The first Theta Trap

22. The Body in Pawn

23. The Body Builder

24. The Jiggler

25. The Whirler

26. The Bouncer

27. The Spinner

28. The Rocker

29. The Boxer

30. The Faller

31. The Education

32. The Fly Trap

33. The DED

34. The DEDEX

35. The Misassist

36. The first geographical location the thetan took on Earth

37. Glare Fights

38. The first time he ran into a Report Station

39. Implant Station

"The actual goal of this process is to bring the preclear to tolerate any viewpoint."

SOP 8-D

15 April 1954

SOP 8-D

THIS PROCEDURE is for use by a trained Scientologist. It can be used in conjunction with Advanced Course Procedure and its primary goal is the delivery of heavy cases. However, it can be extensively applied to all cases. It is better to run a Step I well on 8-C before using this process upon him.

Opening Procedure:

Have preclear move his body around the room locating spots in MEST space. Have him locate many such spots and designate them with his finger. Have him do this until he can do it very well and until he obeys an auditor's directions easily.

Step I:

Ask preclear to be three feet back of his chair. This is the total step. The auditor does not press the matter further even if the preclear is.

Step II:

Have preclear look at his environment and whatever he sees, have him duplicate it many times. Then have him duplicate a nothingness he makes or finds many times.

Step III:

Have preclear hold the two back corners of the room (two minutes at least or two or more hours). Then have him locate spots in space where he is not.

Step IV:

(An E-Meter step.) Give preclear a full assessment by putting him on an E-Meter at this point and asking him to name the people with whom he has been associated since birth. The auditor writes these down and indicates, by a symbol after each name, whether the action of the needle is stuck, small, medium or violent. On a consistently stuck needle, use next-to-last list of *Self Analysis* until needle frees. Then choose that person who got the biggest reaction on the meter and, using this person, have preclear find spots or spaces where this person would be safe. The preclear must be certain of the fact. The auditing command is:

"Find some places where _____ would be safe."

One continues this, until the needle shows no further reaction, on just this first person.

Then one goes to Opening Procedure and starts all the way through the steps again. Now one takes the same person as the auditor first chose and runs this processing question only:

"Spot some things which your _____ does not own."

This is the total question. (One- to two-hour communication lag may not be unusual.) The auditor continues to ask this question, and the preclear continues to spot things which this person does not own, until the needle is relatively inactive. Then the auditor goes to Opening Procedure (above) and continues through the steps. But now he takes a new assessment and proceeds exactly as before.

"Places where _____ would be safe," is Universe Processing.

"Things _____ does not own," is Ownership Processing.

No variations of command of any kind whatsoever should be used by the auditor as these are not dichotomies and variation can be very hard on the preclear, even making him ill. The auditor should add, "The spirit of man," "The spirit of woman," "God" and "the body."

STUDY THIS PROCESS WELL BEFORE USING IT. DO NOT DEPART FROM IT OR VARY IT UNTIL PRECLEAR IS STABLY EXTERIORIZED. THE ACTUAL GOAL OF THIS PROCESS IS TO BRING THE PRECLEAR TO TOLERATE ANY VIEWPOINT.

SCIENTOLOGY,

"Scientology has accomplished the goal of religion expressed in all Man's written history: the freeing of the soul by wisdom."

ITS GENERAL BACKGROUND

(Outline of Professional Course Lectures)

July 1954

SCIENTOLOGY, ITS GENERAL BACKGROUND (OUTLINE OF PROFESSIONAL COURSE LECTURES)*

Scientology, Its Background

Or a history of Knowledge

Scientology

The Western Anglicized continuance of many earlier forms of wisdom. *Scio*–study.

Earliest Version—The Veda

Knowingness or sacred lore

The most ancient sacred literature of the Hindus, comprising over a hundred extant books. One or all four of the canonical collection of hymns, prayers and formulas which are the foundation of the Vedic religion.

The Rig-Veda

Yajur-Veda

Sama-Veda

Atharva-Veda

The Cycle-of-Action

---

*Lectures of 19 July 1954, *Scientology, Its General Background* and 20 July 1954, *Bridge Between Scientology and Civilization.*

The meaning of Veda–Knowingness

Mention of the Book of Job as oldest *written* work–from India

The Tao–The Way

The realization of the mystery of mysteries–i.e., the way to attain knowingness

The *Tao Teh King* by Lao-tzu (604–531 B.C.) taught conformity with the cosmic order and simplicity in social and political organization.

Entirely concentrated on the mind and its discipline

Contemporary with Confucius

The principle of wu-wei (non-assertion or non-compulsion) control by permitting Self-determinism

Dhyana–Knowingness and Lookingness

From mythical times. Named from the legendary Hindu Sage, Dharma, whose many progeny were the personifications of virtue and religious rights.

We are most familiar with the Dhyana in the form of Buddhism.

A Bodhi is one who has attained intellectual and ethical perfection by human means, comparable to our Theta Clear in Scientology.

Gautama Sakyamuni (563–483 B.C.)

Looked upon as founder of the Dhyana.

Never claimed to be anything but a human being, did not profess to bring any revelation from a supernatural source, did not proclaim himself a savior. He professed only to teach men to liberate themselves as he had liberated himself.

From the Dharmapada, a collection of verses said to have been written by Gautama:

"All that we are is the result of what we have thought: it is founded on our thoughts, it is made up of our thoughts.

"By oneself evil is done; by oneself one suffers; by oneself evil is left undone; by oneself one is purified. Purity and impurity belong to oneself; no one can purify another.

"You yourself must make an effort; the Buddhas are only preachers. The thoughtful who enter the way are freed from the bondage of sin.

"He who does not rouse himself when it is time to rise, who, though young and strong, is full of sloth, whose will and thoughts are weak, that lazy and idle man will never find the way to enlightenment.

"Strenuousness is the path of immortality, sloth the path of death. Those who are strenuous do not die; those who are slothful are as if dead already."

The religion of Buddhism, carried by its teachers, brought civilization into the existing barbarisms of India, China, Japan and the Near East – or about two-thirds of Earth's population. Here was the first broadcast wisdom which summated into high cultures.

The Hebrews

Their definition of Messiah is a "teacher or bringer of Wisdom." Their holy work, known to us as the "Old Testament," leans heavily on the sources we have already mentioned.

Moses

Giver of wisdom and law

Jesus of Nazareth

The legend of his study in India

Age of 30-33 teaching and healing

Use of parables like Gautama

Buddhist principles of brotherly love and compassion

Death by Crucifixion

Spread of Christianity into the barbarism of Europe

Religion with fur breechcloths

Close of the Trade Routes

Western Seekers of Wisdom

The separation of science and search from religion–artificial division

The Early Greeks

Lucretius

Spinoza

Nietzsche

Schopenhauer

Spencer

Freud

We think of these as beginning our intellectualism. They quickened it. The bulk of their sources were Asiatic.

Scientology—Scio—study 1932–1954

Study in Asia

Barbaric cultures

Nuclear physics

Scientific methodology

Dianetics, a therapy

The bridge from Man's earliest cultural beginnings to know

The enlightened man

The Prophecy about Maitreya

Definition of Religion—Webster

"3. The profession or practice of religious beliefs; religious observances collectively; rites.

"4. Devotion or fidelity conscientiousness."

Religion—religious philosophy

Scientology has accomplished the goal of religion expressed in all Man's written history: the freeing of the soul by wisdom.

It is a far more intellectual religion than that known to the West as late as 1950.

If we, without therapy, simply taught our truths, we would bring civilization to a barbaric West.

A PPENDIX

FURTHER STUDY

BOOKS & LECTURES BY L. RON HUBBARD

The materials of Dianetics and Scientology comprise the largest body of information ever assembled on the mind, spirit and life, rigorously refined and codified by L. Ron Hubbard through five decades of research, investigation and development. The results of that work are contained in hundreds of books and more than 3,000 recorded lectures. A full listing and description of them all can be obtained from any Scientology Church or Publications Organization. (See *Guide to the Materials*.)

The books and lectures below form the foundation upon which the Bridge to Freedom is built. They are listed in the sequence Ron wrote or delivered them. In many instances, Ron gave a series of lectures immediately following the release of a new book to provide further explanation and insight of these milestones. Through monumental restoration efforts, those lectures are now available and are listed herein with their companion book.

While Ron's books contain the summaries of breakthroughs and conclusions as they appeared in the developmental research track, his lectures provide the running day-to-day record of research and explain the thoughts, conclusions, tests and demonstrations that lay along that route. In that regard, they are the complete record of the entire research track, providing not only the most important breakthroughs in Man's history, but the *why* and *how* Ron arrived at them.

Not the least advantage of a chronological study of these books and lectures is the inclusion of words and terms which, when originally used, were defined by LRH with considerable exactitude. Far beyond a mere "definition," entire lectures are devoted to a full description of each new Dianetic or Scientology term—what made the breakthrough possible, its application in auditing as well as its application to life itself. As a result, one leaves behind no misunderstoods, obtains a full conceptual understanding of Dianetics and Scientology and grasps the subjects at a level not otherwise possible.

Through a sequential study, you can see how the subject progressed and recognize the highest levels of development. The listing of books and lectures below shows where *The Creation of Human Ability* fits within the developmental line. From there you can determine your *next* step or any earlier books and lectures you may have missed. You will then be able to fill in missing gaps, not only gaining knowledge of each breakthrough, but greater understanding of what you've already studied.

This is the path to knowing how to know, unlocking the gates to your future eternity. Follow it.

DIANETICS: THE ORIGINAL THESIS • Ron's *first* description of Dianetics. Originally circulated in manuscript form, it was soon copied and passed from hand to hand. Ensuing word of mouth created such demand for more information, Ron concluded the only way to answer the inquiries was with a book. That book was Dianetics: The Modern Science of Mental Health, now the all-time self-help bestseller. Find out what started it all. For here is the bedrock foundation of Dianetic discoveries: the *Original Axioms*, the *Dynamic Principle of Existence*, the *Anatomy of the Analytical* and *Reactive Mind*, the *Dynamics*, the *Tone Scale*, the *Auditor's Code* and the first description of a *Clear*. Even more than that, here are the primary laws describing *how* and *why* auditing works. It's only here in Dianetics: The Original Thesis.

DIANETICS: THE EVOLUTION OF A SCIENCE • This is the story of *how* Ron discovered the reactive mind and developed the procedures to get rid of it. Originally written for a national magazine–published to coincide with the release of Dianetics: The Modern Science of Mental Health–it started a wildfire movement virtually overnight upon that book's publication. Here then are both the fundamentals of Dianetics as well as the only account of Ron's two-decade journey of discovery and how he applied a scientific methodology to the problems of the human mind. He wrote it so you would know. Hence, this book is a must for every Dianeticist and Scientologist.

DIANETICS: THE MODERN SCIENCE OF MENTAL HEALTH • The bolt from the blue that began a worldwide movement. For while Ron had previously announced his discovery of the reactive mind, it had only fueled the fire of those wanting more information. More to the point–it was humanly impossible for one man to clear an entire planet. Encompassing all his previous discoveries and case histories of those breakthroughs in application, Ron provided the complete handbook of Dianetics procedure to train auditors to use it everywhere. A bestseller for more than half a century and with tens of millions of copies in print, Dianetics: The Modern Science of Mental Health has been translated in more than fifty languages, and used in more than 100 countries of Earth–indisputably, the most widely read and influential book about the human mind ever written. And that is why it will forever be known as *Book One*.

DIANETICS LECTURES AND DEMONSTRATIONS • Immediately following the publication of *Dianetics*, LRH began lecturing to packed auditoriums across America. Although addressing thousands at a time, demand continued to grow. To meet that demand, his presentation in Oakland, California, was recorded. In these four lectures, Ron related the events that sparked his investigation and his personal journey to his groundbreaking discoveries. He followed it all with a personal demonstration of Dianetics auditing–the only such demonstration of Book One available. *4 lectures.*

DIANETICS PROFESSIONAL COURSE LECTURES–*A SPECIAL COURSE FOR BOOK ONE AUDITORS* • Following six months of coast-to-coast travel, lecturing to the first Dianeticists, Ron assembled auditors in Los Angeles for a new Professional Course. The subject was his next sweeping discovery on life–the *ARC Triangle*, describing the interrelationship of *Affinity, Reality* and *Communication*. Through a series of fifteen lectures, LRH announced many firsts, including the *Spectrum of Logic*, containing an infinity of gradients from right to wrong; *ARC and the Dynamics;* the *Tone Scales of ARC;* the *Auditor's Code* and how it relates to ARC; and the *Accessibility Chart* that classifies a case and how to process it. Here, then, is both the final statement on Book One Auditing Procedures and the discovery upon which all further research would advance. The data in these lectures was thought to be lost for over fifty years and only available in student notes published in Notes on the Lectures. The original recordings have now been discovered making them broadly available for the first time. Life in its highest state, *Understanding*, is composed of Affinity, Reality and Communication. And, as LRH said, the best description of the ARC Triangle to be found anywhere is in these lectures. *15 lectures.*

SCIENCE OF SURVIVAL–*PREDICTION OF HUMAN BEHAVIOR* • The most useful book you will ever own. Built around the *Hubbard Chart of Human Evaluation*, Science of Survival provides the first accurate prediction of human behavior. Included on the chart are all the manifestations of an individual's survival potential graduated from highest to lowest, making this the complete book on the Tone Scale. Knowing only one or two characteristics of a person and using this chart, you can plot his or her position on the Tone Scale and thereby know the rest, obtaining an accurate index of their *entire* personality, conduct and character. Before this book the world was convinced that cases could not improve but only deteriorate. Science of Survival presents the idea of different states of case and the brand-new idea that one can progress upward on the Tone Scale. And therein lies the basis of today's Grade Chart.

THE SCIENCE OF SURVIVAL LECTURES • Underlying the development of the Tone Scale and Chart of Human Evaluation was a monumental breakthrough: The *Theta-MEST Theory*, containing the explanation of the interaction between Life–*theta*–with the physical universe of Matter, Energy, Space and Time–*MEST*. In these lectures, delivered to students immediately following publication of the book, Ron gave the most expansive description of all that lies behind the Chart of Human Evaluation and its application in life itself. Moreover, here also is the explanation of how the ratio of *theta* and *en(turbulated)-theta* determines one's position on the Tone Scale and the means to ascend to higher states. *4 lectures.*

SELF ANALYSIS • The barriers of life are really just shadows. Learn to know yourself–not just a shadow of yourself. Containing the most complete description of consciousness, Self Analysis takes you through your past, through your potentials, your life. First, with a series of self-examinations and using a special version of the Hubbard Chart of Human Evaluation, you plot yourself on the Tone Scale. Then, applying a series of light yet powerful processes, you embark on the great adventure of self-discovery. This book further contains embracive principles that reach *any* case, from the lowest to the highest–including auditing techniques so effective they are referred to by Ron again and again through all following years of research into the highest states. In sum, this book not only moves one up the Tone Scale but can pull a person out of almost anything.

ADVANCED PROCEDURE AND AXIOMS • With new breakthroughs on the nature and anatomy of engrams–"Engrams are effective only when the individual himself determines that they will be effective"–came the discovery of the being's use of a *Service Facsimile:* a mechanism employed to explain away failures in life, but which then locks a person into detrimental patterns of behavior and further failure. In consequence came a new type of processing addressing *Thought, Emotion* and *Effort* detailed in the "Fifteen Acts" of Advanced Procedure and oriented to the rehabilitation of the preclear's *Self-determinism.* Hence, this book also contains the all-encompassing, no-excuses-allowed explanation of *Full Responsibility,* the key to unlocking it all. Moreover, here is the codification of *Definitions, Logics,* and *Axioms,* providing both the summation of the entire subject and direction for all future research. *See Handbook for Preclears, written as a companion self-processing manual to Advanced Procedure and Axioms.*

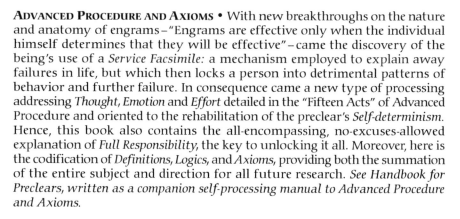 **THOUGHT, EMOTION AND EFFORT** • With the codification of the Axioms came the means to address key points on a case that could unravel all aberration. *Basic Postulates, Prime Thought, Cause and Effect* and their effect on everything from *memory* and *responsibility* to an individual's own role in empowering *engrams*–these matters are only addressed in this series. Here, too, is the most complete description of the *Service Facsimile* found anywhere–and why its resolution removes an individual's self-imposed disabilities. *21 lectures.*

FURTHER STUDY

HANDBOOK FOR PRECLEARS • The "Fifteen Acts" of Advanced Procedure and Axioms are paralleled by the fifteen Self-processing Acts given in Handbook for Preclears. Moreover, this book contains several essays giving the most expansive description of the *Ideal State of Man*. Discover why behavior patterns become so solidly fixed; why habits seemingly can't be broken; how decisions long ago have more power over a person than his decisions today; and why a person keeps past negative experiences in the present. It's all clearly laid out on the Chart of Attitudes—a milestone breakthrough that complements the Chart of Human Evaluation—plotting the ideal state of being and one's *attitudes* and *reactions* to life. *In self-processing, Handbook for Preclears is used in conjunction with Self Analysis.*

THE LIFE CONTINUUM • Besieged with requests for lectures on his latest breakthroughs, Ron replied with everything they wanted and more at the Second Annual Conference of Dianetic Auditors. Describing the technology that lies behind the self-processing steps of the *Handbook*—here is the *how* and *why* of it all: the discovery of *Life Continuum*—the mechanism by which an individual is compelled to carry on the life of another deceased or departed individual, generating in his own body the infirmities and mannerisms of the departed. Combined with auditor instruction on use of the Chart of Attitudes in determining how to enter every case at the proper gradient, here, too, are directions for dissemination of the Handbook and hence, the means to begin wide-scale clearing. *10 lectures.*

SCIENTOLOGY: MILESTONE ONE • Ron began the first lecture in this series with six words that would change the world forever: "This is a course in *Scientology*." From there, Ron not only described the vast scope of this, a then brand-new subject, he also detailed his discoveries on past lives. He proceeded from there to the description of the first E-Meter and its initial use in uncovering the *theta line* (the entire track of a thetan's existence), as entirely distinct from the *genetic body line* (the time track of bodies and their physical evolution), shattering the "one-life" lie and revealing the *whole track* of spiritual existence. Here, then, is the very genesis of Scientology. *22 lectures.*

THE ROUTE TO INFINITY: TECHNIQUE 80 LECTURES • As Ron explained, "Technique 80 is the *To Be or Not To Be* Technique." With that, he unveiled the crucial foundation on which ability and sanity rest: *the being's capacity to make a decision.* Here, then, is the anatomy of "maybe," the *Wavelengths of ARC*, the *Tone Scale of Decisions*, and the means to rehabilitate a being's ability *To Be* ... almost *anything. 7 lectures. (Knowledge of Technique 80 is required for Technique 88 as described in Scientology: A History of Man—below.)*

SCIENTOLOGY: A HISTORY OF MAN • "A cold-blooded and factual account of your last 76 trillion years." So begins A History of Man, announcing the revolutionary *Technique 88*–revealing for the first time the truth about whole track experience and the exclusive address, in auditing, to the thetan. Here is history unraveled with the first E-Meter, delineating and describing the principal incidents on the whole track to be found in any human being: *Electronic implants, entities,* the *genetic track, between-lives incidents, how bodies evolved* and *why you got trapped in them*–they're all detailed here.

TECHNIQUE 88: INCIDENTS ON THE TRACK BEFORE EARTH • "Technique 88 is the most hyperbolical, effervescent, dramatic, unexaggeratable, high-flown, superlative, grandiose, colossal and magnificent technique which the mind of Man could conceivably embrace. It is as big as the whole track and all the incidents on it. It's what you apply it to; it's what's been going on. It contains the riddles and secrets, the mysteries of all time. You could bannerline this technique like they do a sideshow, but nothing you could say, no adjective you could use, would adequately describe even a small segment of it. It not only batters the imagination, it makes you ashamed to imagine anything," is Ron's introduction to you in this never-before-available lecture series, expanding on all else contained in History of Man. What awaits you is the whole track itself. *15 lectures.*

SCIENTOLOGY 8-80 • The *first* explanation of the electronics of human thought and the energy phenomena in any being. Discover how even physical universe laws of motion are mirrored in a being, not to mention the electronics of aberration. Here is the link between theta and MEST revealing what energy *is,* and how you *create* it. It was this breakthrough that revealed the subject of a thetan's *flows* and which, in turn, is applied in *every* auditing process today. In the book's title, "8-8" stands for *Infinity-Infinity,* and "0" represents the static, *theta.* Included are the *Wavelengths of Emotion, Aesthetics, Beauty and Ugliness, Inflow and Outflow* and the *Sub-zero Tone Scale*–applicable only to the thetan.

SOURCE OF LIFE ENERGY • Beginning with the announcement of his new book–Scientology 8-80–Ron not only unveiled his breakthroughs of theta as the Source of Life Energy, but detailed the *Methods of Research* he used to make that and every other discovery of Dianetics and Scientology: the Qs and Logics–methods of *thinking* applicable to any universe or thinking process. Here, then, is both *how to think* and *how to evaluate all data and knowledge,* and thus, the linchpin to a full understanding of both Scientology and life itself. *14 lectures.*

FURTHER
STUDY

THE COMMAND OF THETA • While in preparation of his newest book and the Doctorate Course he was about to deliver, Ron called together auditors for a new Professional Course. As he said, "For the first time with this class we are stepping, really, beyond the scope of the word *Survival*." From that vantage point, the Command of Theta gives the technology that bridges the knowledge from 8-80 to 8-8008, and provides the first full explanation of the subject of *Cause* and a permanent shift of orientation in life from MEST to *Theta*. *10 lectures.*

SCIENTOLOGY 8-8008 • The complete description of the behavior and potentials of a *thetan*, and textbook for the Philadelphia Doctorate Course and The Factors: Admiration and the Renaissance of Beingness lectures. As Ron said, the book's title serves to fix in the mind of the individual a route by which he can rehabilitate himself, his abilities, his ethics and his goals–the attainment of *infinity* (8) by the reduction of the apparent *infinity* (8) of the MEST universe to *zero* (0) and the increase of the apparent *zero* (0) of one's own universe to *infinity* (8). Condensed herein are more than 80,000 hours of investigation, with a summarization and amplification of every breakthrough to date–and the full significance of those discoveries form the new vantage point of *Operating Thetan*.

THE PHILADELPHIA DOCTORATE COURSE LECTURES • This renowned series stands as the largest single body of work on the anatomy, behavior and potentials of the spirit of Man ever assembled, providing the very fundamentals which underlie the route to Operating Thetan. Here it is in complete detail–the thetan's relationship to the *creation*, *maintenance* and *destruction of universes*. In just those terms, here is the *anatomy* of matter, energy, space and time, and *postulating* universes into existence. Here, too, is the thetan's fall from whole track abilities and the *universal laws* by which they are restored. In short, here is Ron's codification of the upper echelon of theta beingness and behavior. Lecture after lecture fully expands every concept of the course text, Scientology 8-8008, providing the total scope of *you* in native state. *76 lectures and accompanying reproductions of the original 54 LRH hand drawn lecture charts.*

THE FACTORS: ADMIRATION AND THE RENAISSANCE OF BEINGNESS • With the *potentials* of a thetan fully established came a look outward resulting in Ron's monumental discovery of a *universal solvent* and the basic laws of the theta *universe*–laws quite literally senior to anything: *The Factors: Summation of the Considerations of the Human Spirit and Material Universe.* So dramatic were these breakthroughs, Ron expanded the book Scientology 8-8008, both clarifying previous discoveries and adding chapter after chapter which, studied with these lectures, provide a postgraduate level to the Doctorate Course. Here then are lectures containing the knowledge of *universal truth* unlocking the riddle of creation itself. *18 lectures.*

The Creation of Human Ability—*A Handbook for Scientologists* • *(This current volume.)* On the heels of his discoveries of Operating Thetan came a year of intensive research, exploring the realm of a *thetan exterior.* Through auditing and instruction, including 450 lectures in this same twelve-month span, Ron codified the entire subject of Scientology. And it's all contained in this handbook, from a *Summary of Scientology* to its basic *Axioms* and *Codes.* Moreover, here is *Intensive Procedure,* containing the famed Exteriorization Processes of *Route 1* and *Route 2*—processes drawn right from the Axioms. Each one is described in detail—*how* the process is used, *why* it works, the axiomatic technology that underlies its use, and the complete explanation of how a being can break the *false agreements* and *self-created barriers* that enslave him to the physical universe. In short, this book contains the ultimate summary of thetan exterior OT ability and its permanent accomplishment.

Phoenix Lectures: Freeing the Human Spirit • Here is the panoramic view of Scientology complete. Having codified the subject of Scientology in Creation of Human Ability, Ron then delivered a series of half-hour lectures to specifically accompany a full study of the book. From the *essentials* that underlie the technology—*The Axioms, Conditions of Existence* and *Considerations and Mechanics,* to the processes of *Intensive Procedure,* including twelve lectures describing one-by-one the thetan exterior processes of *Route 1*—it's all covered in full, providing a conceptual understanding of the *science of knowledge* and *native state OT ability.* Here then are the bedrock principles upon which everything in Scientology rests, including the embracive statement of the religion and its heritage—*Scientology, Its General Background.* Hence, this is the watershed lecture series on Scientology itself, and the axiomatic foundation for all future research. *42 lectures.*

Dianetics 55!—*The Complete Manual of Human Communication* • With all breakthroughs to date, a single factor had been isolated as crucial to success in every type of auditing. As LRH said, "Communication is so thoroughly important today in Dianetics and Scientology (as it always has been on the whole track) that it could be said if you were to get a preclear into communication, you would get him well." And this book delineates the *exact,* but previously unknown, anatomy and formulas for *perfect* communication. The magic of the communication cycle is *the* fundamental of auditing and the primary reason auditing works. The breakthroughs here opened new vistas of application—discoveries of such magnitude, LRH called Dianetics 55! the *Second Book* of Dianetics.

The Unification Congress: Communication! Freedom & Ability • The historic Congress announcing the reunification of the subjects of Dianetics and Scientology with the release of *Dianetics 55!* Until now, each had operated in their own sphere: Dianetics addressed Man *as Man*—the first four dynamics, while Scientology addressed *life itself*—the Fifth to Eighth Dynamics. The formula which would serve as the foundation for all future development was contained in a single word: *Communication.* It was a paramount breakthrough Ron would later call, "the great discovery of Dianetics and Scientology." Here, then, are the lectures, as it happened. *16 lectures and accompanying reproductions of the original LRH hand-drawn lecture charts.*

Further Study

Scientology: The Fundamentals of Thought–*The Basic Book of the Theory and Practice of Scientology for Beginners* • Designated by Ron as the *Book One of Scientology*. After having fully unified and codified the subjects of Dianetics and Scientology came the refinement of their *fundamentals*. Originally published as a résumé of Scientology for use in translations into non-English tongues, this book is of inestimable value to both the beginner and advanced student of the mind, spirit and life. Equipped with this book alone, one can begin a practice and perform seeming miracle changes in the states of well-being, ability and intelligence of people. Contained within are the *Conditions of Existence, Eight Dynamics, ARC Triangle, Parts of Man*, the full analysis of *Life as a Game*, and more, including exact processes for individual application of these principles in processing. Here, then, in one book, is the starting point for bringing Scientology to people everywhere.

Hubbard Professional Course Lectures • While Fundamentals of Thought stands as an introduction to the subject for beginners, it also contains a distillation of fundamentals for every Scientologist. Here are the in-depth descriptions of those fundamentals, each lecture one-half hour in length and providing, one-by-one, a complete mastery of a single Scientology breakthrough–*Axioms 1-10; The Anatomy of Control; Handling of Problems; Start, Change and Stop; Confusion and Stable Data; Exteriorization; Valences* and more–the *why* behind them, *how* they came to be and their mechanics. And it's all brought together with the *Code of a Scientologist*, point by point, and its use in actually creating a new civilization. In short, here are the LRH lectures that make a *Professional Scientologist*–one who can apply the subject to every aspect of life. *21 lectures.*

ADDITIONAL BOOKS CONTAINING SCIENTOLOGY ESSENTIALS

Work

THE PROBLEMS OF WORK–*SCIENTOLOGY APPLIED TO THE WORKADAY WORLD* • Having codified the entire subject of Scientology, Ron immediately set out to provide the *beginning* manual for its application by anyone. As he described it: life is composed of seven-tenths work, one-tenth familial, one-tenth political and one-tenth relaxation. Here, then, is Scientology applied to that seven-tenths of existence including the answers to *Exhaustion* and the *Secret of Efficiency.* Here, too, is the analysis of life itself–a game composed of exact rules. Know them and you succeed. Problems of Work contains technology no one can live without, and that can immediately be applied by both the Scientologist and those new to the subject.

Life Principles

SCIENTOLOGY: A NEW SLANT ON LIFE • Scientology essentials for every aspect of life. Basic answers that put you in charge of your existence, truths to consult again and again: *Is It Possible to Be Happy?*, *Two Rules for Happy Living*, *Personal Integrity*, *The Anti-Social Personality* and many more. In every part of this book you will find Scientology truths that describe conditions in your life and furnish *exact* ways to improve them. Scientology: A New Slant on Life contains essential knowledge for every Scientologist and a perfect introduction for anyone new to the subject.

Axioms, Codes and Scales

SCIENTOLOGY 0-8: THE BOOK OF BASICS • The companion to *all* Ron's books, lectures and materials. This is *the* Book of Basics, containing indispensable data you will refer to constantly: the *Axioms of Dianetics and Scientology; The Factors*; a full compilation of all *Scales* –more than 100 in all; listings of the *Perceptics* and *Awareness Levels*; all *Codes* and *Creeds* and much more. The senior laws of existence are condensed into this single volume, distilled from more than 15,000 pages of writings, 3,000 lectures and scores of books.

Scientology Ethics:
Technology of Optimum Survival

INTRODUCTION TO SCIENTOLOGY ETHICS • A new hope for Man arises with the first workable technology of ethics–technology to help an individual pull himself out of the downward skid of life and to a higher plateau of survival. This is the comprehensive handbook providing the crucial fundamentals: *Basics of Ethics & Justice; Honesty; Conditions of Existence; Condition Formulas* from Confusion to Power; the *Basics of Suppression* and its handling; as well as *Justice Procedures* and their use in Scientology Churches. Here, then, is the technology to overcome any barriers in life and in one's personal journey up the Bridge to Total Freedom.

Purification

CLEAR BODY, CLEAR MIND–*THE EFFECTIVE PURIFICATION PROGRAM* • We live in a biochemical world, and this book is the solution. While investigating the harmful effects that earlier drug use had on preclears' cases, Ron made the major discovery that many street drugs, particularly LSD, remained in a person's body long after ingested. Residues of the drug, he noted, could have serious and lasting effects, including triggering further "trips." Additional research revealed that a wide range of substances–medical drugs, alcohol, pollutants, household chemicals and even food preservatives–could also lodge in the body's tissues. Through research on thousands of cases, he developed the *Purification Program* to eliminate their destructive effects. Clear Body, Clear Mind details every aspect of the all-natural regimen that can free one from the harmful effects of drugs and other toxins, opening the way for spiritual progress.

REFERENCE HANDBOOKS

WHAT IS SCIENTOLOGY?

The complete and essential encyclopedic reference on the subject and practice of Scientology. Organized for use, this book contains the pertinent data on every aspect of the subject:

• The life of L. Ron Hubbard and his path of discovery

• The Spiritual Heritage of the religion

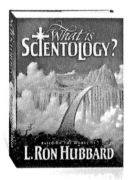

• A full description of Dianetics and Scientology

• Auditing–what it is and how it works

• Courses–what they contain and how they are structured

• The Grade Chart of Services and how one ascends to higher states

• The Scientology Ethics and Justice System

• The Organizational Structure of the Church

• A complete description of the many Social Betterment programs supported by the Church, including: Drug Rehabilitation, Criminal Reform, Literacy and Education and the instilling of real values for morality

Over 1,000 pages in length, with more than 500 photographs and illustrations, this text further includes Creeds, Codes, a full listing of all books and materials as well as a Catechism with answers to virtually any question regarding the subject.

You Ask and This Book Answers.

THE SCIENTOLOGY HANDBOOK

Scientology fundamentals for daily use in every part of life. Encompassing 19 separate bodies of technology, here is the most comprehensive manual on the basics of life ever published. Each chapter contains key principles and technology for your continual use:

• Study Technology

• The Dynamics of Existence

• The Components of Understanding– Affinity, Reality and Communication

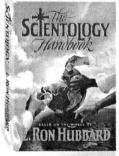

• The Tone Scale

• Communication and its Formulas

• Assists for Illnesses and Injuries

• How to Resolve Conflicts

• Integrity and Honesty

• Ethics and Condition Formulas

• Answers to Suppression and a Dangerous Environment

• Marriage

• Children

• Tools for the Workplace

More than 700 photographs and illustrations make it easy for you to learn the procedures and apply them at once. This book is truly the indispensable handbook for every Scientologist.

The Technology to Build a Better World.

ABOUT L. RON HUBBARD

"To really know life," L. Ron Hubbard wrote, "you've got to be part of life. You must get down and look, you must get into the nooks and crannies of existence. You have to rub elbows with all kinds and types of men before you can finally establish what he is."

Through his long and extraordinary journey to the founding of Dianetics and Scientology, Ron did just that. From his adventurous youth in a rough and tumble American West to his far-flung trek across a still mysterious Asia; from his two-decade search for the very essence of life to the triumph of Dianetics and Scientology—such are the stories recounted in the L. Ron Hubbard Biographical Publications.

Presenting the photographic overview of Ron's greater journey is *L. Ron Hubbard: Images of a Lifetime*. Drawn from his own archival collection, this is Ron's life as he himself saw it.

While for the many aspects of that rich and varied life, stands the Ron Series. Each issue focuses on a specific LRH profession: *Auditor, Humanitarian, Philosopher, Artist, Poet, Music Maker, Photographer* and many more including his published articles on *Freedom* and his personal *Letters & Journals*. Here is the life of a man who lived at least twenty lives in the space of one.

FOR FURTHER INFORMATION VISIT

www.lronhubbard.org

GUIDE TO THE MATERIALS

YOU'RE ON AN ADVENTURE!
HERE'S THE MAP.

- All books
- All lectures
- All reference books

All of it laid out in chronological sequence with descriptions of what each contains

Your journey to a full understanding of Dianetics and Scientology is the greatest adventure of all. But you need a map that shows you where you are and where you are going.

That map is the Materials Guide Chart. It shows all Ron's books and lectures with a full description of their content and subject matter so you can find exactly what *you* are looking for and precisely what *you* need.

Since each book and lecture is laid out in chronological sequence, you can see *how* the subjects of Dianetics and Scientology were developed. And what that means is by simply studying this chart you are in for cognition after cognition!

New editions of all books include extensive glossaries, containing definitions for every technical term. And as a result of a monumental restoration program, the entire library of Ron's lectures are being made available on compact disc, with complete transcripts, glossaries, lecture graphs, diagrams and issues he refers to in the lectures. As a result, you get *all* the data, and can learn with ease, gaining a full *conceptual* understanding.

And what that adds up to is a new Golden Age of Knowledge every Dianeticist and Scientologist has dreamed of.

To obtain your FREE Materials Guide Chart and Catalog, or to order L. Ron Hubbard's books and lectures, contact:

WESTERN HEMISPHERE:
**Bridge
Publications, Inc.**
4751 Fountain Avenue
Los Angeles, CA 90029 USA
www.bridgepub.com
Phone: 1-800-722-1733
Fax: 1-323-953-3328

EASTERN HEMISPHERE:
**New Era Publications
International ApS**
Store Kongensgade 53
1264 Copenhagen K, Denmark
www.newerapublications.com
Phone: (45) 33 73 66 66
Fax: (45) 33 73 66 33

Books and lectures are also available direct from Churches of Scientology.
*See **Addresses**.*

Addresses

S cientology is the fastest-growing religion in the world today. Churches and Missions exist in cities throughout the world, and new ones are continually forming.

To obtain more information or to locate the Church nearest you, visit the Scientology website:

www.scientology.org
e-mail: info@scientology.org

or

Phone: 1-800-334-LIFE
(for US and Canada)

You can also write to any one of the Continental Organizations, listed on the following page, who can direct you to one of the thousands of Churches and Missions world over.

L. Ron Hubbard's books and lectures may be obtained from any of these addresses or direct from the publishers on the previous page.

CONTINENTAL CHURCH ORGANIZATIONS:

UNITED STATES
CHURCH OF SCIENTOLOGY
CONTINENTAL LIAISON OFFICE
WESTERN UNITED STATES
1308 L. Ron Hubbard Way
Los Angeles, California 90027 USA
info@wus.scientology.org

CHURCH OF SCIENTOLOGY
CONTINENTAL LIAISON OFFICE
EASTERN UNITED STATES
349 W. 48th Street
New York, New York 10036 USA
info@eus.scientology.org

CANADA
CHURCH OF SCIENTOLOGY
CONTINENTAL LIAISON OFFICE
CANADA
696 Yonge Street, 2nd Floor
Toronto, Ontario
Canada M4Y 2A7
info@scientology.ca

LATIN AMERICA
CHURCH OF SCIENTOLOGY
CONTINENTAL LIAISON OFFICE
LATIN AMERICA
Federacion Mexicana de Dianetica
Calle Puebla #31
Colonia Roma, Mexico D.F.
C.P. 06700, Mexico
info@scientology.org.mx

UNITED KINGDOM
CHURCH OF SCIENTOLOGY
CONTINENTAL LIAISON OFFICE
UNITED KINGDOM
Saint Hill Manor
East Grinstead, West Sussex
England, RH19 4JY
info@scientology.org.uk

AFRICA
CHURCH OF SCIENTOLOGY
CONTINENTAL LIAISON OFFICE AFRICA
6th Floor, Budget House
130 Main Street
Johannesburg 2001, South Africa
info@scientology.org.za

AUSTRALIA, NEW ZEALAND & OCEANIA
CHURCH OF SCIENTOLOGY
CONTINENTAL LIAISON OFFICE ANZO
16 Dorahy Street
Dundas, New South Wales 2117
Australia
info@scientology.org.au

Church of Scientology
Liaison Office of Taiwan
1st, No. 231, Cisian 2nd Road
Kaoshiung City
Taiwan, ROC
info@scientology.org.tw

EUROPE
CHURCH OF SCIENTOLOGY
CONTINENTAL LIAISON OFFICE EUROPE
Store Kongensgade 55
1264 Copenhagen K, Denmark
info@scientology.org.dk

Church of Scientology
Liaison Office of Commonwealth
of Independent States
Management Center of Dianetics
and Scientology Dissemination
Pervomajskaya Street, House 1A
Korpus Grazhdanskoy Oboroni
Losino-Petrovsky Town
141150 Moscow, Russia
info@scientology.ru

Church of Scientology
Liaison Office of Central Europe
1082 Leonardo da Vinci u. 8-14
Budapest, Hungary
info@scientology.hu

Church of Scientology
Liaison Office of Iberia
C/Miguel Menendez Boneta, 18
28460 – Los Molinos
Madrid, Spain
info@spain.scientology.org

Church of Scientology
Liaison Office of Italy
Via Cadorna, 61
20090 Vimodrone
Milan, Italy
info@scientology.it

Become a Member
of the International
Association of Scientologists

The International Association of Scientologists is the membership organization of all Scientologists united in the most vital crusade on Earth.

A free Six-Month Introductory Membership is extended to anyone who has not held a membership with the Association before.

As a member, you are eligible for discounts on Scientology materials offered only to IAS Members. You also receive the Association magazine, *IMPACT,* issued six times a year, full of Scientology news from around the world.

The purpose of the IAS is:

"To unite, advance, support and protect Scientology and Scientologists in all parts of the world so as to achieve the Aims of Scientology as originated by L. Ron Hubbard."

Join the strongest force for positive change on the planet today, opening the lives of millions to the greater truth embodied in Scientology.

Join the International Association of Scientologists.
To apply for membership,
write to the International
Association of Scientologists
c/o Saint Hill Manor, East Grinstead
West Sussex, England, RH19 4JY
www.iasmembership.org

Editor's Glossary

of Words, Terms and Phrases

absolute(s): that which is free from all doubt or uncertainty; positive, perfectly certain. Page 255.

acceptance level: what the preclear himself accepts, what the people around him in mock-up form accept and what others will accept from others and, included as well, what others have wanted him to accept and what he has wanted others to accept. Page 122.

Acceptance Level Processing: *Acceptance Level Processing* is that process which discovers the lowest level of acceptance of the individual and discovers there the prevailing hunger and feeds that hunger by means of mock-ups until it is satiated (completely satisfied). One has the preclear *mock-up, no matter how blackly or how crudely, items for himself to accept*, then have *others in his mock-ups mock-up things for them to accept* and *others to mock-up things for others to accept*. In Acceptance Level Processing this bracket extends to having the preclear also *mock-up things for others to accept* and *others to mock-up things for him to accept*. Thus there are five stages in the bracket. Page 140.

admiration: admiration is approving attention given to; regard toward; looking on with pleasure. The particle called the admiration particle is seen to be that particle necessary to the construction of a communication line. Page 279.

Advanced Clinical Course units, seven: the seven Advanced Professional Auditor Courses preceding and culminating in *The Creation of Human Ability* and its processing centerpiece, Intensive Procedure. The first through seventh Clinical Courses were delivered by LRH between October 1953 and July 1954. ACCs instructed select professionals on the latest advances of technology and in the full scope of theory. Page 1.

Advanced Course Procedure: a series of codified auditing procedures developed in the first five Advanced Clinical Courses. Hence, the name *Advanced Course Procedure.* Page 397.

airy: like air in its (apparently) intangible or empty character; unsubstantial, unreal, imaginary. Page 275.

alloyed: lowered, impaired or debased; corrupted by mixture. An *alloy* is a metal that is formed by mixing two types of metal together or by mixing metal with another substance thought of as not pure. Page 12.

all up: at or very near an end; with death, defeat or failure hopelessly or unalterably approaching. Page 152.

anchor points: those points which demark the outermost boundaries of the space or its corners are called, in Scientology, *anchor points.* An anchor point is a specialized kind of dimension point. Page 40.

ancients, the: the civilized peoples, nations or cultures of ancient times. Page 312.

androgen: any of several chemical substances naturally produced in the male body that are responsible for the development of male sex organs and for other male sexual characteristics. Page 308.

Anglicized: adapted in customs, manners, speech, outlook or philosophy to the culture of the English-speaking world. Page 413.

antipathetic: in opposition; contrary in nature or character. Also having a strong or deep-rooted dislike. Page 172.

aplomb: self-confident assurance and composure, especially in difficult or challenging circumstances. Page 63.

appreciable: possible to estimate, measure or perceive; large or important enough to be noticed. Page 42.

art: systematic application of knowledge or skill in effecting a desired result. Page 311.

aspect: nature, quality or character. Page 24.

astrology: the study of how the position of the Sun, Moon, planets and stars are supposedly related to and influence life and events on the Earth. *Astrology* is based on the belief that the heavenly bodies form patterns that can reveal a person's character or future. Page 285.

Atharva-Veda: one of the four books of the *Veda*, the ancient sacred writings that contain the first written expression of Man's relationship to the universe and the cycle-of-action of life–birth, life and death. Page 413.

at length: after some time; in the end; eventually. Page 113.

avalanches: the avalanche effect is simply the fact that the MEST universe has pounded the individual for seventy-six trillion years until a point where the person has a terrific appetite for it. The individual has an avalanche to be triggered. It's there. One has the preclear mock-up heavy dense masses–Earths, suns, dark stars and so on and has him avalanche them outward at a mad rate. After a while it slows down and one makes the individual inflow lots of stars, planets, suns, etc., that he is mocking-up. In doing this you work out the automaticity of this type of havingness in its entirety. Avalanches are described in the LRH lecture of 2 February 1954 "Havingness: Comm Lines" in the 3rd American ACC and LRH lecture of 16 March 1954 "Outline of Processes" in the 4th American ACC. Page 378.

back alley(s): a dirty, sordid or clandestine path. Page 275.

backing up: accumulating; holding back. Page 139.

band(s): a more or less well-defined range of something, as a level on a scale. Page 62.

Bard of Stratford-on-Avon: William Shakespeare (1564–1616), English poet and dramatist. So called from his birthplace, Stratford-on-Avon, a town in central England on the Avon River. "All the world's a stage and all the men and women merely players" is from the play, *As You Like It.* (A bard is a poet.) Page 205.

beastliness: quality or behavior of a *beast,* that is, brutish or savage; below the dignity of reason or humanity; marked by or indicating inhuman or immoderate instincts or desires. Page 313.

becomingness: the state or quality of *becoming,* growing or coming to be. Page 281.

Bedlam: an old insane asylum (in full, St. Mary of Bethlehem) in London, known for its inhumane treatment and filthy environment. Inmates were chained to the walls or floor and when restless or violent were beaten, whipped or dunked in water. Page 289.

beget: to bring into being; create, generate, cause. Page 299.

beheld: observed, perceived or seen. Page 138.

behold: 1. used in formal writing when expressing a command calling attention to something. Page vii.
2. to perceive, observe, look at or see. Hence, comprehend. Page 140.

bent: determined to take a course of action; resolved. Page 304.

Black V: a heavily occluded case characterized by no mock-ups, only blackness. The term "Black V (five)" came from application of SOP 8 (Standard Operating Procedure 8), wherein the auditor tests the preclear at each step from Step I on, until he finds a step the preclear can do and begins processing at that step. A preclear who had to be started at Step V of the process was called a "Case V." This level of case could not get mock-ups but only blackness, hence "Black V." Page 232.

Body Recruitment: the phenomenon in which a body part becomes the thetan's orientation-point in existence. It is the thing that is really safe. The main reason why your preclear can't find himself is he is in some outrageous location in the body. Hence, "'*Body Recruitment*' *of the thetan by some part of the body."* Page 123.

Book of Job: a story in the Bible about Job, a man whose faith was severely tested by Satan, with God's permission. Job was prosperous and happy and faithful to God. In order to get Job to curse God, Satan destroyed all that Job owned, killed his children and gave Job sores on his body from head to foot. However, Job would not curse God and, as a reward, God healed Job, giving him twice as much as he had before. Page 414.

boots (someone) out of: moves, ejects or kicks a person out of some state or condition. Page 205.

borne home to: made clear or evident to; clarified or emphasized for. Page 207.

bracket(s): one runs things in *brackets*. The word "bracket" is taken from the artillery, meaning to enclose within a salvo (sudden burst of bullets or other projectiles) of fire. A bracket is run as follows: First, one gets the concept as *happening to the preclear.* Then, one gets the concept of *the preclear making it happen (or thinking or saying it) to another.* Then one gets the concept as *being directed by another at others.* Page 174.

breechcloths: garments made of material wrapped around the breech (buttocks) and hips, often as the sole article of clothing worn by primitive peoples. Page 416.

Buddha, Gautama: Gautama Siddhartha Buddha (563–483 B.C.), Indian religious philosopher and the founder of Buddhism, one of the world's great religions. After experiencing enlightenment for himself, Buddha sought the same for others, advising them to free themselves of all desires and material things. *Buddha* means "Enlightened One." Page 23.

Buddhism: a world religion based on the teachings of Gautama Siddhartha Buddha (563–483 B.C.), Indian religious philosopher and founder of Buddhism. Buddhism emphasizes liberation from the physical world and the breaking of the endless chain of births and deaths. Page 414.

butchery: rough treatment of something or somebody. Used figuratively. Page 144.

445

buttered: smeared or spread out; distributed over a surface or space; likened to the action of spreading butter over something. Page 124.

by-routes: courses, ways or roads that are indirect. Used figuratively. Page 165.

by the hour: describing something done over a period of hours rather than minutes or seconds, as in *"This is a process which is done by the hour."* Page 87.

by the way: along the road or path being taken; in one's course of travel. *Way* in this sense refers to a road, street or path. Page vii.

Camden Indoctrination Course B: the second of two courses given in Camden, New Jersey, in 1953. These became known as the 1st and 2nd Advanced Clinical Courses. Page 348.

cannot help but: to be unable to prevent or avoid something. Page 311.

canonical: of or having to do with a *canon*, any officially recognized set of sacred books. Page 413.

capital: a reference to capitalists collectively and their money, influence, political interests, etc. Page 319.

capitalist(s): a supporter of capitalism or a participant in it. *Capitalism* is an economic system in which a country's businesses and industry are controlled and run for profit by private owners rather than by government, and where money (capital) is invested or loaned in return for a profit. Page 227.

cardinal: of fundamental importance; chief. Page 124.

carried home: *carried* means conveyed, imparted or gotten across to. *Home* means to the vital center or seat, to the very heart or root of the matter. Hence, fully impinged or had a full effect on. Page 289.

case in point: a relevant or good example of what is being considered or spoken of. Page 395.

catch: a hidden element or something concealed which catches or trips one up. Page 225.

chalking up: achieving or accumulating (something). From the idea of using chalk to record a score or points in a game. Page 394.

Change of Space Processing: Change of Space Processing is fully described in Chapter Five, Intensive Procedure, R1–9. Page 66.

check, in: restrained from free movement or action; under control. Page 313.

circle(s): an exclusive group of people with shared characteristics or interests; a class of society consisting of persons who associate together. Page 286.

clairvoyance: the apparent power of perceiving things or events in the future or beyond normal sensory contact. Page 146.

clinical: having to do with a clinic or with methods used in a *clinic*, a place, as in connection with a school or other training facility, which services the public and where students are trained on advanced data and are expected to produce results, often through direct work with individuals or under a trained professional. Distinguished from experimental or laboratory study. Page 1.

coal heaver(s): a person who carries or shovels coal; a laborer, used in reference to the many different items that can be run in R2–21, Granting of Beingness, including the different strata of society, as in *"cats, dogs, kings and coal heavers."* Page 97.

coincidence: exact agreement or correspondence in substance, nature, character, etc. Page 295.

coincident: occupying the same place or position in space. Page 318.

Commander Thompson: Joseph Cheesman Thompson (1874–1943), a commander and surgeon in the United States Navy, who studied Freudian analysis with Sigmund Freud in Vienna for the purpose of introducing the theory and practice of psychoanalysis into the US Navy. Page 310.

common parlance: the speech or writing used by people in general. Page 206.

Communication Formula: the Formula of Communication is defined in Axiom 28, Chapter Four, A Summary of Scientology. Page 96.

communication lag: the interval of time intervening between a posed question and the actual and precise answer to that question.

Communication lag is a manifestation of two-way communication. Whether the interval is filled with speech or silence, the definition of communication lag still holds true. Page 6.

complexes: in psychoanalysis, groups of interrelated impulses, ideas and emotions of which the individual is unaware, but which strongly influence his attitudes, feelings and behavior in a particular activity. Page 310.

compromise: to lessen or devalue; partially surrender one's own position or principles or standards. Page 12.

computation on the case: the computation technically is that aberrated evaluation and postulate that one must be consistently in a certain state in order to succeed. The computation thus may mean that one must entertain in order to be alive or that one must be dignified in order to succeed or that one must own much in order to live. Page 326.

comrade: a person who shares in one's activities, occupation, fortunes or experiences; close friend or companion. Page 12.

concepts: a reference to *Concept Running*, processing where the preclear "gets the idea" of "knowing" or "not being" and holds it, the while looking at his time track. The concept runs out or the somatic it brings on runs out and the concept itself is run. It is not addressed at individual incidents but at hundreds. Concept Running is described in *Scientology 8-80*. Page 178.

concourse: communication; interchange. From *con* meaning together, and *course* meaning to flow. Page 281.

condensation, rarefaction: a reference to a flow of energy such as in electrical flow or sound waves. When such energy travels down a wire, it isn't particles that move along the path (like water through a pipe) but a rhythmic pattern of compressing (condensing) and expanding (rarefying) waves. The wave is carried along by molecules bumping into their neighboring molecules. No molecules actually travel down the path, only the energy is carried along. The repetition of these condensation and rarefaction cycles is referred to as vibration and how many of them take place per unit of time is referred to as frequency. See illustration below. Page 295.

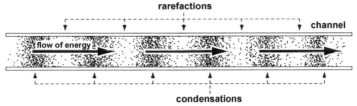

condensing: making more dense or more compact; creating less space. In application to the Know to Sex Scale, Know deteriorates into Look, Look deteriorates into Emotion, Emotion condenses into Effort, Effort condenses into Thinkingness, Thinkingness condenses into Symbols (because Symbols are just packages of thought) and Symbols condense into Eating, and Eating condenses into Sex. Page 52.

Confucius: (ca. 551–479 B.C.) Chinese philosopher and teacher whose philosophy of ethics stressed two virtues: the rules of proper conduct, and love for humanity. His teachings dealt with high ethical and moral standards and the role of individuals in society. Page 414.

conscientiousness: the quality of being loyal to one's conscience or sense of right and wrong. Page 417.

consigned: assigned or turned over to an undesirable position, activity or condition. Page 206.

constancy: the state or quality of being unchanging. Page 53.

convention: a rule, method or practice established as a standard or procedure. Page 311.

cosmic order: the Taoist concept that there is an underlying pattern and power of the universe (light and darkness, day and night, summer and winter, heat and cold) that represents all that is correct, normal or right in the universe and that the individual should seek only to conform with this orderly and harmonious whole. Page 414.

Couéism: a form of "therapy" developed by French psychotherapist Émile Coué (1857–1926). In Couéism, a sort of self-hypnosis is employed where the individual repeats verbal messages to himself such as, "Every day in every way I am getting better and better." Page 165.

counsel, keep one's own: consult with oneself, advise oneself as to actions or matters of right and wrong. Page 13.

cousin: a thing related or similar in some respects to something else. Page 237.

cream off life and leave the skimmed milk, take the upper: obtain or have the best of existence, leaving behind the things of lower quality. Literally, *cream* is the thick, light yellow portion of milk from which butter is made. Because it is lighter than the remainder of the milk, cream will slowly rise to the surface and can be separated by scooping (skimming) it from the top leaving behind the other components, referred to as skim milk. Cream is considered rich tasting and hence, the most excellent part of something. Page 139.

Creative Processing: processing which has the preclear make, out of energy of his own creation, various forms, objects, distances and spaces referred to as *mock-ups*. Creative Processing is fully described in *Scientology 8-8008*. Page 148.

curse word: a word that signifies a source or cause of evil, harm or misery. Page 165.

datum: a *datum* would be anything of which one could become aware, whether the thing existed or whether he created it. Page 218.

dead energy: energy which is not live, flowing, etc. Page 183.

debauchery: extreme or excessive yielding to one's desires or one's appetites, especially for sensual pleasure. Page 276.

deeper significances: deeper meanings as searched for by a person who never sees something for what it actually is. He constantly looks for hidden significances or influences that lie beyond what he is looking at. Page 130.

DEI cycle: a cycle-of-action. First, one merely desires to have. And that is simply *wishes* or *wants*. And then that deteriorates to *have to have*, which is enforced. And then that goes immediately to *inhibited*, which is can't have. Page 217.

Description Processing: Description Processing is fully described in Chapter Five, Intensive Procedure, R2–34. Page 43.

despatch: the act of sending off or out of something (as to a specific destination). Page 316.

Dewey: John Dewey (1859-1952), American philosopher, psychologist and educator who considered science was a method to inquire into the behavior of things and that knowledge was a means of controlling the environment in the hope of improving the quality of life. Page 23.

Dharma: the moral and religious law of Buddhism and Hinduism, each of which has its own Dharma. In Buddhism, the Dharma is reflected in the teachings of Buddha, governing daily life and showing the way to salvation. In Hinduism, the Dharma establishes rules of duty and ethical conduct for all people. Page 23.

Dhyana: in Buddhism and Hinduism, the practice of achieving spiritual enlightenment through meditation and yoga (a school of Hindu philosophy advocating and setting forth a course of physical and mental disciplines for attaining freedom from the material world and union of the self with the Supreme Being). Page 414.

diagnostic: serving to identify or characterize; being a precise indication (of the nature of someone or something). Page 126.

dimension: a measure of spatial extent, such as length, width or height. Page 27.

dimension point: any point in a space or at the boundaries of space. Page 277.

Dirty 30: a reference to *Procedure 30*. (See **Procedure 30.**) Because this process is very arduous to run on people below Boredom on the Tone Scale, and because in its earliest days it was often used on people on whom it should not have been used, it was sometimes called, colloquially, "Dirty 30." Page 263.

dirty words: words or phrases that are considered morally unclean or impure and offensive to accepted standards of decency. Page 325.

disciples: the twelve original followers of Jesus Christ. A *disciple* is one who accepts the teachings of another and assists in spreading or implementing them. Page vii.

drank deep: took into the mind or experienced something in depth. Page 275.

due course, in: in the proper or natural order of events; after the lapse of an appropriate period of time. Page 303.

early-type: of, relating to or characteristic of a period of time near the beginning of a course of events. Specifically, in this sense, related to Dianetics auditing from 1950 to 1951. Page 329.

easy sex: sexual relations that are easily obtained due to environment, types of people, attitude, position of authority, etc. Page 163.

ecstasies: high-spirited states of intense feeling which so dominate the person that he sometimes loses consciousness or self-control. Page 276.

effected: 1. made the effect of. Page 290.
2. brought about; accomplished; made happen. Page 319.

8-C: short for *Opening Procedure of 8-C* which is fully described in Chapter Five, Intensive Procedure, R2–16. The "C" in 8-C stands for "clinical." Page 42.

eight stars: of extremely high quality. This alludes to a system of rating the quality of something by placing a number of stars next to its name or title, normally the highest being five stars. Page 229.

election of Cause: the action whereby individuals designate or select other things Cause than themselves. In the process, Electing Cause, preclears run out the machinery which elects other things Cause than themselves. The center of all their machinery will run out. Page 232.

electronic structure: that structure of anchor points which demark the space in which the illusion of atoms, molecules and functioning structure will occur. *Electronic structure* is a piece of space which demarks the limits of a functioning illusion. A functioning illusion is what is commonly called the body. Page 73.

electropsychometry: the use of an *electropsychometer,* the full name for an E-Meter. (*Electro* means electric or electricity, *psycho* means soul, and *meter* means measure.) Page 310.

Elementary Straightwire: a basic process which consists of *"Something you wouldn't mind remembering"* and *"Something you wouldn't mind forgetting"* and ARC Straightwire just as given in the next-to-last list of *Self Analysis*. Page 46.

emote: to show or express emotion. Page 63.

Emotingness: the condition of showing or expressing emotion. Page 30.

endocrine: having to do with the secretion of chemical substances (hormones) from certain organs and tissues which travel through the blood to all parts of the body. After a hormone arrives at the organ or tissue it affects, it causes certain actions to occur. Hormones regulate such body processes as growth, development, reproduction, response to stress, etc. Page 191.

enjoined: directed to do or not do something. Page 151.

enterprise: an undertaking or project, especially one that is important or difficult or that requires boldness or energy. Page 96.

Envoi: (also spelled *envoy*) the final section of a book or play, or a short section at the end of a poem, used for summing up or as a dedication. *L'* is French for "the" and *envoi* means "a sending." Page 251.

estrogen: a hormone that develops and maintains feminine characteristics in the body. Page 308.

ethnology: the science that analyzes and compares human cultures, especially in regard to social structure, language, religion, technology and historical development. Page 311.

Excalibur: a manuscript written by L. Ron Hubbard in 1938. Although unpublished, the body of information it contained has since been released in Dianetics and Scientology materials. Page 118.

Expanded GITA: a process run to remedy contra-survival abundance and scarcity. *GITA* is short for *Give and Take Processing*. Expanded GITA is described in Step IV of Standard Operating Procedure 8 in This Is Scientology, The Science of Certainty. Page 186.

exteriorization: the act of moving the thetan outside of the body. Page 1.

extrapolation(s): the act of figuring out, from evidence and reasoning, an unknown from something that is known. Page 310.

eye to eye, sees: is in entire agreement; agrees without exception. Page 11.

Fac One: *Facsimile One,* a name given to a whole track implant found in everyone's bank. It is called "Facsimile One" because it is the first proven-up whole track incident which when audited out of a long series of people was found to eradicate a host of ills. Fac One is described in *Scientology: A History of Man.* Page 325.

fader questions: questions to which, because of the characteristics of the mind, there is no possible answer. One of these is *"Give me an unknown time."* As soon as the preclear starts to answer such a question, he of course has As-ised a certain amount of unknownness and will know the time. There are relatively few of these questions. Page 214.

fakir: Muslim or Hindu men who spend their lives in prayer and meditation and who practice extreme self-denial as part of their religion. A certain class of fakirs collect charity by publicly demonstrating skills sometimes thought of as miraculous, such as the ability to walk on fire, perform hypnotism, recline on a bed of nails and carry out tricks requiring quick and clever movements of the hands. Page 376.

fidelity: the quality of being faithful; firm and unchanging loyalty to a person, organization, principle, etc. Page 417.

field: the space a preclear sees or observes with his eyes closed. Page 125.

five-star: of the highest quality. This alludes to a system of rating the quality of something by placing a number of stars next to its name or title, normally the highest being five stars. Page 168.

fixity: the quality or state of being unmoving and unchanging. Page 154.

flatten (a process): continue to run a process as long as it produces change. If a process is producing no change one goes on to the next process. Page 255.

flattened (a communication lag): continued to ask the auditing question until one obtained an even spacing of reply from a preclear. Page 39.

flicking: moving as if with a quick, sharp jerk. Page 390.

force screen: big heavy force fields—which actually are nothing more or less than wave emanations like you get out of a headlight of a car. You change the wavelength of a headlight of a car and speed it up enough and hit somebody with it and it will knock him down. That is an electronic field. That is a force screen. Page 66.

force (something) home: *force* means to make something happen by using physical or mental pressure. *Home* means to the vital center or seat; to the very heart or root of the matter. Hence, compel by pressure into close contact with or make something impinge. Page 184.

Formula H: a technique that deals with the effort to reach and withdraw, to grasp and let go of oneself, of others for themselves, of oneself for others and others for oneself and others for others. For example, as applied to present time, one would ask the preclear to run the effort to reach and to withdraw into and from present time in terms of force, in terms of admiration and in terms of perception. For force, perception and admiration when run resolve the tenacity of engrams. Formula H was developed as a basic resolution in terms of emotion and effort of insane impulses, neuroses, obsessions and compulsions. The "H" stands for hope. Formula H is fully described in Professional Auditor's Bulletin 9 of September 1953, "Formula H" in the Technical Bulletins volumes. Page 363.

fourfold: consisting of four parts or divisions. Page 28.

four-star: of excellent quality. This alludes to a system of rating the quality of something by placing a number of stars next to its name or title, normally the highest being five stars. Page 194.

framework: the set of ideas, facts or circumstances within which something exists or with which one thinks or acts. Page 25.

Freud, Sigmund: (1856-1939) Austrian founder of psychoanalysis who emphasized that hidden, unconscious memories of a sexual nature control a person's behavior. Page 310.

Gautama Sakyamuni: (563–483 B.C.) a name of the *Buddha,* the Indian religious philosopher and founder of Buddhism. The name consists of the family name Gautama and the name Sakyamuni, "Sage of the Sakyas," referring to the warrior caste (Sakyas) which Buddha's father headed. A *caste* is a social class in society separated from others by hereditary rank, profession or wealth. A *sage* is someone who exhibits wisdom and calm judgment. Page 414.

general semantics: a philosophical approach to language, developed by Alfred Korzybski (1879–1950), which sought a scientific basis for a clear understanding of the difference between words and reality and the ways in which words themselves can influence and limit Man's ability to think. Korzybski believed that men unthinkingly identify words with the objects they represent and have nonoptimum reactions to words based on past experiences. Page 203.

generator(s): a machine that converts one form of energy into another, especially mechanical energy into electrical energy. In an electrical generator, the solid iron base of the generator fastened to a floor or table imposes time and space upon two terminals. Without this imposition of time and space, no energy could be possible. A great deal of mechanical motion must be put into an electrical generator because an electrical generator is discharging between the dichotomy of Effort and Matter. Page 41.

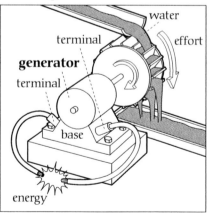

gold balls: anchor points (golden balls) which compose that framework of the body, which permits the body to exist. This framework is composed of a number of gold sparks or little tiny balls or large gold balls. If they are in an excellently well-arranged pattern, and if they are in *the* pattern which creates the illusion of the body, then the body's in good shape. And if they are out of line or if they are disturbed or shattered or gone, then the body is distorted at those points where they are distorted. Page 73.

Grand Tour: Grand Tour is fully described in Chapter Five, Intensive Procedure, R1-9. Page 40.

grant beingness: admit the existence of; give life to. *Grant* means to give, hand out, etc. *Beingness* means existingness in a form. Page 7.

guardian angel: a supernatural being believed to protect a particular person, as from danger or error. Page 207.

hanging up: becoming halted or suspended in progress. Page 84.

hangover: a remaining effect from a previous experience or previous knowledge. Page 136.

hang-ups: things that are halted or suspended. Page 139.

hardly: with energy, force or strenuous exertion; vigorously. Page 276.

HAS: abbreviation for *Hubbard Association of Scientologists*, the organization that served as the central dissemination center, guaranteed the excellence of the technology, processed public and was the central training center for Dianetics and Scientology. See *Addresses* for current organization locations. Page 354.

HAS Clinical Center: an organization (1954-1955) operated by the Hubbard Association of Scientologists (HAS) that trained auditors and offered processing. Page 353.

hazardings: tentative or uncertain explanations or guesses about something. Page 24.

He: God. The word *He* is capitalized in this sense following the practice of capitalizing the word *God*. Page 162.

hews: conforms strictly or adheres (to a line, rule, principle, etc.). Page 82.

Hindu(s): a member of the Hindu religion of India that emphasizes freedom from the material world through purification of desires and elimination of personal identity. Hindu beliefs include reincarnation. Page 413.

hit upon: came upon; reached, found suddenly or by chance. Page 311.

Home Universe: a universe the thetan and several others, or just himself, built once. Page 401.

humdrum: commonplace; unexcitedly routine; lacking variety; boring. Page 139.

hung up: halted or snagged; not moving forward. Page 84.

identification: 1. the determination of one's identity; the recognition of an individual as being what he or she is; the action or process of determining what a thing is. Page 30.
2. orientation and close association of oneself with the qualities, characteristics, etc., of something. Page 126.
3. (said of thought) the action of making one thing equal with another thing, when in fact it is not identical. Such think was discovered to be a function of the reactive mind whereby when past painful incidents are restimulated (brought into action again due to similar things or occurrences in the present environment), they are wholly equated with the present. The reactive mind does not reason, it thinks in identities and can be summed up as everything equals everything equals everything, as fully described in *Dianetics: The Modern Science of Mental Health*. Page 183.

if not, nothing: used to emphasize a particular quality that something has; above everything; undoubtedly. Page 291.

impunity: exempt from consequences, penalty or punishment. Page 313.

in check: restrained from free movement or action; under control. Page 313.

Indian rope trick: a magic trick, Oriental in origin, in which a magician suspends a rope in midair which a person then climbs up and seemingly disappears. Page 312.

Infinite Mind: the mind of the All, present everywhere and independent of time and space; the source and foundation of existence, possessed of all possible power, wisdom and excellence. The Infinite Mind is individualistic. All Mankind does not depend upon or share a portion of the Infinite Mind. Page 170.

infrared: a form of light considered invisible, having a wavelength just longer than that of red light. (Red light has the longest wavelength of visible light detected by the human eye.) Scientists describe a range or spectrum into which visible light can be divided, called a color spectrum, a rainbowlike series of colors, in the following order: violet, blue, green, yellow, orange and red. Each color has a different wavelength, red being the longest then progressing through the colors to violet (at the opposite end) being the shortest. Page 384.

intellectualism: the exercising or engaging of the power or faculty of reason or rational thought. Page 417.

interest: attention with an intention to give or attract attention. Page 93.

interiorize: the action of moving into something (such as the body). Page 73.

interplay: the way in which two or more things repeatedly act on, influence and react to each other. Page 213.

interpositions: things that assume an intervening position or that are situated between (other things). Page 30.

intimate: closely connected or associated. Page 285.

into the teeth of: in direct opposition to, in defiance of. Page 275.

intricate: containing many interrelated details, elements, parts, patterns or factors. Page 84.

inversion: a reversal of position, order, sequence, relation or importance. Page 25.

jarring: having a disagreeable or disturbing effect upon the feelings, thoughts, etc. Page 255.

Journal of Scientology: a magazine published twice monthly by the Hubbard Association of Scientologists from 1952 to 1955 which carried technical articles, information of broad interest to members of the association, general news and the like. Each publication had an issue number followed by the letter "G" which designated "general" for distribution to all Scientologists. Page 271.

jumpily: in a manner characterized by jumps or sudden movements from one thing or state to another. Page 251.

Jung: Carl Gustav Jung (1875-1961), Swiss psychiatrist and psychologist who was a student of Freud but came to disagree with Freud's emphasis on sex and developed his own theory of a "collective unconscious" which contains universal symbols and memories from an ancestral past shared by all humanity. Jung theorized that it was important to understand how the personal unconscious integrates with the collective unconscious. Page 317.

Kant: Immanuel Kant (1724-1804), German philosopher who attempted to answer such concerns as whether there is a God, whether the soul lives on after death and whether people act freely or if their actions are determined by the laws of the world. Page 23.

keep one's own counsel: consult with oneself, advise oneself as to actions or matters of right and wrong. Page 13.

keyed against: set up to trigger in relation to or with respect to (something). In the sentence, *"The machine is keyed against something the thetan may think,"* the machine is set up so it will be activated automatically when the thetan thinks a thought. Literally, *keyed* means set up with a device for opening or closing or switching on electric contacts to activate or energize an appliance, machine, etc. Page 75.

kingdom of God: the spiritual reign of God as supreme king. Page vii.

Know-Sex-Mystery Scale: *see* **Know to Sex Scale**.

Know to Sex Scale: a Scale of Behavior, patterned on the Tone Scale, which starts at the top with Know and goes down to Sex at the bottom. Mystery was added at the bottom of this scale in May 1954, and it became known as the Know to Mystery Scale. For a description of the Know to Mystery Scale see Axiom 25 in Chapter Four, A Summary of Scientology. Page 52.

Krishna: an important Hindu god who appeared as an incarnation (living being embodying a deity or spirit) of Vishnu, one of the three main gods of the Hindu religion. In a sacred Hindu text describing Krishna, it is stated that human life is meant for self-realization (and eternal life) which is good. However, as long as the soul is encased in a body (which will go through birth, growth, old age and disease), human life is bad. Thus, one must take the good with the bad. Page 140.

Ladd, Alan: (1913-1964) a popular American actor who starred in many action and Western films from the 1940s to the early 1960s. Page 205.

lamaseries: monasteries of *lamas*, priests or monks of a branch of Buddhism that is practiced in certain areas of China. Page 23.

lambs among wolves: a *lamb* is a young sheep and, as wolves typically enjoy eating lambs, to *"send you forth as lambs among wolves"* means to send those who are innocent or peaceful among those who are dangerous and evil. Page vii.

Lao-tzu: Chinese philosopher of the sixth century B.C. and founder of *Taoism*, a Chinese philosophy that advocates a simple life and a policy of noninterference with the natural course of things. Page 23.

ledger, side of the: a reference to one of the two sides of a *ledger*, a book in which a summary of monies or assets is recorded. The credits, showing an addition or gain, are noted on one side and the debits, showing any losses or debts, are recorded on the opposite side. Used figuratively. Page 231.

L'Envoi: (also spelled *envoy*) the final section of a book or play, or a short section at the end of a poem, used for summing up or as a dedication. *L'* is French for "the" and *envoi* means "a sending." Page 251.

libido theory: a theory originated by the Austrian founder of psychoanalysis, Sigmund Freud (1856-1939), that the energy or urges motivating behavior are sexual in origin. Page 311.

licensed: given a reason or excuse to do something. Strictly, a *license* is a formal, usually printed or written permission from an authority to do something, for example, to marry, to print or publish a book, to carry on some trade, etc. Page 225.

line of sight: an imaginary line from the observer's eye to a perceived object. Page 104.

loose: 1. to let go of a hold (of something); to weaken the attachment of. Hence, to make unstable or insecure in position. Page 96.
2. to discharge, release or let fly. Page 276.

lore: accumulated facts, traditions or beliefs about a particular subject. Page 413.

Lucretius: (ca. 98-55 B.C.) Roman poet, philosopher and author of the unfinished instructional poem in six books, *On the Nature of Things*, which set forth in outline a complete science of the universe. Lucretius believed everything, even the soul, is made up of atoms controlled by natural laws. Page 416.

luxury: of or like something that is not demanded or required but is desirable. Page 11.

machine(s): in order to have more attention to control other things, one sets up the things he is already controlling as automatic. Having done so, he has given to them a determinism of their own. And having so given them their own determinism they can, if he ceases thus to control them, attack him. Thus we have the *machines* of a thetan. These machines work only so long as they are in control of the individual and then begin to work against the individual. Page 41.

Maitreya: in Buddhism, the *future Buddha* who will be reborn in a period of decline to renew the doctrine of the founder of Buddhism, the Buddha. Page 417.

makes like: behaves like; imitates. Page 235.

Marx: Karl Marx (1818-1883), German political philosopher whose works formed the basis of twentieth-century *communism*, the political theory or system in which all property and wealth is owned by all the members of a classless society and a single party with absolute power runs the economic and political systems of the state. Page 227.

master trick: a coined term from *master* meaning highly skilled or proficient and *trick* meaning an act involving or requiring skill and effectiveness. A *master trick* in this sense is a highly competent and skilled idea or performance of something. Page 203.

(MC) USN: abbreviation for *Medical Corps United States Navy.* Page 310.

mean: an intermediate position, the middle; a condition, quality or course of action that is equally removed from two opposite extremes. Page 298.

mechanical: **1.** concerned with or involving material objects or physical conditions or forces, as in *"Total ARC would bring about the vanishment of all mechanical conditions of existence."* Page 30.
2. from the word *mechanics* which means the procedural or operating details (of something). When applied to theories, *mechanical* means explaining phenomena by the assumption of mechanical action; the explanation of how something works, as in *"But senior to this granting of life is the mechanical matter of orientation-point and symbol."* Page 96.

mechanical definition: called *mechanical* as it is defined in terms of distance and position. *Mechanical* in this sense means "Interpreting or explaining the phenomena of the universe by referring to causally determined physical forces; mechanistic." A being can put out objects to view (or anchor points) and also put out points which will view them, even while the being himself is elsewhere. Thus one can achieve space. "Mechanical" also applies to "acting or performing like a machine–automatic." Thus a *mechanical definition* would be one which defined in terms of space or location such as "the car over by the old oak tree" or "the man who lives in the big house." Here "the old oak tree" and "the big house" are fixed objects and the unfixed objects ("car," "man") are a sort of viewpoint. One has identified things by location. Page 33.

mechanism: the agency or means by which an effect is produced or a purpose is accomplished, likened to the structure or system of parts in a mechanical device for carrying out some function or doing something. Page 128.

mechanistic: of or pertaining to *mechanics,* which means the procedural or operating details (of something). When applied to theories, *mechanistic* means explaining phenomena by the assumption of mechanical action; the explanation of how something works. Page 286.

meeting ground: a common area of knowledge or interest. Page 284.

might as well: used to say that the effect of an action or situation is the same as if it were another one. Page 140.

millstones: things that grind or crush, likened to the pair of circular stones between which grain or another substance is ground, as in a mill. Page 202.

mirror mazes: systems of paths lined with mirrors, built for amusement and designed to confuse persons trying to find their way out. Page 284.

modus operandi: the way of doing or accomplishing something; a method of operating or functioning. Page 81.

mooning: engaging in listless or aimless contemplation. Page 165.

mount: to go upwards; climb; ascend. Page 288.

much less: used to characterize a statement or suggestion as still more unacceptable than one that has been already denied; and certainly not. Page 262.

murderous: characterized by extreme difficulty. Page 201.

musty: (of immaterial things, ideas, etc.) stale or outdated. Hence, lacking newness, originality or interest. *Musty* means smelling old, damp and stale because of not having been used or exposed to fresh air for a long time. Page 276.

mystic: a person who claims to attain, or believes in the possibility of attaining, insight into mysteries transcending ordinary human knowledge, as by direct communication with the divine or immediate intuition in a state of spiritual ecstasy. Page 93.

mysticism: the belief that it is possible to achieve knowledge of spiritual truths and God through contemplation or through deep and careful thought. Page 285.

mythical: relating or pertaining to an imaginary or fictitious thing or person. Page 207.

naught: nothing at all. Used in formal writing. Page 276.

Near East: a region comprising countries of southwest Asia and generally thought to include Turkey, Iraq, Israel, Saudi Arabia, as well as nations in northeastern Africa. Page 415.

necromancy: the practice of attempting to communicate with the spirits of the dead in order to predict or influence the future. Page 312.

next-to-last list: the second-to-last list in the book *Self Analysis*, which asks the preclear to recall a time which really seems real to him, a time when he felt real affinity from someone, a time when someone was in good communication with him, etc. Page 309.

Nietzsche: Friedrich Wilhelm Nietzsche (1844–1900), German philosopher and poet who asserted that traditional values had lost their power in the lives of individuals and that a person could affirm life and create new values to replace the traditional ones. Page 23.

nigh: near in place, time or relationship. Used chiefly in poetic or religious writings. Page vii.

Nirvana: the goal of the Hindus. Hindu beliefs are that "Reality is One" and that ultimate salvation, and release from the endless cycle of birth to death, is achieved when one merges or is absorbed into the "one divine reality" with all loss of individual existence. Page 146.

no savvy: informal for "does not understand." Page 229.

nothing if not: used to emphasize a particular quality that something has; above everything; undoubtedly. Page 291.

nothingness: an absence of quantities and locations. A complete absence of quantities and location would be an absolute nothingness. Page 31.

nuclear physics: the branch of physics that deals with the behavior, structure and component parts of the center of an atom (called the nucleus), which constitutes almost all of the mass of the atom. Page 23.

nuthin': informal pronunciation of nothing, meaning not anything, a zero amount. Page 235.

objectively: in a manner that addresses the environment and not the thinkingness of the person. Page 142.

obsessively: excessively, especially extremely so. Page 5.

Occident: the West; the countries of Europe and America. Page 23.

occult: practices involving supernatural influences, agencies or phenomena such as magic or witchcraft; something mysterious or supernatural such as hidden or secret knowledge which is said to be beyond normal understanding and not bound by the strict laws of science. Page 93.

odds: superiority in numbers or resources; differences in favor of one of two people, groups, etc., who are in competition, battle, etc. Page 146.

Officer 666: the title of a 1912 Broadway play in which a wealthy businessman returns from out of town to find he is being impersonated by a burglar living in his house. He gives a police officer (Officer 666) $500 for the loan of his uniform to catch the burglar himself. Page 206.

Old Testament: the first part of the Bible, that tells the history of the Jews before the birth of Christ, their relationship with God and their beliefs, such as in the future appearance of the *Messiah*, the King of the Jews who will bring an age of peace and freedom. A *testament* is a covenant (binding agreement) between human beings and God. The *Old Testament* is the Christian name for the Jewish Bible as they believe that its laws and prophecies are fulfilled in the person of Jesus, whose mission is described in the New Testament. Page 415.

Opening Procedure by Duplication: Opening Procedure by Duplication is fully described in Chapter Five, Intensive Procedure, R2–17. Page 42.

Opening Procedure of 8-C: Opening Procedure of 8-C is fully described in Chapter Five, Intensive Procedure, R2-16. The "C" in 8-C stands for "clinical." Page 42.

Operating Thetan: the state of Operating Thetan means that the person does not need a body to communicate or work. The goals

466

and abilities of Operating Thetan are fully described in SOP 8-O, Goals of Operating Thetan. Page 321.

Orient: the countries of eastern Asia, especially China and Japan. Page 23.

orientation-point: that point in relation to which others have location. It is also that point from which the space containing the locations is being created. Page 95.

Other-determinism: a condition of having one's actions determined by someone or something other than oneself; assigning cause elsewhere. Other-determinism is other-cause. Page 25.

out of touch: lacking in awareness or understanding (in regards to something); not in communication or agreement with. Page 84.

out the window: out of use, effect or consideration. Page 145.

outthrust: to extend or cause to extend outward; push outwards. Page 278.

PABs: abbreviation for *Professional Auditor's Bulletins,* a series of issues written by L. Ron Hubbard between 10 May 1953 and 15 May 1959. The contents of the bulletins were technical and promotional. Available in the Technical Bulletins volumes. Page 140.

pains, take no: make no special effort or take no extra trouble to do something. Page 116.

Pan-determinism: is the ability to regulate the considerations of two or more identities, whether or not opposed. Page 44.

parables: simple stories illustrating or teaching truths or moral lessons. Page 416.

paradox: something that (apparently) has contradictory or inconsistent qualities. Page 350.

parity: the state or condition of being the same in power, value or rank; equality. Page 171.

patty-caked: handled in a weak or ineffective manner, such as running a process shallowly. *Patty-caked* comes from the children's game "Pat-a-cake," in which a child claps hands along with another child while chanting a nursery rhyme. (A usual form of the rhyme is:

Pat-a-cake, pat-a-cake, baker's man! Bake me a cake as fast as you can....) Page 170.

penicillin: a drug that kills bacteria and is used to treat a wide range of infections. Page 286.

periodic chart: a table of the *elements*, Earth's most basic substances such as gold, lead, calcium and oxygen that cannot be broken down into simpler substances by ordinary chemical means. The chart is constructed in vertical columns with elements of similar or recurring properties and in horizontal rows by increasing weight. Page 295.

periphery: the space, region or area surrounding something; the outer boundary; the outside of something thought of as a circle. Page 101.

personifications: persons regarded as embodying or typifying a quality, idea or the like. Page 414.

pertinencies: relevant and applicable datums, principles, laws, etc. Page 24.

Philadelphia Lecture Series: a series of lectures by LRH, sixty-two of which were delivered in December 1952 in Philadelphia, Pennsylvania, with another fourteen supplementary lectures delivered in London in January 1953, making seventy-six lectures in all. Known as the *Philadelphia Doctorate Course*, these lectures stand as the largest single body of work on the anatomy, behavior and potentials of the spirit of Man. Page 171.

phobia: a strong unreasonable compulsion; a persistent, excessive anxiety or preoccupation with something. Page 376.

Phoenix International Congress: an international congress of Dianeticists and Scientologists held in Phoenix, Arizona, from 28 December to 31 December 1953. During twenty-two lectures, LRH released a new version of SOP 8-C and the full technology of how to be a Group Auditor. Page 348.

physical sciences: any of the sciences, such as physics and chemistry, that study and analyze the nature and properties of energy and nonliving matter. Page 23.

pious: acting or talking in a falsely moralizing way in order to impress others. Page 163.

Plato: (427–347 B.C.) Greek philosopher who argued that the reason an ideal society does not come about is because men are greedy, ambitious, competitive and jealous. Page 313.

plot: to lay out or show some process, condition or course of something, as if with the precision used to chart the course of a ship, draw a map of an area, etc. Page 300.

power plants: buildings where electrical power is generated; power stations. Page 41.

predicated (on): (said of a statement or action) based or established (on). Page 335.

Prelogic(s): the Prelogics are those five Logics which precede The Logics as written in *Advanced Procedure and Axioms.* The Prelogics concern themselves with this fact: that theta locates objects in space and time and creates space and time in which to locate things. Page 355.

pressing: urging strongly or insistently. Page 111.

prime motivator: the chief force that impels or moves to action. *Prime* in this sense means first in degree or rank in comparison with other things. *Motivator* here is something that initiates or is a stimulus to action or behavior. Page 310.

Procedure 30: a procedure comprised of Opening Procedure by Duplication (R2-17), Problems and Solutions (R2-20) and Granting of Beingness (R2-21) run one right after another. It is called "30" because 30 is a call sign that is used on radio. It means "the end, finished, through, done." And it finishes a lot of cases. It's also called "30" because it has 3 parts for a thetan, which is the "0." Page 87.

Professional School: a Scientology training center located in Phoenix, Arizona, which provided Scientology auditor training in 1953. See *Addresses* for current locations. Page 321.

profit: benefit, gain, progress made. Page 96.

profitable: of use, benefit or advantage. Page 226.

prophets: those who speak by divine inspiration or as the interpreters through whom the will of a god is expressed. Page vii.

Psychoanalysis, Terminable and Interminable: a reference to "Analysis, Terminable and Interminable," a paper written by Sigmund Freud (1856-1939) in which Freud pessimistically writes of psychoanalysis and how its outcome must always fall short of the ideal, designating it the impossible profession. In the paper, he discusses case histories and patients who finished their therapy but eventually suffered a relapse. Page 311.

psychotherapy: 1. from *psyche* (soul) and *therapy* (to cure), a means of improving an individual's mental or spiritual condition, as in *"The earliest known psychotherapy consisted of getting a patient to laugh."* Page 113.
2. the supposed treatment of disorders of the mind, as in psychoanalysis. Page 351.

Q and Aing: *Q and A* stands for "Question and Answer." The answer to the question or the question to the answer are both the same, because this is identification. Page 5.

qualify: make suitable, eligible or fit for something. Page 156.

quasi-: seeming; having a likeness to something; resembling. Page 322.

queasiness: the state or condition of being subject to or affected with *nausea*, a feeling of sickness in the stomach. Page 89.

Rain: the title of the theatrical and movie adaptation of "Miss Thompson," a short story written by English author W. Somerset Maugham (1874-1965) that tells of a Scottish missionary who, during the rainy season on a South Sea island, attempts to convert a prostitute to religion. Page 206.

randomity: it is a ratio: the amount of predicted motion in ratio to the amount of unpredicted motion which the individual has. He likes to have about 50 percent predicted motion and about 50 percent unpredicted motion. Page 146.

rarefaction, condensation: a reference to a flow of energy such as in electrical flow or sound waves. When such energy travels down a wire, it isn't particles that move along the path (like water through a pipe) but a rhythmic pattern of compressing (condensing) and expanding (rarefying) waves. The wave is carried along by molecules bumping into their neighboring molecules. No molecules actually travel down the path, only the energy is carried along. The repetition of these condensation and rarefaction cycles is referred to as vibration and how many of them take place per unit of time is referred to as frequency. See illustration below. Page 295.

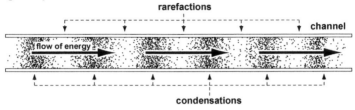

record: a phonograph record, a vinyl disc (normally twelve inches in diameter) with grooves in it, on which music, voice or other sounds are permanently recorded. Page 105.

reject: kick out; push out; get rid of. Hence, *"Have him pitch things away in 'mock-up' until you find something he can 'reject' "* refers to the fact that some individuals are compulsively trying to reject and require their rejection level handled before their acceptance level can be addressed. The individual must be worked until he can reject things in an avalanche and only then will he be able to accept things. Page 378.

rejection level: what is rejectable by the preclear. Page 122.

relegation: the act of assigning to a specific position, place or condition as insignificant. Page 389.

Remedy of Havingness: processing that makes the individual capable of accepting or rejecting anything. The preclear is asked to either mock something up and throw it away or mock something up and pull it in on himself. Page 41.

remote viewpoint: that thing which a person puts out remotely to look through; a system of remote lookingness. It is a specialized kind of viewpoint. The place from which the individual is himself looking we call viewpoint. *Viewpoint* means something an individual puts out to look through and the point the individual looks through. Page 136.

Report Station: a reference to the location where the thetan "reports in" between lives and receives an implant. Page 403.

residual: present or existing, often with the sense of being a quantity left over at the end of a series of actions, conditions, etc. Page 159.

ridge(s): a ridge is essentially suspended energy in space. It comes about by flows, dispersals or ridges impinging against one another with a sufficient solidity to cause an enduring state of energy. A dispersal from the right and a dispersal from the left, colliding in space with sufficient volume, create a ridge which then exists after the flow itself has ceased. The duration of ridges is quite long. Page 133.

Rig-Veda: a collection of hymns; the oldest and most important of the four books of the *Veda*, the ancient sacred writings that contain the first written expression of Man's relationship to the universe and of the cycle-of-action of life—birth, life and death. *Rig* is from an ancient Indian word meaning praise and *veda* means knowledge. Page 413.

root of all evil: the source of all wrongdoing. From lines in the Bible which state, "For the love of money is the root of all evils." Page 310.

rut: a fixed or established manner of doing something or way of being, usually unvarying, dull or unpromising, likened to being in a groove. Page 147.

sage: a wise man; a person of profound wisdom. Page 414.

Sama-Veda: one of the four books of the *Veda*, the ancient sacred writings that contain the first written expression of Man's relationship to the universe and of the cycle-of-action of life—birth, life and death. *Sama* is from an ancient Indian word meaning chant and *veda* means knowledge. Page 413.

Satanists: ones who follow or worship Satan (or the Devil). In Christian tradition, Satan was the leader of the angels who rebelled against God and who were cast out of heaven. He and his followers are seen to be the source of evil in the world. Page 162.

savvy: understand or know. The phrase *no savvy* is informal for "does not understand." Page 229.

Schopenhauer: Arthur Schopenhauer (1788-1860), German philosopher who believed that the will to live is the fundamental reality and that this will, being a constant striving, cannot be satisfied and only causes suffering. Page 23.

science: knowledge; comprehension or understanding of facts or principles, classified and made available in work, life or the search for truth. A science is a connected body of demonstrated truths or observed facts systematically organized and bound together under general laws. It includes trustworthy methods for the discovery of new truth within its domain and denotes the application of scientific methods in fields of study previously considered open only to theories based on subjective, historical or undemonstrable, abstract criteria. The word *science*, when applied to Scientology, is used in this sense–the most fundamental meaning and tradition of the word–and not in the sense of the *physical* or *material* sciences. Page 18.

Science of Human Affairs: a science that deals with the concerns, occurrences, matters and interests characteristic of and involving people. Page 23.

scientific method: the principles and processes of discovery and demonstration considered characteristic of or necessary for scientific investigation. Page 275.

scrip: a small bag, wallet or satchel, especially carried by a traveler, a shepherd or a beggar. Page vii.

seamier: less pleasing, less worthy or less presentable; having unpleasant qualities associated with a degraded way of living. From the rough side of a garment where the seams show. Page 314.

sees eye to eye: is in entire agreement; agrees without exception. Page 11.

Self Analysis in Scientology: an edition of the original *Self Analysis* that included Creative Processing. Page 309.

Self-determinism: a condition of determining the actions of self. Self-determinism is a First Dynamic determinism. That is, "I can determine my own actions." Page 12.

senior survival: anything which wins; which is to say, demonstrates that it has more force, more power, more survival capability than the preclear. Page 398.

seven Advanced Clinical Course units: the seven Advanced Professional Auditor Courses preceding and culminating in *The Creation of Human Ability* and its processing centerpiece, Intensive Procedure. The first through seventh Clinical Courses were delivered by LRH between October 1953 and July 1954. ACCs instructed select professionals on the latest advances of technology and in the full scope of theory. Page 1.

short-circuits: becomes inoperable, fails or ceases working (in the manner of a short circuit). A *circuit* is a system of electrical components and wires forming a complete path around which an electrical current can flow and which carries out a specific function. A *short circuit* is electricity following a shorter, less resistive path rather than the main pathway of wires and parts intended. It leads to excessive electrical flow (without resistance, electricity flows uncontrollably, creating overload) and normally shuts down the equipment it is associated with. Page 236.

Short 8: a short form of *Standard Operating Procedure 8*. Short 8 is fully covered in This Is Scientology, The Science of Certainty. Page 309.

shotgun: covering a wide area or field. A shotgun fires many small pellets (shot) that spread out to cover a wide area. Page 334.

sign: something that suggests or represents the presence or existence of something else, such as a condition, fact, etc., as in *"and then, not repostulating the static, mooning over the lie or the sign."* Page 165.

singular: of unusual quality; remarkably good; exceptional. Page 144.

16-G: the 16th issue of the *Journal of Scientology*, entitled "This Is Scientology, The Science of Certainty." (The *Journal of Scientology* was a magazine published twice monthly by the Hubbard Association of Scientologists from 1952 to 1955 which carried technical articles, information of broad interest to members of the association, general news and the like. Each publication had an issue number followed by the letter "G" which designated "general" for distribution to all Scientologists.) This Is Scientology, The Science of Certainty is contained in the References section. Page 271.

Six Ways to Nothing: a series of steps to process nothingness including looking through and finding barriers, black space and nothingness. The steps are repeated in six directions: straight forward, straight back, to the right, to the left, above and below. For example: "Now in front of you find the first barrier. Now look through that and find the next barrier, and look through that and find the next barrier. Now find black space. Now find nothingness. And sit back and know." Six Ways to Nothing is described in the LRH lecture of 17 May 1954 "Simple Processes" in the 6th American ACC. Page 361.

slew: (past tense of *slay*) struck down; killed somebody or something. Page 301.

snapping: moving rapidly or abruptly onto something or into a position of closure with something else. Page 397.

so called: used to suggest that the word or words used to describe somebody or something are not appropriate. Page 319.

some little time: an unspecified, but possibly considerable length of time. Page 63.

son of peace: a peaceful man; a man of peace. Page vii.

SOP 8: Standard Operating Procedure 8. SOP 8 is fully described in the References section, This Is Scientology, The Science of Certainty. Page 186.

SOP 8-C: Standard Operating Procedure 8-C is fully described in the References section, SOP 8-C: The Rehabilitation of the Human Spirit. The "C" in 8-C stands for "clinical." Page 271.

SOP 8-D: Standard Operating Procedure 8-D was issued on 15 April 1954 and is a version of SOP 8. The "D" indicates that it is next in sequence to SOP 8-C. Standard Operating Procedure 8-D is fully described in the References section, SOP 8-D. Page 43.

SOP 8-O: a technique which drills up the capabilities, on a gradient scale, of the thetan so he can see, hear, speak, get out electricity, throw out postulates, control bodies other than his own, and do other things which are well within his abilities. The "O" stands for Operating Thetan. SOP 8-O is fully described in the References section, SOP 8-O. Page 348.

so to speak: phrased in this way; that is to say. Used to indicate that one is expressing something in an unusual way or expressing an unusual concept. Page 315.

speculations: conclusions, opinions, reasons, etc. Also, contemplations or considerations of a subject as well as the conclusions reached from that. Page 23.

Spencer, Herbert: (1820-1903) English philosopher known for his attempted application of the doctrines of evolution to philosophy and ethics. Page 23.

Spinoza: Baruch Spinoza (1632-1677), Dutch philosopher who believed that "God or Nature" was the only substance and all that existed. He believed that God and Nature are the same thing. All objects and thought are forms or manifestations of God. Page 416.

spiral: a term of lives or a term of existences or a single existence which bears an intimate relation, one to the other. Page 401.

spiralings: a spiral is a line in the form of a curve that winds around a central point, at the same time moving in toward, or farther out, from the center. Hence figuratively, any thought process or idea resembling such a spiral pattern as in going round and round, etc. Page 275.

Starr, Meredith: (1891-1971) English writer, poet, psychotherapist and resident of Cyprus, he was involved in mysticism, in various "new" methods of psychology and was a devoted follower of Meher Baba (1894-1969), Indian mystic and spiritual teacher. Page 317.

St. (Saint) Luke: the third book of the New Testament of the Bible—the Gospel According to Luke. A *Gospel* is one of the first four books of the New Testament, describing the life, death and resurrection of

Jesus and recording his teaching. Saint Luke was an early Christian follower of Jesus Christ. Page vii.

straits: a position of difficulty, distress or need. Page 328.

stretched: extended to its full length, breadth and depth, capacity and dimension. Page 69.

subjective: a reference to subjective processes, those processes which intimately address the internal world of the preclear. Page 84.

subscribed to: supported or agreed with. Page 17.

suppositions: the mental acts of believing or assuming something to be the case or ideas that result from believing or assuming, especially as opposed to ideas based on firm evidence. Page 289.

Swizzle-Stick: Swizzle-Stick Processing is for the preclear who just sits there and stirs it around and around and around and isn't going to get any place. First and foremost, he believes at the most, maybe, that there was one person in the world who really wanted him to live and he believes maybe that person is now gone and his (own) chances of survival are zero. *Swizzle-stick* is a humorous reference to the small stick used for stirring mixed drinks. The process consists of three parts: 1) "Give me an incident in your past you wouldn't mind owning" or "Something in your past you wouldn't mind owning." 2) "Who are you being (whatever it is) for?" such as "Who are you eating for?" "Who are you sleeping for?" "Who are you being tired for?" "Who are you being sick for?" and so on. Such an individual hasn't got such a thing as his own problem: it's totally other people's problems, so anything he's doing, he's doing it "for." 3) The individual is trying to survive but he is using succumb as a mechanism to survive. We ask him "Well, who do you want to survive? Who have you wanted to survive? What have you tried to make survive?" "Who has wanted you to survive?" A full description of Swizzle-Stick Processing can be found in the lectures 14 June 1954, "General Lecture, Part II" and 14 June 1954, "Survival" available in the 6th American ACC. Page 98.

syphilis: an infectious sexually transmitted disease, that in its final stage may attack the brain, spinal cord and other parts of the body, causing blindness, deafness, mental illness, heart failure, paralysis and bone deformities. Page 215.

take no pains: make no special effort or take no extra trouble to do something. Page 116.

take rank over: to surpass or be superior to in importance. Page 24.

takes exception to: makes objection to; finds fault with; disapproves of. Page 392.

take the upper cream off life and leave the skimmed milk: obtain or have the best of existence, leaving behind the things of lower quality. Literally, *cream* is the thick, light yellow portion of milk from which butter is made. Because it is lighter than the remainder of the milk, cream will slowly rise to the surface and can be separated by scooping (skimming) it from the top leaving behind the other components, referred to as skim milk. Cream is considered rich tasting and hence, the most excellent part of something. Page 139.

Tao: the Tao Teh King, the doctrine and philosophy written by Lao-tzu (604–531 B.C.) in verse form. It literally means "The Way" and is the foundation of *Taoism*, a Chinese philosophy that advocates a simple life and a policy of noninterference with the natural course of things. Page 23.

Tar Baby: a tar doll appearing in a well-known story by American journalist and author Joel Chandler Harris (1848–1908). In the *Tar Baby Story*, a fox makes a doll out of tar and sets it up by a roadside to catch Br'er (brother) Rabbit (a character in the book). Br'er Rabbit approaches the tar doll and starts asking it questions. The doll never responds ("She says nuthin'"). Angered by this, Br'er Rabbit strikes the doll and gets his hands, feet and head stuck in the tar doll. Page 235.

teletypewriters: instruments resembling a typewriter used in a form of long-distance communication. The striking of the keys produces electrical impulses that travel over wires and are printed at the receiving end. Page 75.

tendered: offered formally in writing; offered freely as for acceptance. Page 282.

ten-star: having a quality superior to all others; very exceptional. This alludes to a system of rating the quality of something by placing a number of stars next to its name or title, normally the highest being five stars. Page 121.

thee: a formal way of saying *you*, used in poetic, religious and other writings. Page 218.

theta body: a thetan isn't a point in this particular universe, he just thinks he is. He has a theta body, a composite of all sorts of things: engrams, masses of effort ridges, screens, etc. Page 185.

Theta Clear: this is a relative, not an absolute term. It means that the person, this thought unit, is clear of his body, his engrams, his facsimiles, but can handle and safely control a body. Page 322.

30: the "30" in *Procedure 30*. It is called "30" because 30 is a call sign that is used on radio. It means "the end, finished, through, done." And it finishes a lot of cases. It's also called "30" because it has 3 parts for a thetan, which is the "0." *See also* **Procedure 30**. Page 87.

thrust down the throat: to force someone to agree to or accept (something). Page 276.

time-continua: plural of *time-continuum*. A *continuum* is a continuous extent, series or whole, no part of which can be distinguished from neighboring parts except by arbitrary division. A *time-continuum* is an agreed-upon uniform rate of change. Page 146.

trade routes: the routes taken between Europe and Asia by merchants on ships and by land that closed up around A.D. 1000. Page 416.

treats: deals with in order to achieve some particular result. Page 23.

tubes: *vacuum tubes*, devices once broadly used in electronics to control flows of electrical currents. Called vacuum tubes because they are sealed glass tubes or bulbs from which almost all the air has been removed in order to improve electrical flow. Page 75.

turbulent masses: the anatomy of mystery consists of, in this order: unpredictability, confusion and chaos, covered up because it cannot be tolerated. The anatomy of a mystery runs like this: we have an individual who has two or more particles in motion and he says he "can't predict them." And having said that he couldn't predict them, therefore, he conceives them to be a confusion. And having conceived them to be a confusion, he draws a curtain across them and says, "That's a mystery. That's unknowable now." Turbulent masses are the confusion preceding mystery. Page 62.

24-G: the 24th issue of the *Journal of Scientology,* entitled "SOP 8-C: The Rehabilitation of the Human Spirit." (The *Journal of Scientology* was a magazine published twice monthly by the Hubbard Association of Scientologists from 1952 to 1955 which carried technical articles, information of broad interest to members of the association, general news and the like. Each publication had an issue number followed by the letter "G" which designated "general" for distribution to all Scientologists.) SOP 8-C: The Rehabilitation of the Human Spirit is contained in the References section. Page 271.

Turner, Lana: (1920–1995) a blonde American actress who became a well-known example of Hollywood glamour. Page 205.

ultimate: beyond which no advance can be made; forming a final stage concerning nature or quality; fundamental or elemental. Page 32.

units: plural of *unit,* a single group, usually regarded as a whole part of something larger, such as a self-contained part of an educational program. *See also* **seven Advanced Clinical Course units.** Page 1.

universal solvent: that which has the power to solve anything, such as to cause any problem, situation, etc., to be resolved, disappear or vanish. The *universal solvent* was a substance sought by alchemists that was supposedly capable of dissolving all substances, particularly metals and leading to the transformation of any metal into gold and, as well, able to give immortality to human beings. An alchemist is one who studied *alchemy,* a predecessor to chemistry practiced in the Middle Ages. *Universal* in this sense means applicable to, operative or valid in all cases. Page 300.

universe: a universe is defined as a "whole system of created things." There could be and are many universes and there could be many kinds of universes. We are, for our purposes here, interested in two particular universes. The first of these is the MEST *universe,* that agreed-upon reality of matter, energy, space and time which we use as anchor points and through which we communicate. The other is our *personal universe*, which is no less a matter of energy and space. These two universes are entirely distinct and it could be said that the principal confusion and aberration of the individual stems from his having confused one for the other. Page 1.

unknowns: unknowns are described in Chapter Five, Intensive Procedure, R2-52. Page 180.

unlimited technique: unlimited techniques are fully described in Standard Operating Procedure 8, Appendix to SOP 8 No. 1. Page 309.

unseemly: contrary to accepted standards of good taste or appropriate behavior. Page 19.

unto: used to indicate that something is said, given or done to somebody. Page vii.

USN: abbreviation for *United States Navy.* Page 310.

valor: boldness or determination in facing great danger, especially in battle; heroic courage; bravery. Page 139.

Veda: the Vedic Hymns, the earliest recorded philosophic writings. They are the most ancient sacred literature of the Hindus (the natives of India) comprising over a hundred books still in existence. They tell about evolution, about Man coming into this universe and the curve of life, which is birth, growth, degeneration and decay. The word *veda* means knowledge. Page 23.

Velocity: one of the component parts of communication, including the velocity of the impulse or particle. *Velocity* is the rate of speed with which something happens or moves. Page 31.

vested interests: those who seek to maintain or control an existing activity, arrangement or condition from which they derive private benefit. Page 275.

vicissitudes: the sudden or unexpected changes, shifts, ups and downs, often encountered in one's life, activities or surroundings. Page 275.

Viewpoint Straightwire: Viewpoint Straightwire is described in Chapter Five, Intensive Procedure, R2-25. Page 62.

vindicated: justified or proven as being correct or valid, especially in light of later developments. Page 311.

wavelength: *wavelength* is the relative distance from node (crest) to node (crest) in any flow of energy. In the MEST universe, wavelength is commonly measured by centimeters or meters. The larger the number, the lower the wavelength is considered to be on the gradient scale of wavelengths. The smaller the number, the higher the wavelength is considered to be on the gradient scale. Node, as used here, refers to the crest (topmost part) of the wave. Page 27.

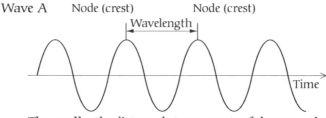

The smaller the distance between crests of the wave, the higher the wavelength is considered to be on the gradient scale of wavelengths.

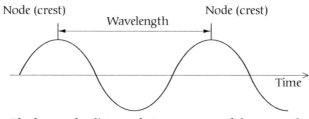

The larger the distance between crests of the wave, the lower the wavelength is considered to be on the gradient scale of wavelengths.

waves: paths of flow or patterns of flow. When any object vibrates, its motion causes an energy flow to move out and away from this vibrating source. This energy flow is a wave. For instance, dropping a rock in a pond sends waves out from the point where the rock contacts the water. Page 197.

Western civilization: the type of culture and society developed by the countries of Western Europe and the Americas. Page 23.

Western Hills: a range of hills in China, situated northwest of Beijing (the capital of China). The range is known for its many temples and has long been a religious retreat. Page 23.

wide-open case: a case which is possessed of full perception except somatic. *Wide-open* does not refer to a high-tone individual but to one below 2.0 who should be easy to work but is often inaccessible and who finds it difficult to regain a somatic and simple to regain perception. The wide-open case is fully described in the lecture series Technique 88: Incidents on the Track Before Earth. Page 200.

wild variable: a factor in a situation or problem that behaves in an uncontrolled, strange or unpredictable fashion. *Variable* is most commonly used in mathematics and science where it represents something unknown or unpredictable. A variable is often contrasted with a constant which is known and unchanging. Page 286.

worked over: subjected to thorough treatment; dealt with completely. Page 71.

worry machine: the phenomenon whereby people who have blackness predominantly are trying to keep something bad from happening. They are trying to uncreate a condition before it occurs. They spend all their time uncreating non-existent conditions. And this is a definition of worry. It is a worrying machine that uncreates before it creates. Page 232.

wu-wei: (Chinese, literally meaning nonaction) in the Chinese philosophy of Taoism, the principle of yielding to others as the most effective response to the problems of human existence. *Wu-wei* is natural, nonaggressive (but not passive) behavior that compels others (through shame, if for no other reason) to desist voluntarily from violence or overly aggressive conduct. *Wu-wei* is thus regarded as the secret to human happiness, for through "nonaction" all things can be accomplished. Page 414.

Yajur-Veda: one of the four books belonging to the *Veda,* the ancient body of sacred writings that is the first recorded writing on Man's relationship to the universe and the endless cycle of birth, life and death. The Yajur-Veda is a textbook of sacrifices. *Yajur* is from an ancient Indian word meaning sacrifices, and *veda* means knowledge. Page 413.

ye: a special form of the word *you*, employed in poetic and religious writings. Page vii.

Zen Buddhism: a form of Buddhism that emphasizes meditation and personal awareness rather than doctrine and the study of scripture. The word *Zen* is the Japanese equivalent of the Sanskrit *Dhyana*, which means "knowingness" and "lookingness." Page 289.

INDEX

A

490

election of, 232

Pan-determinism and, 169

potential source of flow, 359

unwillingness to be, 362

Cause and Effect, 304

basic commands, 119

certainty and, 332

process, 118

Cause-point

communication and, 359, 391

cautions

follow the Auditor's Code, 47

certainty, 283–291, 331

clarity of observation, 286

delivered by blows, 290

easily obtained, 286

increase power to observe with, 296

knowledge and, 281

of communication, 1

of impact, 289

opposite negative certainty, 334

people at low levels of awareness and, 289

positiveness of observation, 302

road to, 317–320

sanity and, 286

self-determined, 289

Certainty Processing, 331–339

fixations of attention resolved by, 336

overall basic technique, 335

preclear who doesn't respond, 338

change, 230

considerations, 189, 202

failed to, 230, 231

ideas upwards, 191

last effort, 169

mind, 312

of auditors, 6

postulates, 389, 390

primary manifestation of time, 27

process and preclear, 5

Change of Space (Processing), 66–68, 394, 400

exteriorized, 393

goal of, 393

Grand Tour, 394

list to be run, 401

R2-18 and, 88

Changing Minds

R2-50, 189–190

Chart of Attitudes, 164, 166, 335

buttons, 167, 191

Chart of Human Evaluation, 30, 153

scarcity of attention and, 101

Chart of Processes, 46

chemistry

periodic chart of, 295

childhood home, 96

exteriorization, 1, 348, 351, 353, 393

always "here" and never "there," 126

attention and, 377

Beingness Processing and, 126

changing mind and, 189

description, 351

difficulty with, 126, 353

for other purposes, 322

from actual physical universe objects, 110

Gradient Scale of Exteriorization, 124

higher Pan-determinism and, 153

in the case of certain, 370

low-step cases and, 310

preclear difficult to exteriorize, 152

preclear exteriorized and knows it, 323

recruitment and, 123

remedy which results in, 150

top goal in processing, 376

variability, 125

When he is exteriorized and knows it thoroughly, 323

Exteriorization by Attention, 101

Exteriorization by Distance, 43

preclear found it unreal, 120

R2-24, 107–110

Exteriorization by Scenery, 326, 342

F

facsimile, 66, 336–338

definition, 336

Duplication and, 342

loss and, 210

solid, 198

thinking by, 201

facsimile bank, 267

Facsimile One, 402

Factors, The, 277–282, 321

human spirit, material universe and, 277

SOP 8 and, 321

"fader" questions, 214

failure

biggest lock on Alter-isness, 230

inexplicable, 286

safe if your parents did, 239

source of in SOP 8-C, 364

Faller, 403

fatness, 215

fear

hurting in a just cause, 12

Fifth Dynamic, 294

Fighting

Games Processing and, 204

Q

R

S

sanity, 287

assist for recovery of, 118

certainty, 283, 286

road to, 286

dangerousness of environment and, 118

direct index of, 376

keynote of, 183

R2-16 until full, 85

Satan, 162

Scale of Action, 289

scale of attitude, 30

Scale of Awareness, 289

going up, 302

scale of behavior, 391

Scale of Substitutes Acquired by Reason of Loss, 210–211

Scale of Tolerance of Viewpoints, 391

scarcity, 280

Expanded GITA and, 324

of attention, 101

of games, 246

of opponents, 184, 207

of roles, 206

of universes, 319

of viewpoints, 322

thus comes about, 280

Schopenhauer, 23, 416

science

definition, 318

scarcity of universes, 319

Science of Human Affairs, 23

science of knowing how to know, 23, 276

science of knowledge, 283

Scientologist

Code of a, 17–19

one who understands life, 26

Scientology

basic series of assumptions, 25

definition, 24

description, 351

Dianetics and, 285

its background, 413

religion, 417

Science of Human Affairs, 23

science of knowing how to know, 23, 347

science of knowledge, 283

summary of, 23–35

two divisions, philosophic and technical, 24

use of, 18

Scientology 8-8008, 164, 217, 363

Standard Operating Procedure 8, 321

"Scientology, Its General Background," lectures, 413

Second Dynamic, 294, 310

second postulate, 32, 162, 163, 165, 200

Security Processing

R2-72, 239

Self Analysis, 327, 342

next-to-last list, 309, 314, 327, 341, 397, 408

Short 8, 341, 342

primary source of untruth, 34

R2-16, R2-17 and, 141

why persists, 165

time-continua, 146

time, place, form and event, 33

Time Tolerance

R2-29, 121

tolerance

auditor, 70

for the physical universe, 1

in viewing and experiencing, 112

occupying same space, 70

of nothingnesses and somethingnesses, 120

of space, 392

preclear, 70

scale of tolerance of, 391

time, R2-29, 121

Tolerance of Space, 391

tone

stuck in, 231

Tone 0.0

total unawareness and, 296

Tone 40, 296

Tone Scale, 63, 234, 295–298, 312, 315, 391

ARC and, 234

bottom of, description, 297

evil below 2.0 on, 213

observer is very low on, 312

processes and, 46

scale of Desire-Enforce-Inhibit and, 186

see also **DEI Scale**

spirals and, 296

top of, description, 296

tooth trouble, 148

total Knowingness

consists of, 29

Touching

R2-64, 229

Triangle

Affinity, Reality and Communication, 295

Certainty of Awareness, 288

Space-Be, Energy-Do, Time-Have, 363

truth, 32

definition, 33

exact consideration, 33

Scientology and, 24

time, place, form and event, 33

Turner, Lana, 205

two-terminal universe, 299

two-way communication, 31, 39, 46, 51

establishing, 52

maintain with preclear, 7

where on Tone Scale, 46

U

ugliness, 32, 139, 279

gradient scale of, 322

"unsolvable problem," 34

upward spiral, 296

Use of Problems and Solutions, 195

    R2-20, 92–94

    second step for Procedure 30, 92

V

valences

    packages of abilities, 129

    thetan is trying to avoid, 128

Veda, 23, 413

    means knowingness, 414

Velocity, 96, 121

    component part of Communication, 31, 51

    of impulse, 51

        or particle, 31

velocity

    increase of, 52

Via

    processing of Processes, 209

    R2-41, 165–167

via

    curse word of existence, 165

    definition, 165

vicissitudes, 275

victory

    stuck in, 177

Viewpoint

    R2-25, 111

viewpoint, 277–282, 298–299, 391

    any thing better than no thing, 281

    can never perish, 280

    command the continuing attention, 300

    Communication requiring, 294

    definition, 305

    description, 278

    interchange amongst, 278

    knowing, from many places, 304

    loss of a, 307

    psychotic and past, 328

    reactive mind and, 305

Viewpoint ARC Straightwire, 111

    R2-25, 111

Viewpoint Straightwire, 111

    basic theory behind, 62

    goal of, 62

    R2-25, 111

vision, 150

W

war, 207

waste, 314

    DEI Scale and, 187

    description, 323

    Expanded GITA, 323

    fighting, 174, 175, 187

    Healthy Bodies, 342